Hope & Recovery

A Twelve Step guide
for healing from
compulsive
sexual behavior

Excerpts quoted from *Alcoholics Anonymous* ©1976 and *Twelve Steps and
Twelve Traditions* © 1981. Reprinted by permission of Alcoholics Anonymous
World Services, Inc.

Library of Congress Cataloging-in-Publication Data
Hope & recovery.

   1. Psychosexual disorders—Case studies.   2. Compulsive behavior—
Case studies.   I. Title: hope and recovery.   [DNLM: 1. Compulsive
Behavior—therapy—popular works.   2. Psychotherapy—popular works.
3. Sex disorders—therapy—popular works. WM 611 H791]
RC556.H67 1987   616.85'83   87-6773
ISBN 0-89638-102-1

Inquiries, orders, and catalog requests should be addressed to:

CompCare Publishers
2415 Annapolis Lane
Minneapolis, Minnesota 55441
Call toll-free 800/328-3330
(Minnesota residents 612/559-4800)

6   5   4   3   2

92   91   90   89   88   87

To all our sisters and brothers in Twelve Step Programs throughout the world, especially the untold numbers of sex addicts who preceded us — people who lived lonely, driven lives without the saving grace of the Twelve Steps. May these people and the addicts who still suffer be in our thoughts and prayers.

The Twelve Steps of A.A.

1. We admitted we were powerless over (problem)—that our lives had become unmanageable.

2. Came to believe that a Power greater than ourselves could restore us to sanity.

3. Made a decision to turn our will and our lives over to the care of God *as we understood Him.*

4. Made a searching and fearless moral inventory of ourselves.

5. Admitted to God, to ourselves, and to another human being the exact nature of our wrongs.

6. Were entirely ready to have God remove all these defects of character.

7. Humbly asked Him to remove our shortcomings.

8. Made a list of all persons we had harmed, and became willing to make amends to them all.

9. Made direct amends to such people wherever possible, except when to do so would injure them or others.

10. Continued to take personal inventory, and when we were wrong, promptly admitted it.

11. Sought through prayer and meditation to improve our conscious contact with God *as we understood Him*, praying only for knowledge of His will for us and the power to carry that out.

12. Having had a spiritual awakening as a result of these steps, we tried to carry this message to addicts and to practice these principles in all our affairs.

(Reprinted for adaptation with permission of AA World Services, Inc.)

The Twelve Traditions of A.A.

1. Our common welfare should come first; personal recovery depends upon A.A. unity.

2. For our group purpose there is but one ultimate authority—a loving God as He may express Himself in our group conscience. Our leaders are but trusted servants; they do not govern.

3. The only requirement for A.A. membership is a desire to stop drinking.

4. Each group should be autonomous except in matters affecting other groups or A.A. as a whole.

5. Each group has but one primary purpose—to carry its message to the alcoholic who still suffers.

6. An A.A. group ought never endorse, finance, or lend the A.A. name to any related facility or outside enterprise, lest problems of money, property and prestige divert us from our primary purpose.

7. Every A.A group ought to be fully self-supporting, declining outside contributions.

8. Alcoholics Anonymous should remain forever nonprofessional, but our service centers may employ special workers.

9. A.A., as such, ought never be organized; but we may create service boards or committees directly responsible to those they serve.

10. Alcoholics Anonymous has no opinion on outside issues; hence the A.A. name ought never be drawn into public controversy.

11. Our public relations policy is based on attraction rather than promotion; we need always maintain personal anonymity at the level of press, radio, and films.

12. Anonymity is the spiritual foundation of all our traditions, ever reminding us to place principles before personalities.

Notes From the Publisher

Two dozen men and women contributed time, talent, and wisdom to the creation of this book. Some of these men and women were among the first members of specialized Twelve Step groups established to help people deal with obsessive thoughts and compulsive behaviors related to sex. These special groups were formed when people sharing similar problems came together and worked a Program of recovery based on the Twelve Steps of Alcoholics Anonymous. Some of these people first became aware of their sex addiction through participation in other Twelve Step groups (Alcoholics Anonymous, Overeaters Anonymous, Gamblers Anonymous, and Emotions Anonymous.) As they learned more about the addictive process in these other Twelve Step groups, they began to see the addictive nature of their own thoughts and behaviors relative to sex. These people who already were active in the Twelve Step fellowship brought many valuable things with them to this new group: belief in the power and wisdom of the Twelve Steps, support of other Twelve Step groups, guidance from the Twelve Traditions, and a variety of responsible and useful publications. These written materials, particularly *Alcoholics Anonymous* and *Twelve Steps and Twelve Traditions*, formed the philosophical foundation for the Twelve Step group concept that continues to offer hope and help to sex addicts of all ages and backgrounds.

Excerpts from *Alcoholics Anonymous* (the Big Book) and *Twelve Steps and Twelve Traditions* are reprinted by permission of Alcoholics Anonymous World Services, Inc. The page references to the Big Book are from the Third Edition, twenty-sixth printing, 1986. The page references to *Twelve Steps and Twelve Traditions* ("Twelve and Twelve") are from the thirty-second printing, 1986.

Notes From the Authors

The Twelve Steps tell us that we need to carry the message of recovery to other sex addicts. This book is a part of that mission. But regardless of the circumstances that led you to this book, we hope that you will come to see that *anyone* can achieve the promises of the title in his or her life:

- If you are concerned about your own obsessive thoughts and/or compulsive sexual behaviors, this book may provide some valuable opportunities for you to see whether or not your life is similar to the lives of sex addicts.

- If you are currently (or have been) involved in a relationship with someone who you think might be a sex addict, you may find special help in the personal stories included in this book. One of these personal stories was written by a co-dependent person whose experiences you might recognize.

- If you are a helping professional, this book may provide you and your clients with more information about sex addicts and sex addiction. Having a basic familiarity with Twelve Step language and the personal stories of those who have suffered may help you better understand the pain, loneliness, and isolation that your clients have experienced or continue to struggle with, and the help that is available to everyone.

- If you have come to realize that you do, in fact, have concerns or unresolved issues regarding your sexual thoughts and/or behaviors, we believe that this book can help you learn how and where to start on the road to recovery. *This book was written for sex addicts in all stages of recovery.*

Through our personal stories and the text itself, we have tried to provide as much genuine reassurance and guidance to readers as possible. We know from our own experiences that, early in the recovery process, most people have many fears and many questions. We hope that this book will give every sex addict who reads it an opportunity to learn from those who have preceded them. Some people may wish to study the text before they attend a Twelve Step meeting. Doing this may help stimulate their thinking and help them maximize the benefits of discussions that take place at meetings. People already attending Twelve Step meetings on a regular basis may find this book helpful as they learn how to use the Twelve Steps and the Twelve Traditions to heal from the pain and scars of obsessive thinking and compulsive sexual behavior. When faced with individual or Twelve Step group problems, people can turn to this book for guidance and read how others have acted in similar situations. Readers who do not have access to Twelve Step groups especially for sex addicts will find information in this book that will help them establish and maintain their own groups. Oldtimers in the Program may find that this book is, among other things, a useful reminder to them of where they came from, what their lives used to be like, and how different their lives are now. Reminders like this can help every one of us remain humble and grateful for all that the Program has allowed us to do and become.

Preface

After years of working with self-help literature created by and for other Twelve Step groups, it became increasingly clear to us that the time was right to develop a text of our own based on personal experiences. Even though the material from other Twelve Step groups was extremely helpful to us, we could see that newcomers to our specialized groups always had some difficulty "translating" this material in order to apply it to their own specific problems with sex addiction. A few years ago, someone asked when we were going to write our own book. The collective answer to that question came in a single word: *"Tomorrow."* At the time, we didn't realize the complexity of the task we were undertaking or the degree of patience we would have to exercise in order to see a book through to publication. More than once during the writing and editing processes, we agreed that if we'd known just how difficult and time-consuming the project would be, we would have been reluctant to begin at all. But it seems that each time our frustration peaked, we received yet another request for help from someone and our commitment was renewed and strengthened once again.

The overwhelming number of requests for guidance that we received from people throughout the country helped us set our primary goal for this book: we decided that it must be comprehensive and practical enough so that it would enable any two people using it to form a working group and effectively adapt the Twelve Steps to the problem of sex addiction. We decided that it would be essential to include personal stories of *recovering* addicts and we also felt that these stories should illustrate not only the shame and pain of addiction, but also the struggle, hope, and joy of recovery. We trust that these stories will encourage people and show them—with real-life examples—that they are not alone and that recovery, especially the early phase, is hard work for *everyone*.

When twenty-four people work together on a sensitive and personal project such as this book, conflicts and disagreements are bound to arise. Of course we *did* have problems from time to time, but we never allowed these problems to undermine our working relationships with each other. When we *did* have conflicts and disagreements, we worked through them—not for the sake of trying to "win" an argument, but in the spirit of trying to build and reinforce mutual support and understanding. The manuscript for this book was reviewed by long-term members of various Twelve Step groups as well as by people who are not members of *any* Twelve Step group. Everyone involved in this project feels that in keeping with the Twelve Traditions, it is very important for us to remain anonymous. We also agree that it is important to remain anonymous *within the Program* regarding our work on this book. We feel that this complete anonymity helps to ensure that we will not be treated differently just because our personal stories are in print. We find that it is both encouraging and humbling to remind ourselves that we were simply in the right place at the right time to write this book...and that if *we* hadn't written it, another group of people almost certainly *would have*. The title of this book came to us one night after a lengthy discussion during which dozens of titles were suggested and subsequently rejected. Remembering an important Program slogan, "Keep It Simple," also helped us remember that the book deserved a title that made a clear and simple statement: *anyone can experience a new life of hope and recovery*.

Contents

Personal Stories of Addiction, Hope & Recovery

"Even though my recovery record is not a perfect one, the past two years have given me more of a sense of belonging as well as more peace and serenity than I ever thought possible."

"Living sanely means accepting where I've been and using that information to proceed to a new destination."

"I grew up and started admitting how I felt."

"Finding the Program was like having a ton of bricks lifted off my chest."

"What a relief it was not to be alone anymore and to finally turn my will over to my Higher Power."

"At last I was able to let go of the burden of resentment, one person at a time."

"...I would never exchange the honest imperfections of my life today for my old life of lies and delusions."

"Slowly, I'm learning that I don't need to be alone and I don't need to reject intimacy in an effort to protect myself."

"...forgiveness begins with ourselves, then grows to include those who have hurt us."

Appendix

The Twelve Steps*

Step One
We admitted we were powerless over our compulsive sexual behavior—that our lives had become unmanageable.

Step Two
Came to believe that a Power greater than ourselves could restore us to sanity.

Step Three
Made a decision to turn our will and our lives over to the care of God as we understood God.

Step Four
Made a searching and fearless moral inventory of ourselves.

Step Five
Admitted to God, to ourselves, and to another human being the exact nature of our wrongs.

Step Six
Were entirely ready to have God remove all these defects of character.

Step Seven
Humbly asked God to remove our shortcomings.

Step Eight
Made a list of all persons we had harmed and became willing to make amends to them all.

Step Nine
Made direct amends to such people wherever possible, except when to do so would injure them or others.

Step Ten
Continued to take personal inventory and when we were wrong promptly admitted it.

Step Eleven
Sought through prayer and meditation to improve our conscious contact with God, as we understood God, praying only for knowledge of God's will for us and the power to carry that out.

Step Twelve
Having had a spiritual awakening as the result of these Steps, we tried to carry this message to other sex addicts and to practice these principles in all of our activities.

* The Twelve Steps reprinted for adaptation with permission of AA World Services, Inc. © 1972.

The Twelve Steps As
a Program of Recovery

The Twelve Steps: special words that helped us recover from obsessive thinking and compulsive sexual behavior. Having this limited amount of material to work with was a real advantage for those of us who tended to complicate our lives. The Twelve Steps are very powerful and versatile tools—simple and straightforward enough to help the newcomer, yet substantive enough so that oldtimers in the Program can always gain new insights from them.

When we came to the Program, we were told that people from all backgrounds had used the original Twelve Steps of Alcoholics Anonymous—as well as the adaptations—to deal effectively with their addictions. And through our work in the Program, we discovered that the only thing people need to bring with them to the Program is a desire to change. We also were told that the Twelve Steps describe a fundamental recovery process that had worked effectively for other addicts. Looking back, we all agree that recovery is the most important thing we ever did for ourselves. But we needed to learn that we had to be patient and go slowly with recovery because it involves a very difficult process: changing patterns of thought and behavior that had controlled our lives. And it was important for us to remember that life changes don't happen quickly or easily. Our addiction kept us too blind to see the path of recovery without guidance from others, so we learned the Twelve Steps and how to work them both from and *with* other addicts.

The numbering of the Twelve Steps and the logical order in which they are presented helped us greatly, especially when we first began our work in the Program. Being compulsive people, we always wanted to reach our goals and "fix" things *immediately*—the faster the better. The following true story illustrates how we addicts tend to rush things: Two recovering addicts met with another addict not yet in the Program in order to explain the Program and the Twelve Steps to him. As it turned out, the man these recovering addicts talked to was eager and willing to begin a new way of life by learning the Twelve Steps and getting involved in the Program. After they met, the three people exchanged phone numbers and parted. Then, when one of the men returned home, he found on his recording machine the following message from the addict he had Twelve-Stepped less than an hour before: "I've finished Steps One through Four, *now what do you want me to do tomorrow?*" Indeed, many of us wanted to begin making amends and carrying the message to others *before* we had taken a really honest look at ourselves and our addiction. But we discovered that we could not make amends until we had completed our personal inventories. We also discovered that it was very difficult to ask God, as we understood God, to remove our shortcomings before we'd even had an opportunity to *identify* those shortcomings. When we finally understood that recovery is a lifelong, day-at-a-time process, we realized that we had as much time as we needed, and we began working at a pace that was most appropriate and comfortable for us.

Once we had worked through each of the Twelve Steps, we were able to conceptualize and use them together as a kind of "tool kit." It follows, then, that if we had worked on Steps One through Three only, we would have had only those three tools to choose in working the Program. When we were familiar with all of the Steps, we found that we were better able to choose the Steps that were best suited to the specific problems we were having. Steps One, Two, and Three helped us heal our relationship with the God of our understanding. Once this healing process began, we used Steps Four, Five, Six, and Seven to repair our relationship with ourselves. Steps Eight and Nine helped us to repair relationships with other people and Steps Ten, Eleven, and Twelve served us well as guidelines for our long-term maintenance program. We continue to work the Steps; we never *complete* them. For this reason, we refer to ourselves as recover*ing* rather than recover*ed* sex addicts.

We find that it is helpful to think of the Twelve Steps in the following way throughout our recovery: instead of finishing *the* Fifth Step, for example, we try to think in terms of finishing *a* Fifth Step. In fact, we continue to work the Fifth Step periodically throughout recovery, just as we continue to work many of the Steps. We remind ourselves that we can begin the process of recovery each and every morning of our lives. In the past, most of us found sufficient time to act out in some way every day. We had to learn to find time *for recovery* each day instead. Our question to ourselves changed and rather than asking "Can I afford to work on recovery today?" we began asking "Can I afford *not* to work on recovery today?" We also learned to be disciplined, not compulsive, in relation to our work in the Program. We began to see that when we were being compulsive about something, we were rigid and driven, but that when we were acting in a disciplined manner, we were flexible and much more willing to spend some extra time considering the options that were most appropriate for us.

The longer we were in recovery, the easier it became. But it was still important for us to be aware of and to practice the principles of recovery every day because *addiction does not permit us the luxury of procrastination.* We worked hard to resist any temptation to take half-measures and/or postpone our recovery. In the past, the consequences of our acting-out behaviors had always ensured that we'd never have enough time to focus our resources and energies on recovery. When we grew in recovery, we stopped using our jobs, our families, our health, and all other elements and situations in our lives as excuses for not being able to get on with the work of the Program. The Twelve Steps—as well as the Twelve Traditions—ultimately became a way of life for us. These concepts were not something we thought about only in meetings and applied only to our sexual behaviors; these concepts actually became an integral part of our philosophy of life. *Recovery cannot be rushed.* It was only with time and practice that we were able to fully integrate the Steps into our lives.

The Twelve Steps*

Step One
We admitted we were powerless over our compulsive sexual behavior—that our lives had become unmanageable.

Step Two
Came to believe that a Power greater than ourselves could restore us to sanity.

Step Three
Made a decision to turn our will and our lives over to the care of God as we understood God.

Step Four
Made a searching and fearless moral inventory of ourselves.

Step Five
Admitted to God, to ourselves, and to another human being the exact nature of our wrongs.

Step Six
Were entirely ready to have God remove all these defects of character.

Step Seven
Humbly asked God to remove our shortcomings.

Step Eight
Made a list of all persons we had harmed and became willing to make amends to them all.

Step Nine
Made direct amends to such people wherever possible, except when to do so would injure them or others.

Step Ten
Continued to take personal inventory and when we were wrong promptly admitted it.

Step Eleven
Sought through prayer and meditation to improve our conscious contact with God, as we understood God, praying only for knowledge of God's will for us and the power to carry that out.

Step Twelve
Having had a spiritual awakening as the result of these Steps, we tried to carry this message to other sex addicts and to practice these principles in all of our activities.

* The Twelve Steps reprinted for adaptation with permission of AA World Services, Inc. © 1972.

1

Am I Really Out of Control?

"Sex Addict"—the words conjured up terrible images in our minds and reminded us of other words like "sick," "pervert," and "fiend." Most of us agree that the fear of being labelled sex addicts made us very reluctant to examine our sexual behaviors. But the Twelve Steps address this common fear directly. Note that the First Step begins with the word *We*; the words reassure us that others know what we have suffered and that the cause of our suffering and desperation can be identified.

When we understood and accepted the words "sex addict," we also gained new insights about our thoughts and behaviors. We learned that we were not hopelessly demented, wicked, or forever damned; *we were addicts*. And as sex addicts, we were people who continued to act out sexually, even as our lives continued to be negatively affected by our sexual behaviors. Much to our relief, we learned that addiction is not a symptom of weak will power or a lack of self-discipline. Indeed, many of us evidenced great self-discipline and will power in other areas of our lives. But we came to see that trying to control sex addiction with will power is like trying to *think away a broken leg*. Try as we might and however good our intentions, will power is just not effective in dealing with the complex problem of sex addiction. *Besides, most of us had unsuccessfully tried to use our will power to fight our sex addiction many times.*

The use of the pronoun *We* in the First Step also reinforces the fact that addicts cannot recover alone. Addicts need the help of other addicts in order to stop their acting-out behaviors. We learned through experience that when it came to dealing with our sex addiction we were powerless as individuals, but that as a fellowship we had power. Our addiction had isolated us from other people emotionally, if not physically. But we came to understand that in order to recover, we had to be with other people and share with them.

We also learned not to confuse our admission/acknowledgment that we were powerless with the sense of being fundamentally bad people. Instead, our admission is merely a statement that we understand our problem realistically. We believe that "admitted" is another way of saying that we are aware of or have conceded the truth. *Essentially, we had to surrender to something more powerful than ourselves.* Continuing on with our fight would have brought certain destruction. For many of us, our choices finally came down to: incarceration, insanity, or untimely death from disease, homicide, or suicide. But the Program taught us that we had another choice as well: *surrender and subsequent recovery*. We learned that there was absolutely *no reason* to be ashamed of wanting to change our lives and make them better.

The process involved in gaining new insights about ourselves and our addiction was very painful. For so long, our acting-out behaviors had successfully helped us avoid or numb our feelings. We learned that acting out was, for us, *any* sexual behavior or obsessive thinking that we engaged in to deny our feelings or distract ourselves from our feelings. Some of us came to see, for example, that even if we cruised for six hours and *did not* pick up a sex partner, we were still acting out—that our compulsive cruising was an acting-out behavior in and of itself because of the way we used it. When we began the First Step process by carefully looking at our thought and behavior patterns, some of us were able to see for the first time the hurt, loneliness, guilt, and shame that we had so desperately tried to avoid or deny. Many of us attempted to escape these insights by returning to addictive thinking. But we learned that this was only another sign that we needed to have other addicts around us during our First Step work. We needed these people around to help deter us from acting out in reaction to the pain of our insights.

After admitting our powerlessness, some of us then tried to use it as an excuse to continue acting out. ("Well, what else do you expect of me? I can't help it; remember, I'm an addict and I'm powerless.") But we learned that *powerless does not mean helpless*. Once we came to know the Twelve Steps and the fellowship, it seemed we no longer had any excuses left for not attending to our recovery. In working the First Step, we learned some important concepts that became vital to our healing. First of all, we learned that we were not to blame for becoming sex addicts; we did not consciously *choose* this addiction. We were, however, responsible for our recovery and for repairing the damage we had done to ourselves and to others through our acting-out behaviors. Powerlessness will never be an excuse for continuing acting-out behaviors.

At first, most of us desperately tried to convince ourselves (and others) that we were somehow different from other people and that what *appeared* to be addiction was not addiction *in our situations*. Many of us told ourselves that other people had, after all, done many of the same things *we* had done, yet *they* weren't considered sex addicts. Some of us told ourselves that we weren't addicts because our particular acting-out behaviors began out of curiosity or simply in the spirit of fun and adventure. But the Program helped us see that it really didn't matter *how or why* our behaviors started in the first place. The fact is, *we had become addicts*; exploring the hows and whys of our addiction would not be enough to make us stop. The fact is, our addiction had taken on a powerful, uncontrollable life of its own. Some of us searched our individual stories in desperate but futile attempts to determine when we might have crossed some invisible line and become addicts. But insight could only *motivate* us to seek change; insight couldn't *make* us change. We could not think our way out of our situation; *we had to act*

3

our way into a new pattern of thinking instead. It was definitely time for action.

At first we found that our minds were working overtime, frantically trying to make sense of the insanity that is addiction. Some of us even imagined that we could eventually regain control of our sexual behavior without any help or support. But as we look back, we realize that many of us knew that our sexual behavior was controlling our lives. Within the Program, we had to progress to a point where we could accept the fact that we could *not* stop what we were doing on our own. In fact, we came to see that we could stop what we were doing only when we acknowledged and accepted this paradox. As long as we continued to derive satisfaction from the times when it merely *looked as if* we were in control, we simply weren't ready to stop our addictive behaviors.

Those of us who spent time and energy pointing out to ourselves and others how our sexual behaviors were not creating problems only succeeded in avoiding the real issues. *Isolated incidents of control were not important*. We came to see that the most important thing was the overall pattern of our thoughts and behaviors and that, furthermore, certain thoughts and behaviors created problems in our lives. Taking the most objective look we could at things, we saw that if we *had* been in control, we wouldn't have had so many problems: for example, we wouldn't have had to struggle so much and risk jobs, health, friends, family, our very *lives*, in fact, in order to act out. If our acting-out behaviors were just bad habits, then the tremendous problems they created in our lives would have been enough to make us change or stop. But the fact that we continued on with our behaviors *despite* the problems they created in our lives told us that we were addicts. We looked carefully at what we had done and also at the effects these things had on our lives and how we felt about everything. In many cases, our primary problem was not our acting-out behaviors *themselves*, but how they ultimately affected our lives.

Most of us found that our major problem was not stopping our behaviors in the first place, but *staying stopped*. While many of us had relatively long periods of time when we did not act out, we eventually resumed our acting-out behaviors. Countless times we promised ourselves, our loved ones, and our God that we would stop forever and "never do those things again." We realize now that no addict can make such promises. Our failure to keep our word in these matters did not mean we were lying. *We failed in our attempts to maintain our abstinence because of our addiction.* And given our powerlessness as addicts, we simply cannot make forever/never promises of this kind. Countless broken promises to ourselves and others and our compulsive need to place our addictive urges before anything else in our lives led us and those around us to the belief that we had no value as people. This belief then added to our feelings of low self-worth and shame, making it all the more likely that we would act out again. But even as we were caught up in this destructive cycle, we could see that something was terribly wrong. We didn't have a word for what was wrong at the time, or perhaps we tried to blame everything on someone or something else. In our hearts, though, many of us sensed all along that our sexual behavior was related to our feelings that things were wrong. People in our lives may have tried to tell us that they could see our pain, but we were always too frightened, too angry, too numb to really "hear" them.

At first, most of us were actually more fearful of living life without our acting-out behaviors than we were of continuing to live the painful lives of active sex addicts. *But when the pain of acting out became so debilitating that recovery seemed easier, we were finally able to admit our powerlessness.* For so long, we denied having any problems at all, even when others could see so clearly what was happening to us. We looked back

5

fondly on the "good times" and remembered the "highs" we'd experienced during those times. When our problems were finally too devastating to deny or ignore any longer, we were angered at the thought of giving up what we had perceived, in our insanity, to be the best part of our lives. *Our sexual behavior had always been there for us* and we truly believed that it would never let us down. We were angry that our behavior had progressed from being simply a way to escape pain to become *the primary source of pain in our lives*. We were angry and wanted to blame other people in our lives for our problems: ("If he/she wouldn't dress that way!" "They made me act like that!" "It's their fault!" "You saw how she came on to me; what else could I do?") We were able to think of many things to blame our behavior on—everything, that is, but our addiction. We'd cite our spouse's behavior or our work as reasons for our acting-out behaviors. (Most of us chose to ignore the fact that there were people all around us with challenging relationships and/or similar jobs who did not act out at all).

Many of us were further angered to think that there was a God who would allow us to hurt in the way we hurt as active addicts. *Our anger made sense*; how and where we directed our anger became the primary problem. Once we learned to redirect our anger toward our *addiction*—where it belonged—we used the energy that came from it for *recovery* rather than for useless and nonproductive blaming.

At first we tried to bargain with our sponsors, our families, and ourselves—"Just let me hold on to this part of my past; I'll only engage in this behavior on special occasions!" But it was not our sponsor's responsibility—or anyone else's—to prove to us or convince us that we were sex addicts; *that determination was completely up to us*. We found that in reality it was *our addiction*, not other people, we were attempting to bargain with. But we cannot bargain with addiction. As the Big Book reminds us, "Half measures availed us nothing" (p. 59).

When we really saw our powerlessness, many of us initially felt an almost overwhelming sense of hopelessness. Seemingly, there was no way out of this trap we were in. In *choosing* to recover, we were giving up more than just our acting-out behaviors. Indeed, we found that in order to progress in recovery, we also needed to let go of some of our friends, some of our activities, some of our favorite places to relax and socialize, even some of our humor. It was extremely difficult for most of us to let go of these things, but our sponsors and other group members helped us work through our fears and the adjustments we needed to make. As we talked with others, we could see for ourselves that as recovering sex addicts, our lives could be filled with wonderful things and genuine feelings that we could face and deal with effectively. They told us that we would not always feel so depressed and they reassured us that in recovery we would make gains and grow in ways that we could only *imagine* when we first came to the Program. We began to trust and accept the support that these recovering addicts offered us.

Of course the problems we faced as sex addicts were not limited to our sexual behaviors. Most of us could see that our overall health—physical, mental, and spiritual—had been adversely affected by our sex addiction. In fact, the second half of the First Step addresses this total, whole-person involvement. We came to see that *unmanageability* was the price we paid in order to continue acting out. Note that the First Step uses a hyphen rather than the word *and* between the words powerless/ unmanageable. We have come to see that this is because powerlessness and unmanageability do not represent two separate elements, but two interrelated elements of the same relentless progression of addiction. In fact, we see this hyphen functioning much like an equal sign. When we were acting out (*our powerlessness*)—we suffered the consequences of our acts (*our unmanageability*.) Likewise, when we allowed our lives to become unmanageable (dysfunctional, unorganized, and out of

7

balance), we began acting out again. This cycle continued on and eventually a pattern was established: in order to bury the pain/shame we were feeling because of our acting-out behaviors, we acted out again. *It began to look and feel as if we were trapped*. We couldn't stop acting out. We found that it simply didn't work to think that if we only straightened out our lives, we could resume our acting-out behaviors and never struggle with problems again. *We had to address each and every area of our lives*. Just as our addiction affected every area of our lives, so would recovery affect every area of our lives.

One of our primary goals in working on the First Step is to gain understanding and acceptance of our addiction. But we discovered that this understanding and acceptance had to be much more than intellectual acceptance, it had to be *emotional acceptance* as well. We knew that we had achieved this emotional acceptance when we finally admitted that we were addicts and felt free to speak about our addiction to other addicts without feeling ashamed. In order to gain a full emotional understanding of how our addiction had affected us, we wrote histories of our own acting-out behaviors that focused on our feelings and the consequences related to our actions. In the process of recording this history, many memories and feelings were stirred up that we'd hoped never to have to deal with again. At this point, many of us slipped into a euphoric recall and so-called *stinkin' thinkin'* and actually began considering ways we could resume our old acting-out behaviors. We'd say things like "It really wasn't that bad," and "Gosh, I miss all the fun I used to have." After working on our histories, we all agreed to call another recovering addict each day. This commitment to communicate with other addicts served as a kind of insurance that we wouldn't set ourselves up to act out again. As we talked on the phone with other addicts about how we were thinking and feeling at those times, we began to realize once more that words like "fun" and "excitement" were not accurate descriptions of what we had been through. Kneeling in the stall of a public toilet, having sex with someone we disliked, or waking up next to a total stranger are activities more accurately described with words like "fear," "loneliness," "desperation," and "shame."

We shared our stories with our sponsors and/or groups; in turn, our sponsors and groups pointed out patterns they could see in our lives and asked us questions about facts they felt we may have glossed over or omitted completely in attempts to avoid embarrassment, shame, or pain. Sharing our personal stories with others was a terribly frightening thing to do at first. Above all, we feared rejection. But we were overwhelmed by the acceptance and affection directed toward us when we shared our most painful secrets. And each time we shared our stories at retreats, meetings, or in the process of making Twelve Step calls, our isolation and shame lessened. We also learned something new each time we told our stories or heard other peoples' stories. And whenever we were reminded of the pain of that way of life, our desire to recover was renewed.

As we recounted our individual stories, we could see the point at which we hit bottom or even the precise moment when we finally said "This is too much; I can't go on. I'll do whatever it takes not to have to live like this anymore." For each of us, that moment came at different times and stages—being arrested, losing still another relationship, being so lonely while surrounded by others, and wanting to die and finally be free of the whole thing. What was it that happened or didn't happen that we finally were ready? Each addict must determine for himself or herself when he or she hits bottom. Some of those who never did hit bottom or change in any way subsequently died painful deaths as active addicts. Our sponsors encouraged us to keep the circumstances and feelings involved in hitting bottom forever in our memories. We were advised to do this so that we could use these feelings as a guide. Each time we were faced with the possibility of acting out, we recalled the details of hitting bottom and asked ourselves the following question: *"Is what I'm about to do worth the pain of resuming that way of life?"* As long as we kept an honest view of the experience of hitting bottom in our minds, the answer to ourselves was always *"No!"*

As soon as we shared our First Step with our sponsors and other group members, we were tempted to share our stories with our friends and families. We were anxious to do this in order to explain our past behaviors to them. But it was better, we found, to wait and share our stories after we'd had more time in recovery and had worked more of the Steps. Even then, we looked to our group conscience to help us decide which people in our lives needed to know what facts about our addiction and how much they needed to know. Being honest does *not* mean manipulating or abusing others by revealing information in ways that might harm them. Most of us had poor boundaries and we could have harmed ourselves and others further by indiscriminately sharing the details of our stories with them. As is true with so many of the elements in the process of recovery, we found that "Easy Does It" was a helpful reminder as we worked the First Step.

The Twelve Steps*

Step One
We admitted we were powerless over our compulsive sexual behavior—that our lives had become unmanageable.

Step Two
Came to believe that a Power greater than ourselves could restore us to sanity.

Step Three
Made a decision to turn our will and our lives over to the care of God as we understood God.

Step Four
Made a searching and fearless moral inventory of ourselves.

Step Five
Admitted to God, to ourselves, and to another human being the exact nature of our wrongs.

Step Six
Were entirely ready to have God remove all these defects of character.

Step Seven
Humbly asked God to remove our shortcomings.

Step Eight
Made a list of all persons we had harmed and became willing to make amends to them all.

Step Nine
Made direct amends to such people wherever possible, except when to do so would injure them or others.

Step Ten
Continued to take personal inventory and when we were wrong promptly admitted it.

Step Eleven
Sought through prayer and meditation to improve our conscious contact with God, as we understood God, praying only for knowledge of God's will for us and the power to carry that out.

Step Twelve
Having had a spiritual awakening as the result of these Steps, we tried to carry this message to other sex addicts and to practice these principles in all of our activities.

* The Twelve Steps reprinted for adaptation with permission of AA World Services, Inc. © 1972.

2

There Is Help

The First Step tells us that we can remove our acting-out behavior. *The Second Step then tells us that we can replace this acting-out behavior with something else.* The first two Steps essentially communicate the following concepts: *"We cannot control our addiction"* and *"We think something else can control our addiction."*

Once we identified our problem and had a name for it as well, we knew that we needed to make some fundamental changes in our lives. Efforts to change were nothing new to most of us because we had already tried to stop or somehow alter our addictive sexual behavior many times. For so long we'd held the belief that sex could fix whatever was wrong in our lives. Once we acknowledged our problem, however, we could see that we had to seek out an entirely different kind of help. *At this point, the key question we had to ask ourselves was this: Am I willing to believe that my addiction can be arrested only if I seek help from a power other than my own will and determination?*

We were ready to work the Second Step once we were truly willing to *believe. Note that the Second Step does not suggest that we ask for faith or trust.* Eventually we came to see that our faith and trust develop naturally as we work the Third Step. In contrast, *the Second Step is a kind of mental inventory that helps us decide for ourselves that there is, indeed, something greater than ourselves that we can believe in.* The Second Step helped us break through a powerful myth that had intensified our shame and fear, a myth that told us our addiction was so powerful that nothing could be done about it and that we were doomed to struggle with our acting-out behaviors for the rest of our lives.

Once we really understood the Second Step, we found that we could no longer take refuge in our ignorance. When we finally realized that the Second Step tells us that there *is* a way out of our dilemma if we choose it, trusted old rationalizations no longer held up ("It's just too much; I've tried everything" or "It's hopeless; I may as well give up and act out all I can!"). And our acting-out behaviors were never quite the same once we learned more about recovery and came to know that we *could recover. Our belief in the Second Step led us to believe in the power it describes.*

"A power greater than ourselves"—those of us who were atheists or agnostics resented this phrase at first because it sounded to us like a reference to God. We were assured, however, that the group itself could be regarded as this Higher Power. At our first few meetings, we looked around us and saw others who had gone through the same torment as we had, yet who were no longer filled with shame and hopelessness as we were. In fact, these people had a serenity that we could have only *wished* for. At meetings we listened to dramatic and inspiring stories about addicts who had been free from obsessive thinking and acting-out behaviors for months, *even years. And there we were, sitting with these people and desperately hoping for just a few hours of freedom from the torment of our addictive urges.* Surely this group of addicts with its collective wisdom, experience, support, objectivity, and success in dealing with a powerful addiction represented a power greater than that of any individual addict; we learned that we could choose to see things in this way if we wanted to. *In order to stop rationalizing our acting-out behaviors, we had to stop denying that there was anything more powerful than we were.* The Big Book summarizes all of this simply and memorably when it says: "We had to quit playing God" (p. 62).

After a time in recovery, we began to wonder if the phenomenon we had always thought of as *luck* was really some kind of *spiritual force*. We often wondered how in the world we had managed to survive everything we'd been through. So many times we had placed ourselves in great danger in the process of acting out, yet somehow we survived.

We have come to see the Second Step as a promise that we can, indeed, recover and return to a natural and healthy state. Essentially the Second Step is a stated promise of future sexual health. At first most of us had some difficulty with the Second Step phrase "restore us to sanity" because of its implication that we had been insane. In time most of us freely admitted that we were sex addicts; admitting to insanity proved to be more difficult for many of us. But as we looked carefully at the First Step, we could see that many of our actions were, in fact, senseless and that *insanity* was a completely accurate description for them. It is *not sane* to repeat self-destructive behaviors; it is *not sane* to make the same mistake several times and expect a different outcome each time; it is *not sane* to believe that sex can solve our problems.

We came to understand that we had continued to act out sexually in desperate efforts to avoid feelings of loneliness, fear, sadness, shame, guilt, anger, and unhappiness. But as we listened to the stories shared by other addicts, we realized that no matter how much we acted out sexually, those behaviors could not prevent or even lessen these feelings. In the end, we found that to squabble over a word we disliked—such as insanity—was to completely miss the hopefulness that develops through working the Second Step.

"Restore us to sanity" also implies that we had been sane. So many of us had come to believe that we were *born defective*. The Program assured us that even though we were wounded and scarred, *we were not defective people*. Our insanity continued on, even as we began to recover. For example, believing that we were different from other addicts, some of us decided that we could probably limit our acting out to *weekends only* or that we could act out *just one time*, then stop through the sheer strength of our will power. Some of us decided that we were somehow different from other people and that the Program just wouldn't work for us. But we learned that these mind games were just further examples of how insidious our addiction was and how it continued to tell us lies, setting us up to act out time and time again.

After we became willing to accept the concept of a Higher Power, we worked to gain more knowledge of that power in order to move on to the Third Step—turning our lives over to our Higher Power. But we realized that we needed to have a practical understanding of our Higher Power in order to make use of that power in the Second Step. As we studied, contemplated, and discussed spirituality with others, we learned to call upon our Higher Power in the Second Step as well as in all subsequent Steps. *Ultimately, the Second Step helped us define spirituality for ourselves.*

At first many of us found it very difficult to distinguish between spirituality and religion. Some of us continued to act out even as we worked hard to study and practice various religions. And because we had prayed yet still were unable to stop acting out, we just assumed that our prayers had been ignored. Until we realized that religious conviction alone does not *guarantee* a spiritual awakening, many of us were deeply distrustful of the concept of a Higher Power and of the entire process of turning our lives over. Our shame led us to believe that even though we sought to have a relationship with God, God apparently didn't want to have anything to do with *us*. Those of us who had no sense of our own spirituality naturally found it very difficult to either write about our beliefs or discuss them with other addicts. Many of us were, however, perfectly willing to talk about what we did *not* believe. This starting point was probably as valid as any we could find. We identified the spiritual concepts that were *least* useful to us, then took that list to recovering addicts and asked them to help us identify the options that remained for us. The guideline most often suggested to us was that our Higher Power ought to be loving, caring, and a power greater than ourselves. *We found new hope and freedom when we came to understand that spirituality is defined from within.*

The Twelve Steps*

Step One
We admitted we were powerless over our compulsive sexual behavior—that our lives had become unmanageable.

Step Two
Came to believe that a Power greater than ourselves could restore us to sanity.

Step Three
Made a decision to turn our will and our lives over to the care of God as we understood God.

Step Four
Made a searching and fearless moral inventory of ourselves.

Step Five
Admitted to God, to ourselves, and to another human being the exact nature of our wrongs.

Step Six
Were entirely ready to have God remove all these defects of character.

Step Seven
Humbly asked God to remove our shortcomings.

Step Eight
Made a list of all persons we had harmed and became willing to make amends to them all.

Step Nine
Made direct amends to such people wherever possible, except when to do so would injure them or others.

Step Ten
Continued to take personal inventory and when we were wrong promptly admitted it.

Step Eleven
Sought through prayer and meditation to improve our conscious contact with God, as we understood God, praying only for knowledge of God's will for us and the power to carry that out.

Step Twelve
Having had a spiritual awakening as the result of these Steps, we tried to carry this message to other sex addicts and to practice these principles in all of our activities.

* The Twelve Steps reprinted for adaptation with permission of AA World Services, Inc. © 1972.

3

Accepting the Help

The First and Second Steps help us acknowledge our sex addiction as well as the fact that help is available. For many of us, *accepting* this help was much more difficult than acknowledging our addiction and the help available. For so long, *our addictive thinking* told us that we should be able to solve our problems by ourselves and that we should—and could—recover on our own.

The Third Step essentially asks us to make a crucial decision: *Do we really want what the Program has to offer?* Our families, friends, lawyers, therapists, sponsors, clergymen, social workers, or probation officers cannot make this decision for us. We must make this decision by and for ourselves based on our freedom of choice. But just making an affirmative decision did not change us; *the actions we took as a result of our decision changed our thinking and our behavior.*

The Third Step asks us to "turn our will over to the care of God." For so long we had been such willful people. Many of us believed that through our will power *alone*, we could stop any thought or behavior or remove ourselves from any situation. But when we worked the first three Steps, we could see for ourselves that even the strongest, most disciplined will power was no match at all for the power of this addiction. Most of us had become accustomed to using our intelligence and ingenuity to justify our thoughts and behaviors to others and to ourselves. As the Big Book says, an addict's life is "self-will run riot" (p. 62). The Program taught us to use whatever skills we have to enhance our recovery rather than to perpetuate our addiction.

We never set a goal to stop thinking about sex entirely, for to do so would have been to completely deny our sexuality. In time we came to see that our major problem was not the fact that we *had* sexual thoughts, but that we engaged in *obsessive* thinking about sex in order to hide from reality and to escape or deny our feelings. In recovery we first began thinking about sex in healthy and self-affirming ways. For instance, instead of replaying past acting-out behaviors or thinking obsessively about the future, *we learned to focus on the here and now.* Of course we continued to have normal sexual urges and desires and some of these urges and desires were healthy to act on. *But we knew that we were really working the Third Step when we were finally relieved of our obsessive sexual thoughts.*

Before we recovered, we were preoccupied even when we weren't acting out because we always allowed our thoughts to drift back to past behaviors or race ahead with plans for our next binge. When we really began working the Program and were no longer preoccupied in this way, we became less self-centered and began to pay attention to the ways that our actions affected us and other people in our lives as well. Soon we found that we were able to think about our behavior and its possible consequences, then carefully choose the course of action that would keep us on a spiritual path. When we finally turned our will and our lives over to our Higher Power, we made a conscious decision to fill our minds with *spiritual thoughts* rather than with obsessive thoughts about sex. This decision meant, of course, that we could no longer hide in a fantasy world of sex and power.

The Third Step refers to turning over our lives to God. We have come to understand that *this phrase really refers to the need to change our behaviors as well as our thoughts. In time, our behaviors did change.* We came to see that we were making a conscious decision to turn our lives over to the care of God each and every time we chose *not to* pick up a pornographic magazine, or chose *not to* drive around the block again and again seeking out an attractive person we saw on the street, or chose *not to* wait by a window in anticipation of watching someone undress. Even when our new behaviors seemed insignificant to us, we trusted those who had preceded us in the Program and tried our best to "act as if" we really *did* believe in the importance of what we were doing. Of course, any new skill we learn requires practice; *recovery is no different.*

After a time in recovery, we began to really *experience* the changes in our thinking and behavior. For example, when we saw an attractive person, we allowed ourselves to acknowledge our feelings and the fact that we felt attracted to him or to her, but we chose not to engage in sexual fantasies about that person. Some of us found it helpful to use a "three-second rule"—we allowed ourselves to appreciate another person's attractiveness for three seconds, then deliberately turned our thoughts to other things. In time we came to know that just because we found other people particularly attractive, we did not *have* to think of those people in sexual terms. We learned that by reaching out to other sex addicts or our Higher Power for help, we could actually *arrest* the addictive cycle before we had the chance to set ourselves up to act out obsessive thoughts. When these kinds of thoughts entered our awareness, we did not dwell on them, nor did we attempt to embellish them. Rather than struggling with efforts to *not* think about our addiction, *we concentrated on our recovery instead.* In fact we came to see that our addictive thoughts intensified when we chastised or punished ourselves for them or attempted to fight them.

In turning "our will and our lives over to the care of God" we were essentially turning over all that we did and all that we were. We knew that a fundamental change like this would require a major commitment on our part and, naturally, we were very frightened. We had no idea what might happen to us if we gave up our basic belief that we were in control. *Who or what would be there to protect us then?* Many of us had grown up without parental support and guidance; consequently, as adults in recovery, we were fearful that God would leave us to the same unpredictability, emptiness, and loneliness that we had become so familiar with as children.

As addicts, we were already well acquainted with one kind of power greater than ourselves: *our addiction*. In many ways we had treated this addiction as a god and we had come to believe that it was the answer to *everything*. Most of us had completely turned our lives over to our addiction. But as we began to work the Program, it became quite apparent to us that the trust we'd had in our addiction was not well placed. We finally recognized the fact that our addiction was not only letting us down, *but destroying us as well*. It is not so surprising, then, that we feared a similar experience if we gave ourselves over to another power greater than ourselves. But the Third Step makes a very important and distinctive promise when it refers to "the *care* of God," rather than the *control* of God. In time we came to see the Third Step as a promise of support and guidance rather than a reference to control and rigidity. We came to believe that *this God would not turn on us*.

Looking back, we can see that initially many of us were skeptical about the spiritual nature of the Program because we'd had negative experiences with religion. But with help from others, we found that we were able to distinguish between *spirituality* and the actions and rituals carried out in the name of God and religion. This clarification not only helped us become less defensive and negative, it also helped us open ourselves up to the real purpose and meaning of the Twelve Steps. On the other hand, those of us who came to the Program with long-held and cherished religious beliefs feared that the Program would somehow require us to choose between recovery and our religious beliefs. We were relieved and pleased to learn that the Twelve Steps—as spiritual suggestions—do not interfere in any way with our religious beliefs.

Tradition Two includes the following phrase: "a loving God as that God may express Himself/Herself in our group conscience." This Tradition, we discovered, essentially tells us that it isn't necessary for everyone in the group to share the same beliefs. Indeed, Tradition Three reminds us that "The only requirement for membership...is a desire to stop compulsive behavior." We also found that the Program gave us freedom to believe whatever was true and meaningful for us. We found that we were able to use whatever image of God worked for us. Anything we surrendered to became our God. "God as we understood God" came to mean that the group, with its strength and guidance, could function as a Higher Power if that concept worked best for us.

The lessons we learned in the process of working the Second Step and the sense of safety we felt at meetings combined to give us courage to work the Third Step fully and effectively. Early on, it was especially comforting to remind ourselves often that the Program works One Day At A Time, and that we only needed to make a decision to "turn our will and our lives over to the care of God" for each twenty-four-hour period of time. We need not think in terms of making a decision for the rest of our lives. In fact, each and every morning of our lives we are free to choose: we can turn that particular day over to the care of God, or we can attempt to recover alone.

When we finally made the decision to become recovering addicts, we learned to ask for help from other addicts and from our Higher Power as well. Sooner or later, we all came to see and believe how vitally important it is to have the help of a Higher Power in order to progress from abstinence (not acting out) to real sobriety (abstinence combined with ongoing spiritual growth). The Big Book wisely reminds us that "Half measures availed us nothing" (p. 59). *The Third Step really addresses not just our addictive behaviors, but our lives as a whole.* We came to know that if recovery was to become a way of life for us, it had to involve much more than just the *absence* of acting-out behavior. This important concept is reinforced by our adapted Twelfth Step ("practice these principles in all of our activities.") In all aspects of our lives—in our jobs and in our relationships with friends and family—we began asking ourselves this question: *What is the most meaningful and effective spiritual course I can choose in this situation?*

As it turned out, some addicts were completely unwilling to go beyond the first two Steps. Even though they admitted their powerlessness and believed that there was help for their addiction, they refused to trust the Program and the process involved in accepting the help they needed. These addicts wanted to recover, but they wanted to recover on their own terms and they wanted to do so without effort or pain. The only thing we could do to help these people was to continue working *our own Program* and offering a reminder that the Steps promise a "spiritual awakening," but *only* "as the result of (working) these Steps." Recovery did not come easily for *any* of us.

Many of us did, in fact, "white-knuckle" our early recovery. We held on tight and tried to control our lives through the strength of our determination and will power. Some of us steadfastly refused to change *anything* about ourselves or our lives, with the exception of our most obvious and destructive acting-out behaviors. But relying on will power alone created some very painful and unpleasant situations for us and for the people around us; in fact our behavior made some of our fellow addicts and family members so uncomfortable that they actually told us to hurry up, have our slip, and get it over with. But contrary to what many of us believed at first, recovery is not a test of our endurance. *Recovery teaches us how to flow with life, not how to fight against life.*

As we began to take the action suggested in order to recover, we usually did so in a fairly compliant manner. We told ourselves that we'd have to go to meetings and call on others. We shared a desire to recover, but most of us resented the effort and personal changes that recovery seemed to require. How quickly we forgot just how much time and energy we had always used to maintain our addictive behavior. But the longer we were familiar with and used the Third Step, the less discomfort and resentment we felt about it and about the Program as a whole.

As we learned to trust the Program unconditionally, we began to surrender to it. We knew that we always had a choice. We did not *have* to do anything, but we did choose to attend meetings. We felt very grateful for the opportunity to recover when we finally began to see recovery as a gift formed from the wreckage of our addiction. We began to see that prayer, meditation, attending meetings, phoning others, and making Twelve Step calls were all clear signs that we were actively working the Third Step. Those of us who now sponsor other recovering addicts encourage those people to write out their Programs and regularly review them in order to see exactly how they are turning their lives over and changing as well. We also encourage these people to be as specific as possible about the components of their Program—from the number of times they pray each day, to the number of meetings they attend each week, to the number of phone calls they make to other addicts.

As part of our ongoing Tenth Step Inventory, many of us maintain a journal detailing how we have turned things over to God each day. We used simple prayers such as "Thy will, not mine, be done" and the slogan "Let Go And Let God" as well as the words of the Eleventh Step—we pray "only for knowledge of God's will for us and the power to carry that out." We have found that the more effort we put into looking for spiritual things, the more spiritual things we see. In time, we came to believe that the benefits of recovery are far greater than the costs of recovery.

The Twelve Steps*

Step One
We admitted we were powerless over our compulsive sexual behavior—that our lives had become unmanageable.

Step Two
Came to believe that a Power greater than ourselves could restore us to sanity.

Step Three
Made a decision to turn our will and our lives over to the care of God as we understood God.

Step Four
Made a searching and fearless moral inventory of ourselves.

Step Five
Admitted to God, to ourselves, and to another human being the exact nature of our wrongs.

Step Six
Were entirely ready to have God remove all these defects of character.

Step Seven
Humbly asked God to remove our shortcomings.

Step Eight
Made a list of all persons we had harmed and became willing to make amends to them all.

Step Nine
Made direct amends to such people wherever possible, except when to do so would injure them or others.

Step Ten
Continued to take personal inventory and when we were wrong promptly admitted it.

Step Eleven
Sought through prayer and meditation to improve our conscious contact with God, as we understood God, praying only for knowledge of God's will for us and the power to carry that out.

Step Twelve
Having had a spiritual awakening as the result of these Steps, we tried to carry this message to other sex addicts and to practice these principles in all of our activities.

* The Twelve Steps reprinted for adaptation with permission of AA World Services, Inc. © 1972.

4

Threshold to Self-Knowledge

Some of us were so afraid of the prospects of examining our thoughts and behaviors that we tried to postpone, delay, or otherwise avoid moving on to the Fourth Step. Some of us thought that by working diligently on the first Three Steps only, or by working all of the other Steps while ignoring the Fourth Step, we might be able to "get by" in the Program. But it didn't take long for us to realize that we simply cannot by-pass any one Step and still work the Program effectively.

We learned that the recovery process works best for us when we follow the path that is suggested by the Twelve Steps. We really need to work the Fourth Step in order to move on to the Fifth Step and admit the exact nature of our wrongs, then proceed to the Sixth and Seventh Steps to identify our character defects and have our shortcomings removed. Completion of the Fourth Step inventory is also very important in our efforts to be thorough and specific in preparing our lists in the Eighth Step and making amends in the Ninth Step. By the time we get to the Tenth Step and the concept of ongoing personal inventories, we can see that without careful attention to the Fourth Step, every Step that follows it is severely weakened.

Our deep feelings of shame made so many of us unwilling to look at the past. Above all, we had come to think of ourselves as defective people; we were fearful that if we were to take a really honest look at ourselves, we'd discover that we were, indeed, the horrible people we had thought ourselves to be. We came to understand that our feelings of shame and low self-esteem had actually *nurtured* our addiction. As long as we held on to these negative beliefs about ourselves, we'd continue to punish ourselves and would therefore be much more likely to act out. Once we understood and overcame our resistance to working on the Fourth Step, we found new freedom from the bondage of the past.

The Fourth Step also gave us the opportunity to finally *put into practice* our decision to turn our lives over to the care of God as we understood God. We learned to *act as if* we believed we would be cared for and we willingly carried out the specific tasks suggested by the Steps. Having completed these tasks suggested by the Steps, we realized that our faith and trust in our Higher Power began to grow. Then each time we worked a Step, our faith and trust grew stronger. We found that the "searching" referred to in this Step meant going to any lengths we had to in order to inventory both our liabilities and our assets. We needed to look at our liabilities not to punish ourselves, but to examine the issues that continued to haunt us. *Only when we faced and accepted ourselves as we were* did we gain the freedom and confidence we needed to choose a different and healthier way of life. *Self-honesty is fundamental to this Program; we really cannot recover without getting to know ourselves.*

As we worked on the Fourth Step, our sponsors and others in our groups encouraged us to be as specific, detailed, and thorough as possible in recounting the patterns of thinking and behavior we had engaged in. One way these people helped was by reminding us that our goal was to rid ourselves of all the negative mental and emotional baggage we had accumulated while we were acting out. Our recovery depends upon our willingness to take responsibility for our past and present actions. We learned that in order to move away from our addiction and on toward freedom and recovery, we needed to move beyond rationalizations, stereotypes, a tendency to minimize, and *the language of denial. In recovery, we found that we could no longer fool ourselves with words*! Shocking as some of these words seemed to us at first, we learned to use them in order to describe accurately our acting-out behaviors. For example, when some of us looked at how we had used coercion and manipulation in order to get others to have sex with us, we came to understand something very important: by using threats, power, or force in order to get people to have sex with us, we were essentially commiting acts of rape. Furthermore, *we needed to use the word rape in describing this kind of acting-out behavior.*

Some of us assumed that we were not yet ready to work the Fourth Step because we were still fearful. *We finally became "fearless" when we no longer allowed our fears to control us or prevent us from doing what we needed to do in order to recover.* But even when we arrived at this "fearless" state, we continued to feel remorse for what we had done. We came to understand that *fearless does not necessarily mean painless.* We had to guard against placing ourselves in situations which might trigger shame and guilt about past behaviors. In the past, we had acted out in order to *avoid* these feelings; in recovery we allowed ourselves to experience our feelings, *then move on.* The Fourth Step tells us that our fears will diminish only after we begin the inventory process, allow ourselves to experience the feelings we have, then move on. *Our fears finally left us when our search began in earnest.*

Somehow, we thought that we would be ready to work this Step only when we no longer felt intimidated by the concept of a moral inventory. But we soon realized that *this day would never come.* Our fear continued to tell us that we were about to begin a very important task and that we would have to be extremely careful in carrying it out. Many of us found, in fact, that perfectionism was one of the major liabilities that interfered with our work on the Fourth Step. As it turns out, many of us had the same thought at first: *If I try hard enough, I can complete an absolutely perfect Fourth Step.* Even as we wrote our Fourth Step, some of us were already jumping ahead to the Fifth Step and considering ways we might say what we needed to say to others and how we might be judged when we did so. Eventually, though, we realized that thoughts like these only make an already difficult task *even more difficult*. Working on a Fourth Step was only that—*working on a Fourth Step*. We came to understand that anything we left out—intentionally or unintentionally—in working our Fourth Step could be addressed in subsequent Fourth Step work.

At first we were tempted to take the inventories of everyone but ourselves and we were also tempted to use the defects of others as excuses for our own behaviors. Our sponsors helped us resolve these issues by reminding us that our inventories are personal and individual. In other words, as we work on our inventories, we must focus on *ourselves* rather than on our lovers, our families, our employers, or on society as a whole. In the process of completing a "moral inventory" we learned that we did, indeed, have values. The guilt we felt about what we had done in the past helped us identify behavior that became completely unacceptable to us as we began to recover. We learned what was and wasn't right for us and this knowledge helped to free us.

Not only did this Step teach us that we were not the terrible people we thought we were, it also helped us identify our strengths and assets and the ways these attributes could help us in recovery. Self-hatred was certainly one of the major liabilities we included in our inventories, along with the shame, self-pity, and self-centeredness that were so much a part of our addiction. But we also learned to note our creativity, our responsiveness to others, our talents, and other gifts that are so much a part of being a whole person. Each day we made a point of working on at least one of our liabilities and one of our assets. Each of us found it helpful to call another addict at the end of the day and discuss with him or her the feelings and emotions that our writing had conjured up for us that day. As an integral part of our Program and recovery, the Fourth Step gives us many opportunities to get back in touch with our human qualities— qualities many of us lost sight of during the times we were acting out.

The Twelve Steps*

Step One
We admitted we were powerless over our compulsive sexual behavior—that our lives had become unmanageable.

Step Two
Came to believe that a Power greater than ourselves could restore us to sanity.

Step Three
Made a decision to turn our will and our lives over to the care of God as we understood God.

Step Four
Made a searching and fearless moral inventory of ourselves.

Step Five
Admitted to God, to ourselves, and to another human being the exact nature of our wrongs.

Step Six
Were entirely ready to have God remove all these defects of character.

Step Seven
Humbly asked God to remove our shortcomings.

Step Eight
Made a list of all persons we had harmed and became willing to make amends to them all.

Step Nine
Made direct amends to such people wherever possible, except when to do so would injure them or others.

Step Ten
Continued to take personal inventory and when we were wrong promptly admitted it.

Step Eleven
Sought through prayer and meditation to improve our conscious contact with God, as we understood God, praying only for knowledge of God's will for us and the power to carry that out.

Step Twelve
Having had a spiritual awakening as the result of these Steps, we tried to carry this message to other sex addicts and to practice these principles in all of our activities.

* The Twelve Steps reprinted for adaptation with permission of AA World Services, Inc. © 1972.

5

From Shame to Acceptance

We actually worked through a portion of the Fifth Step by
working the Fourth Step, because in the process of making a
"searching and fearless moral inventory" we admitted to God
and to ourselves the exact nature of our lives and wrongdoings.
In fact, each of the Steps that precedes the Fifth Step helps
prepare us to tell "another human being" everything about ourselves and what we have done.

Most of us had thought of ourselves as fundamentally defective and shameful people for such a long time. We held onto
the belief that we would never be accepted by those who *really*
knew us and what we had done. Over and over again, our
feelings of shame told us that we were *bad people*. We came
to understand that when we kept our acting-out behaviors secret,
our shame only grew more intense and kept us isolated from
others. But when we finally shared the exact nature of our
wrongs with others, we gained new insights about ourselves
and our behaviors: we could see that we were, in fact, worthwhile people who had done some harmful and abusive things
to ourselves and to others *because of our addiction*. We felt so
free when we finally heard ourselves speak to others and share
our long-held secrets with them. The Fifth Step gave each of
us an opportunity to know what it's like to have another person
respond to us in a positive and nuturing way, even though he
or she knows all of our shameful secrets.

In recovery we still had powerful feelings of guilt about our
past acting-out behaviors, but the Fifth Step motivated us to
move beyond seeing ourselves only as shameful and unworthy
people. By allowing ourselves to feel guilty instead of letting
ourselves be consumed and paralyzed by shame, we could see
more clearly what actions we should take in order to move

ahead in our recovery. Specifically we learned that we needed to take responsibility for our acting-out behaviors and make amends to those we had harmed; Steps Eight and Nine would help us with these actions. As we worked the Fifth Step, however, we were able to work through our feelings of guilt for the first time. The Fifth Step taught us that we had a clear choice: we could continue to let our feelings of guilt develop into paralyzing shame, or we could learn to let our feelings of guilt move us to decisive, healing action.

In choosing "another human being" to hear our Fifth Step, many of us turned to people who had themselves completed this Step. Most of us felt more comfortable sharing this Step with people who were aware of what we were going through. We chose not to ask friends, family members, or partners to hear our Fifth Step because we did not wish to place additional pressure on them. We selected other people we felt particularly safe with, people who we felt would really *listen* to our Fifth Step but not offer judgments, advice, or forgiveness. *A Fifth Step is not supposed to be a confession.* We are, after all, responsible for forgiving ourselves. And everything we need in order to forgive ourselves is within the Twelve Step Program. Some of us chose our sponsors or other recovering addicts who were familiar with our First Step to hear our Fifth Step. Some of us chose members of the clergy to hear our Fifth Step, at least in part because of the confidential aspect of this relationship. But regardless of *whom* we chose to hear our Fifth Step, we made sure that he or she had an understanding of sex addiction *before* we met. (The Fifth Step is not an appropriate time or place in the Program to educate other people about the process of addiction.) Some of us chose *two people* to hear our Fifth Step: one person to listen to us, the other person to provide the emotional support we'd need. Some of us chose different people to hear different portions of our Fifth Step. Those of us who split the Fifth Step up in this way reminded ourselves, however, that our goal was to be able to do the entire Fifth Step with one person.

We have come to see that the word *exact* represents a key concept of the Fifth Step. We found that it is counterproductive to be vague and general as we describe the nature of our wrongs. Looking back, we remember that general statements like "I did some terrible things when I was acting out" only served to intensify our feelings of shame. We actually felt most relieved when we described—as clearly and specifically as possible—*exactly* what we had done. For example, rather than saying "I hurt my family," we'd share the details of specific incidents that had hurt individual members of our families. For example, one recovering addict described the specific nature of his wrongs in the following way: "One time I missed my daughter's school play because I was in a motel room having sex with someone. Later my daughter told me that she was hurt and angry that I'd let her down again by not showing up for her performance that night. I lied to her and told her I'd had car trouble. Then I angrily added that she was ungrateful and always expected too much from me."

In preparing for a Fifth Step, we always choose a setting that is not likely to be distracting to us in any way; we also allow ourselves plenty of time for this opportunity to talk to another person. Some of us pray with those we admit our wrongs to, both before and after our Fifth Step work. Doing this seems to help us learn more about emotional and spiritual intimacy.

As we became more familiar with the Fifth Step, it no longer seemed like the momentous task we assumed it would be at first. Now, whenever we think that working a Fifth Step might help us in our recovery, we do one as soon as possible. And we never feel pressure to do the Fifth Step "exactly right"; the reference to exactness in this Step relates to the specificity of the information we share about our wrongs. We find that we have absolute trust that when we work it honestly and willingly, this Step will *always* be helpful to us. As we tell "another human being" about ourselves and what we have learned, we always have a strong sense of the presence of a Higher Power. Surely this is one of many spiritual experiences we continue to have as we work the Twelve Steps.

The Twelve Steps*

Step One
We admitted we were powerless over our compulsive sexual behavior—that our lives had become unmanageable.

Step Two
Came to believe that a Power greater than ourselves could restore us to sanity.

Step Three
Made a decision to turn our will and our lives over to the care of God as we understood God.

Step Four
Made a searching and fearless moral inventory of ourselves.

Step Five
Admitted to God, to ourselves, and to another human being the exact nature of our wrongs.

Step Six
Were entirely ready to have God remove all these defects of character.

Step Seven
Humbly asked God to remove our shortcomings.

Step Eight
Made a list of all persons we had harmed and became willing to make amends to them all.

Step Nine
Made direct amends to such people wherever possible, except when to do so would injure them or others.

Step Ten
Continued to take personal inventory and when we were wrong promptly admitted it.

Step Eleven
Sought through prayer and meditation to improve our conscious contact with God, as we understood God, praying only for knowledge of God's will for us and the power to carry that out.

Step Twelve
Having had a spiritual awakening as the result of these Steps, we tried to carry this message to other sex addicts and to practice these principles in all of our activities.

* The Twelve Steps reprinted for adaptation with permission of AA World Services, Inc. © 1972.

6

Commitment to Change

Working the first Three Steps on a regular basis helped us achieve the primary goal we set for ourselves when we came to the Program: stopping our acting-out behaviors. When our lives became more manageable, we could see that we needed to make other changes as well—changes that would necessitate the removal of our character defects. But most of us were reluctant to give up our character defects because they had functioned as reliable sources of comfort for us. In fact, some of our character defects, such as lying and grandiosity, had functioned as "old friends," helping us survive the painful reality we had known for so long.

As we approached the Sixth Step, most of us were fearful because we knew how important this Step was to our recovery. Now we can see that the fear we struggled with as we began to work this Step was due, at least in part, to the doubts we had that our character defects would or even *could* be removed. After all, most of us had tried so many times to rid ourselves of our character defects—primarily our addiction—and we failed each time we tried. But we didn't let our fears and doubts deter us from working this Step and it became a powerful new source of clarification and help for us. The Sixth Step helped us understand that we did not have to assume total responsibility for the removal of our character defects. The Sixth Step also helped us understand that being "entirely ready" means being *willing*, not necessarily being overjoyed and enthusiastic. We came to understand that given the One Day At A Time philosophy so important to the Program and recovery, we needed to be only as "entirely ready" as we could possibly be on a given day. In other words, each day we have the opportunity to make a conscious decision that we will be as ready as possible on that day. We found that when we were truly willing, God removed our character defects. The Sixth Step helped us decide for ourselves—on a daily basis—that we were ready to be relieved of our burdens and freed from our self-imposed limitations.

Most of us were realistic and honest about our resistance to change. Early in recovery many of us attempted to buy some time and flexibility by saying things like, "I'm not ready to give this up yet, but I will pray for the willingness to do so." But as our trust in the Program and in our Higher Power began to grow, we became more and more interested in changing old behaviors and having our character defects removed. We were still fearful of change, but in recovery we became aware of a dramatic difference between the short-term pain of *changing* old and harmful behaviors and the long-term, debilitating pain of *holding onto* old and harmful behaviors. Looking back, many of us characterize this difference in the following way: changing old and harmful behaviors is similar to having a hopelessly infected tooth removed. Of course it's painful to have a tooth removed; in fact, just the *anticipation* makes most people very fearful. In the long run, however, *not* having a hopelessly infected tooth removed almost certainly will result in continuing pain, further infection, complications and, inevitably, even more pain.

Some of us have absolutely no idea how or why our addiction developed, nor do we know exactly how our character defects were removed. But we don't allow ourselves to spend time worrying about these things. In fact, when newcomers to the Program ask us why we're not more concerned about the causes of our addiction or the details of how the Program works, some of us use the following analogy as an explanation: In order to benefit from the use of corrective lenses, people don't have to understand all the factors that contribute to the problems they're experiencing with their vision, nor do they need to understand exactly how their corrective lenses were prepared. In a similar way, we found that in order to get the results we want from the Program, we don't have to understand the causes of our addiction, nor do we need to understand exactly how the Program works. We know that the Program *does work. We have seen the Program work; we have experienced the Program working in our lives.* For example, those of us who had our grandiosity removed, then managed to replace that character defect with feelings of genuine self-worth have had many opportunities to *experience* the subsequent changes in our lives. And we know now that this "transformation" was the result of a change in behavior, not just a re-labeling of old behaviors in order to justify them.

One of the most powerful and *disabling* character defects many of us needed to have removed was a tendency to blame the world for our unhappiness and our addiction. We were able to reclaim responsibility for our lives and our actions when we stopped playing negative, self-defeating messages to ourselves and consciously affirmed the fact that—yes—*we could change*, and with our willingness and the help of God *we would change.* We learned through experience that even though the process of changing our behavior is very difficult, that task is still easier, more natural, and many times more possible than trying to change the world around us.

The Twelve Steps*

Step One
We admitted we were powerless over our compulsive sexual behavior—that our lives had become unmanageable.

Step Two
Came to believe that a Power greater than ourselves could restore us to sanity.

Step Three
Made a decision to turn our will and our lives over to the care of God as we understood God.

Step Four
Made a searching and fearless moral inventory of ourselves.

Step Five
Admitted to God, to ourselves, and to another human being the exact nature of our wrongs.

Step Six
Were entirely ready to have God remove all these defects of character.

Step Seven
Humbly asked God to remove our shortcomings.

Step Eight
Made a list of all persons we had harmed and became willing to make amends to them all.

Step Nine
Made direct amends to such people wherever possible, except when to do so would injure them or others.

Step Ten
Continued to take personal inventory and when we were wrong promptly admitted it.

Step Eleven
Sought through prayer and meditation to improve our conscious contact with God, as we understood God, praying only for knowledge of God's will for us and the power to carry that out.

Step Twelve
Having had a spiritual awakening as the result of these Steps, we tried to carry this message to other sex addicts and to practice these principles in all of our activities.

* The Twelve Steps reprinted for adaptation with permission of AA World Services, Inc. © 1972.

7

Asking for Grace

When we came to the Program, many of us somehow associated the concept of humility with *humiliation*. But we learned through the process of recovery that humility has nothing at all to do with humiliation and self-deprecation and everything to do with self-honesty, modesty, serenity, peace of mind, openness, and the willingness to learn. In recovery, we came to know—some of us for the first time in our lives—the difference between arrogance and pride. We also came to know that if were willing to do our part—attend meetings, make calls, pray, and meditate—God would do the things we were powerless to do. *Twelve Steps and Twelve Traditions* succinctly characterizes the humility we develop as we work the Program: "It amounts to a clear recognition of what and who we really are, followed by a sincere attempt to become what we could be" (p. 58).

Just as the Third Step teaches us to ask God to remove our powerlessness, the Seventh Step teaches us to ask God to remove our shortcomings. As we worked this Step, we came to understand that we no longer had to accept the limitations of the past, nor did we have to achieve *perfection* in the present or future. Completing the inventory suggested in the Fourth Step and admitting our wrongs to others as suggested in the Fifth Step helped us become more humble and, therefore, more receptive to new thoughts and behaviors. As a result of our new openness and willingness, we learned what we needed to do in order to recover and we also learned to identify and utilize the personal strengths that would prove to be so helpful to us. In recovery we no longer allowed ourselves to think in extremes, so at last we were able to avoid the traps of shame and grandiosity that for so long had blinded us to both problems and solutions.

43

Asking God to remove our shortcomings is, itself, an act of humility. Instead of daring God and/or demanding certain things as we might have done in the past, we merely asked God to help us. The Seventh Step process is essentially a *collaborative* effort with God. We can see now that the most important part of this collaboration is the fact that *we initiate it ourselves.* Instead of focusing on *if* and *how* God will remove our shortcomings, we came to understand that we need to focus on *whether or not we really are asking God to remove our shortcomings and how we are asking that this be accomplished.* We found that we were able to shift to the more positive and productive focus by asking ourselves questions like this: *Am I seeking the wisdom of other recovering addicts? Do I really listen at meetings and apply the group conscience in my life?* We learned that one way of asking God to remove our shortcomings was to ask other people in our groups to tell us how they saw our recovery proceeding. Indeed, some of these people saw changes in us that we were not yet aware of ourselves. *We had an opportunity to experience the Seventh Step in action each time the people in our groups supported us as we changed our thinking and behaviors.*

We came to understand that the removal of our shortcomings is not an isolated event, but a process we must participate in and not try to control. Just as our addiction did not develop instantly, our shortcomings did not disappear instantly either. We were often impatient during this process because we wanted God to work at *our* pace, but we learned to see this impatience as a helpful warning: whenever we sensed that we were becoming impatient with God's timetable, we'd pray for understanding and acceptance of whatever was or wasn't happening and also for the knowledge of what we could do to facilitate the process.

We learned that we could not ask God to remove our addictive urges if we continued to place ourselves in addictive situations (e.g. spending time in pornographic bookstores, visiting people we had acted out with in the past). Indeed, many of us were told by our sponsors that if we wanted to avoid a slip, we must "stay away from slippery places." On the other hand, we also learned that we could not be passive, sit back, and wait for God to "fix" us.

In time and with our willingness, God sent us the help we needed *through hopeful and encouraging words from other addicts and also through the insights we gained as we meditated.* Soon we found that we were able to do things we had previously thought impossible. Once we experienced this kind of success and began living more manageable lives, we experienced some powerful changes in our thinking and behaviors: our feelings of rage subsided; we no longer felt the need to judge others; and we became more patient and tolerant. We could see these kinds of changes in other group members, and they were able to see similar changes in us. We decided that if the wonderful people who were in our groups really cared about us, then perhaps we were worthwhile and lovable people *after all*. Indeed, AA speaks of this promise in the Big Book: "That feeling of uselessness and self-pity will disappear. We will lose interest in selfish things and gain interest in our fellows. Self-seeking will slip away. Our whole attitude and outlook upon life will change. Fear of people and of economic insecurity will leave us. We will intuitively know how to handle situations which used to baffle us. We will suddenly realize that God is doing for us what we could not do for ourselves" (p. 84).

On a daily basis, we pray to have our shortcomings removed. We repeat the Seventh Step in our prayers and we also meditate for guidance as to how we can continue to facilitate the growth process. *And we pray for patience.* Through the Big Book, AA teaches us to pray: *"My Creator, I am now willing that you should have all of me, good and bad. I pray that you remove from me every single defect of character which stands in the*

45

way of my usefulness to you and my fellows. Grant me strength, as I go out from here, to do your bidding. Amen" (p. 76).

The Twelve Steps*

Step One
We admitted we were powerless over our compulsive sexual behavior—that our lives had become unmanageable.

Step Two
Came to believe that a Power greater than ourselves could restore us to sanity.

Step Three
Made a decision to turn our will and our lives over to the care of God as we understood God.

Step Four
Made a searching and fearless moral inventory of ourselves.

Step Five
Admitted to God, to ourselves, and to another human being the exact nature of our wrongs.

Step Six
Were entirely ready to have God remove all these defects of character.

Step Seven
Humbly asked God to remove our shortcomings.

Step Eight
Made a list of all persons we had harmed and became willing to make amends to them all.

Step Nine
Made direct amends to such people wherever possible, except when to do so would injure them or others.

Step Ten
Continued to take personal inventory and when we were wrong promptly admitted it.

Step Eleven
Sought through prayer and meditation to improve our conscious contact with God, as we understood God, praying only for knowledge of God's will for us and the power to carry that out.

Step Twelve
Having had a spiritual awakening as the result of these Steps, we tried to carry this message to other sex addicts and to practice these principles in all of our activities.

* The Twelve Steps reprinted for adaptation with permission of AA World Services, Inc. © 1972.

8

The End of Isolation

When we were acting out, most of us vehemently denied that
we were harming *anyone*. Some of us were completely *unaware*
of the fact that we had harmed others and some of us had
justified or ignored our wrongdoings through rationalization or
outright dishonesty. Those of us who *did* acknowledge that we
were harming others vowed that we would soon make up for
everything we had done with some extraordinary act. Despite
the fact that we rarely, if ever, got around to carrying out these
acts of contrition, we continued on with our acting-out behavior. By the time we came to the Program, most of us were
so anxious to deal with our guilt and shame that we wanted to
apologize *immediately* to everyone we had ever harmed. Now
we understand that we would have done ourselves and others
more harm than good had we rushed out and apologized to
people *before* we worked the first Seven Steps. *Working these
Steps helped each of us understand that arresting our addictive
behavior was the best and most appropriate amend we could
make.*

Given our experiences with the Fourth Step, we decided that
it was important that our lists of all persons we had harmed be
written lists. As we worked the Fourth Step, we could see that
the written word is sometimes more powerful and real to us
than our thoughts because it is difficult to avoid or minimize.
In deciding who we should include on our lists, we sought and
received guidance from several sources: our sponsors, other
group members, people who had heard our most recent Fifth
Step, and people who were familiar with our stories. At first
most of us struggled with our lists: we wanted to omit some
people from them because we were too ashamed to face them;
we wanted to omit other people from them because we didn't

know how we could possibly make appropriate amends to them. We finally worked through our difficulties with this portion of the Eighth Step by applying two helpful slogans to the tasks at hand. Taking "First Things First" we had to proceed and begin the task of compiling our lists, then we had to remind ourselves to "Keep It Simple" so we wouldn't feel overwhelmed with the idea of completing this important task.

We could see that our lists of the persons we had harmed would not be complete until we added *our own names* to them. In many instances, our addiction had harmed us even more deeply than it had harmed others. Regardless of whether our acting-out behaviors involved others or not, they had been harmful to us emotionally, spiritually, and physically. Stopping our acting-out behaviors and becoming involved in the process of recovery were amends we made to ourselves. We found that we needed to work on ourselves as individuals before we could even *begin* to work on our relationships with other people.

One of the most difficult tasks of recovery is learning to forgive and love ourselves. We had harmed ourselves deeply when we did things that violated our values. Although our acting-out behaviors seemed to indicate that we *had* no morals or ethics, the intense feelings of guilt we struggled with as a result of these behaviors told us otherwise. We knew from our feelings of discomfort that we were somehow in conflict with what we knew was right for us. Those of us who were sexual with married people tried to tell ourselves that the situation was *their problem, not ours*. Of course many of us knew in our hearts that when we willingly took part in an activity we believed to be wrong, *it became our problem*. Those of us who prostituted our bodies desperately wanted to believe that we were in control and powerful, but the pain we felt about the nature of our activities and our powerlessness told us otherwise. In time, we learned that each act that violated the basic dignity and rights of ourselves and/or others belonged on our lists.

In recovery, we began to see that we had been people of extremes when it came to our relationships with others. It seems that most of us either tried to control and dominate others, or we were overly—sometimes pathologically—dependent upon others. When we were acting out, many of us used other people to justify and/or perpetuate our addictions and to help us clean up the wreckage that remained. It was as though we wanted to be viewed as gods yet cared for as children. In all areas involving other people, our acting-out behaviors represented a variety of wrongdoings. Concerning money and our addiction, for example, some of us were careless with the belongings of others and some of us took advantage of the generosity of others; some of us were dishonest with others for the purpose of material gain; some of us used money that didn't belong to us or money that was being saved for some other purpose in order to purchase pornography or sexual favors; some of us stole money from others. But regardless of whether we misused, misrepresented, manipulated, cheated, or actually *stole* money from others, these various acting-out behaviors relative to money could be described in the same way: we were using money and the things we thought money could buy in an effort to fill the emptiness that was causing us so much pain.

We learned that in addition to harming people by the things we did, we also harmed people by *not doing* certain things. For example, we harmed other people in our lives by not following through in our commitments to them and by not being there for them when that was clearly our responsibility. The Eighth Step gave us an opportunity to consider the things we had neglected doing for and with the people in our lives during the time of our active addiction. We simply had not been *there*—physically or emotionally—to offer those we cared about gestures of love and compassion and words of support and comfort that are so important to any relationship.

Our prideful ego was a powerful barrier to the Eighth Step process. Most of us had become accustomed to keeping score and holding on to our resentments. At first some of us assumed that we would make amends to others *only when the people who had harmed us admitted their wrongdoings to us.* But we discovered that we could not afford this luxury in terms of time or process. We came to understand that, as addicts, we could not risk "spiritual suicide" by holding on to the negative energy that is tied up in resentment and self-righteousness. *We simply had too much to lose.* Negative energy can, in fact, completely destroy the vulnerability and honesty that are so vitally important to recovery. The Eighth Step prepared us to be humble in our dealings with others as well as with ourselves.

As time went on, many of us began to see some striking similarities between addiction and resentment. We learned that an important part of the process of developing a willingness to change is the process of looking at how we acted in relationships. We found it helpful to refer back to our Fourth Step to see how our shortcomings had contributed to the painful and unproductive conflicts many of us experienced in those relationships. *Recovery did not prevent us from getting angry within the context of our relationships; recovery taught us that we could no longer afford to let feelings of anger go unresolved and grow into resentment and the isolation that results.* In recovery we learned to express our anger in healthy ways, then let it go.

The Twelve Steps*

Step One
We admitted we were powerless over our compulsive sexual behavior—that our lives had become unmanageable.

Step Two
Came to believe that a Power greater than ourselves could restore us to sanity.

Step Three
Made a decision to turn our will and our lives over to the care of God as we understood God.

Step Four
Made a searching and fearless moral inventory of ourselves.

Step Five
Admitted to God, to ourselves, and to another human being the exact nature of our wrongs.

Step Six
Were entirely ready to have God remove all these defects of character.

Step Seven
Humbly asked God to remove our shortcomings.

Step Eight
Made a list of all persons we had harmed and became willing to make amends to them all.

Step Nine
Made direct amends to such people wherever possible, except when to do so would injure them or others.

Step Ten
Continued to take personal inventory and when we were wrong promptly admitted it.

Step Eleven
Sought through prayer and meditation to improve our conscious contact with God, as we understood God, praying only for knowledge of God's will for us and the power to carry that out.

Step Twelve
Having had a spiritual awakening as the result of these Steps, we tried to carry this message to other sex addicts and to practice these principles in all of our activities.

* The Twelve Steps reprinted for adaptation with permission of AA World Services, Inc. © 1972.

9

Restoring Relationships

After we made lists of all persons we had harmed and became *willing* to make amends to them all, we were ready to make our amends. In order to move ahead, most of us had to confront and overcome a basic fear that people would perceive us as weak if we made amends to them. We finally moved through this obstacle to recovery by reminding ourselves that *we make amends to enhance our own growth and recovery, not to get approval, admiration, or sympathy from others*. We work the Ninth Step to learn to forgive *ourselves*, not to learn how to get other people to forgive us.

Most of us had acted as our own harshest critics, so we were quite surprised to find that many people had actually forgiven us long before we were willing to forgive ourselves. *In order to really recover, we had to let go of our shame and guilt about the past and learn to live in the here and now.* We learned that our primary responsibility was to put forth an honest effort to make amends to those we had harmed. And we came to understand that this honest effort had very little to do with the way people did or didn't respond to us when we made amends to them. We cannot afford to adapt our recovery to the opinions and reactions of others. We found that the very *effort* of reaching out and making amends relieved us of our feelings of shame and provided new opportunities for spiritual growth as well.

Through our own experiences, we learned that it is *usually* best to make direct, face-to-face amends to the people we have harmed. We also learned that it is important to be as specific and appropriate as possible in making these amends. For example, if one of us stole money from someone, our amends to that person involved repaying the exact amount of money in question. Even when our wrongdoings are not material in nature—

and most of them aren't—specificity and appropriateness are still important to the process of making amends. In some instances, however, we found that it was *impossible* to be specific and appropriate in making amends. For example, most of us found that we simply didn't have enough hours in the day to pay our children back for the amount of time we spent away from them while we were acting out. Likewise, we were unable to pay people back for the pain and distress they had to endure whenever they worried about us. In cases such as these, we simply did what we could to stop the behavior that had harmed these people in the first place. *Changing our behavior was the most powerful thing we could do in making amends.*

The Ninth Step does not set down rigid rules and procedures for making amends. In fact, because of the apparent flexibility of this Step, we found that we had to take special care not to misuse it by interpreting it as written encouragement to adopt a casual, inconsistent, or otherwise careless approach to the process of making amends. The phrase "wherever possible" in this Step should not be construed as permission to avoid making amends whenever doing so is inconvenient or uncomfortable for us. Through meditation as well as through the help of our sponsors and groups, we found that "...*wherever possible...*" really means that when we are with people we have harmed and have an opportunity to make amends to them, we should follow through and do so. When we became alert and open to the opportunities for making amends, we found them easily and naturally.

Some of the people we had harmed were unknown to us, others could not be located, and still others were dead by the time we were ready to make amends to them. When we knew for a fact that there was no chance of making direct amends to certain people, we carefully made meaningful symbolic amends to them instead—for example, we'd send a contribution to a particular charity or cause, offer an appropriate prayer, or write a letter. Of course the letters we wrote to these people were never sent; *nevertheless, the very act of becoming willing to make amends was and always will be valuable in helping us forgive ourselves.*

When we approached people we had harmed in order to make amends to them—particularly those people who were still hurting from the effects of our acting-out behavior—we found that we had to exercise patience and understanding in dealing with their reactions and responses to us. We did not, however, allow these people to abuse us in any way. The length and quality of our sobriety spoke louder than any words we could utter, so our growth was *noticeable* to those who knew us well. Naturally we were reluctant to face many of the people we had harmed and many of the people we had harmed were uncomfortable with the idea that we wanted to make amends to them. Some of these people even tried to minimize the effects of our behavior by saying things to us like, "Oh forget it; it wasn't such a big deal." When people tried to dissuade or distract us from making amends, we politely asked them to hear us out, then explained that in addition to the changes in our behavior, *one of the things we needed most in recovery was to hear ourselves being honest and responsible.*

At one time or another, we all had real concerns that in the process of making amends to the people we had harmed, we would only harm them further. Indeed, the second half of the Ninth Step suggests that it *is* possible to injure people in the process of making amends to them. Other people in the Program offered helpful guidance to us as we struggled with decisions about which people in our lives we should make direct, face-to-face amends to and which people in our lives we should make indirect amends to. We came to understand that it is probably not a good idea, for example, to make direct amends to someone by informing him or her that we had been sexual with his or her spouse. Similarily, we came to understand that making

57

amends by telling people that our relationships with them had not been what they thought they were could and probably *would* harm those people further. In these highly sensitive situations, we found that the best amend we could possibly make to the people we had harmed was simply to stop our acting-out behaviors. After all, the word "amend" means to change or to alter. It became clear to us that *changing the way we act in relationships is another powerful way of working the Steps effectively.*

Whenever we felt uncertain about whether or not direct amends would harm certain people further, we proceeded by dividing the Ninth Step into three parts. First, we wrote letters to these people stating that we realized we'd harmed them and we were making efforts to change our behavior and improve ourselves. We did not discuss our addiction in these letters to the people we had harmed, but simply asked if we could meet with them and make amends to them. Next, we called these people to ask if they would be willing to share with us their reactions to the letters they had received from us. If people were not open to sharing their reactions and feelings with us, we did not pursue the issue further with them. But if they *were* willing to share their reactions and meet with us as well, we selected a *neutral* meeting place—in other words, a place that would not bring back feelings of shame about our acting-out behaviors or in any way tempt us to resume those behaviors. (The powerful awareness we had of our addiction and the First Step reminded us to be extremely careful not to set ourselves up to act out again.) When we finally met with these people and made direct amends to them, we felt it was appropriate to tell them about our addiction, but only in *very general terms.*

No matter how we finally make amends to the people we have harmed, we always try to focus on our *recovery* rather than on the details of our acting-out behavior. We find that when our focus is on recovery, we are less likely to shame ourselves or overwhelm the person we are making amends to. Using the Seventh Step for guidance, we always ask our Higher Power to remove our grandiosity before we make amends. In recovery we no longer feel the need to play the role of the all-knowing "perfect person," so we make our amends simply, quietly, and with humility. We always try to keep things as simple as possible. Prior to making amends of any kind, we pray for strength and knowledge of God's will. Then each time we make amends, we find new freedom and further relief from the burdens of shame and guilt.

The Twelve Steps*

Step One
We admitted we were powerless over our compulsive sexual behavior—that our lives had become unmanageable.

Step Two
Came to believe that a Power greater than ourselves could restore us to sanity.

Step Three
Made a decision to turn our will and our lives over to the care of God as we understood God.

Step Four
Made a searching and fearless moral inventory of ourselves.

Step Five
Admitted to God, to ourselves, and to another human being the exact nature of our wrongs.

Step Six
Were entirely ready to have God remove all these defects of character.

Step Seven
Humbly asked God to remove our shortcomings.

Step Eight
Made a list of all persons we had harmed and became willing to make amends to them all.

Step Nine
Made direct amends to such people wherever possible, except when to do so would injure them or others.

Step Ten
Continued to take personal inventory and when we were wrong promptly admitted it.

Step Eleven
Sought through prayer and meditation to improve our conscious contact with God, as we understood God, praying only for knowledge of God's will for us and the power to carry that out.

Step Twelve
Having had a spiritual awakening as the result of these Steps, we tried to carry this message to other sex addicts and to practice these principles in all of our activities.

* The Twelve Steps reprinted for adaptation with permission of AA World Services, Inc. © 1972.

10

Maintaining the Growth

Looking back, many of us realize that when we first came to the Program, we saw it as a refuge from the consequences of our acting-out behaviors. But when we began working Steps One through Nine on a regular basis, we were able to confront and resolve many of the negative thoughts and behaviors that remained from our addiction. As we became more grounded in recovery and less burdened with the shame, guilt, and painful memories that had plagued us, some of us were hopeful that there might even be a time in the future when we'd no longer have to work the Program. But that isn't how the Program and recovery work. We learned that in order to *maintain* recovery and everything we had gained through it, we must continue working the Program.

As we grew in our recovery, we changed some of the expectations we had for ourselves. In other words, some of the behaviors we found acceptable early in our recovery were no longer acceptable to us later on in recovery. In response to our continuing growth, we continued to adjust our inventories as well as the parameters—or boundaries—that helped us identify our own acceptable and unacceptable behaviors. By encouraging us to do a "spiritual housecleaning" on a regular basis, the Tenth Step helps us maintain a healthy relationship with ourselves. Along with Steps Eight and Nine, the Tenth Step helps us acknowledge and own up to the mistakes we've made and it also helps us let go of feelings of guilt before they consume us.

Using the Fourth Step as a guide, we learned to resist getting involved with the inventories of other people. Each of us learned to focus on our own inventory and our own recovery. We also learned to be alert to signs of impatience and defensiveness in our thoughts and behaviors. As time went on, we added to our inventories those things we felt *good* about having done. Looking back over a day of our lives, we'd carefully consider the positive ways we had worked each of the Twelve Steps on that particular day and exactly how we had "practiced these principles" in all areas of our lives. Many of us found it helpful to put our thoughts and feelings in writing as we worked each of the Twelve Steps. Even now, some of us continue to keep journals that trace the process and progress of our recovery. Reviewing our own written impressions in this way gives us yet another opportunity to see what we were like in the past, what we are like now, and how we have changed.

But even in recovery, not one of us is perfect. No matter how long we have been working the Program or how many of our shortcomings have been removed, we continue to make mistakes. In fact, we always will. Note that the Tenth Step says *"when we were wrong,"* not *if we were wrong*. Our Program is based on our willingness to change and our honest efforts to progress; it is not based on compulsive activities carried out in order to achieve moral perfection. Of course we all made plenty of mistakes when we were acting out, but at that time we were either too driven to notice them or we were so consumed with guilt that we were unable to admit them—to ourselves or to anyone else. In recovery, we came to understand that unresolved feelings of guilt have a powerful negative impact on our thoughts and behaviors. We could see that the times we had been burdened with feelings of guilt were the times we were most likely to resume our acting-out behaviors. In recovery, we learned to let our feelings of guilt lead us to decisive action: we'd seek out other people, acknowledge our wrongdoings to them, then forgive ourselves and let go of the guilt. When we finally understood that by harboring guilt, we only set ourselves up for shame, isolation, and self-pity, we learned to deal with it *immediately*.

"To Thine Own Self Be True"—this slogan is particularly helpful as we work the Tenth Step. We often remind ourselves that the Tenth Step says "when we were wrong," *not when we were caught and confronted by someone.* In recovery we learned to admit our wrongs, even when we knew for a fact that other people were completely unaware of them. First we admitted our wrongs to ourselves and our Higher Power, then we made amends according to the principles of Steps Eight and Nine. In recovery we also learned to recognize and understand how and when we had made mistakes or behaved inappropriately, *but we no longer tried to rationalize our actions.* On the other hand, recovery also taught us that "when we were wrong" does *not* mean that we must take responsibility and/or make a blanket admission for all of the problems in the world. *We learned to focus our inventories on our own current behaviors.*

Regarding our wrongdoings, the Tenth Step simply suggests that we *admit* them; it says nothing about being punished for them—by ourselves or by others. Of course, admitting our wrongs is an essential part of being honest with ourselves. We came to see that the words "promptly admitted" do not necessarily mean that we must admit our wrongs to another person. As soon as we admitted our wrongs to *ourselves*, we found that we were free to use the Twelve Steps as a guide for appropriate action. Most of us believe that when we *do* admit our wrongs to others, the process of sharing information about ourselves helps us maintain our humility. This kind of self-disclosure also helps us maintain a realistic perspective about our relationship to others: while we never allow ourselves to minimize the impact of our actions on others, we carefully guard against the kind of grandiose thinking that might tell us we have real power over others. In admitting our wrongs to others, we feel that it's always wise to keep things simple. Instead of making lengthy and complicated explanations for our behaviors, we find that it is most effective to use a simple and straightforward approach like the following: "I acted badly; I made a mistake. I want to say that I'm sorry; I will do everything I can to make sure that I never act that way again."

Many of us find that in addition to a nightly inventory, it is also very helpful to take some "spot-check" inventories throughout the day. Taking inventories each day and then following through with appropriate action helps us transform feelings of helplessness and hopelessness into a growing sense of gratitude.

The Twelve Steps*

Step One
We admitted we were powerless over our compulsive sexual behavior—that our lives had become unmanageable.

Step Two
Came to believe that a Power greater than ourselves could restore us to sanity.

Step Three
Made a decision to turn our will and our lives over to the care of God as we understood God.

Step Four
Made a searching and fearless moral inventory of ourselves.

Step Five
Admitted to God, to ourselves, and to another human being the exact nature of our wrongs.

Step Six
Were entirely ready to have God remove all these defects of character.

Step Seven
Humbly asked God to remove our shortcomings.

Step Eight
Made a list of all persons we had harmed and became willing to make amends to them all.

Step Nine
Made direct amends to such people wherever possible, except when to do so would injure them or others.

Step Ten
Continued to take personal inventory and when we were wrong promptly admitted it.

Step Eleven
Sought through prayer and meditation to improve our conscious contact with God, as we understood God, praying only for knowledge of God's will for us and the power to carry that out.

Step Twelve
Having had a spiritual awakening as the result of these Steps, we tried to carry this message to other sex addicts and to practice these principles in all of our activities.

* The Twelve Steps reprinted for adaptation with permission of AA World Services, Inc. © 1972.

11

Spiritual Intimacy with God

Ours is a spiritual Program, but we have learned that *how* we define spirituality is completely up to us. Many of us first realized that we wanted to have a closer relationship with our Higher Power when we learned to pray and meditate in the process of working the Second and Third Steps. We came to see that prayer and meditation are not ends in themselves, but effective means to achieve a close relationship with God. We find that the Eleventh Step helps us maintain a fulfilling spiritual relationship with the God of our understanding.

Looking at the Twelve Steps, we see that *addiction* is mentioned only in the First Step, while *God* is referred to in the Second, Third, Fifth, Sixth, Seventh, Eleventh, and Twelfth Steps. Indeed, the concept of God is very important to recovery and leads to many opportunities for soul-searching and discussion. When we were still acting out, some of us saw God as an object of fear; some of us saw God as an awesome power to be called upon only in times of crisis; some of us thought of God only as a distant and uncaring figurehead. But regardless of our perceptions, most of us wondered what kind of God would allow us to live with the horror of our addiction. In recovery, we began to feel that we wanted to have a relationship with God—not as an adversary, but as a trusted companion who would nurture us and guide us for the rest of our lives. After a time in recovery, our prayers to God became much more spontaneous and we talked more freely and openly. In fact, we learned to talk with God in much the same way we would talk with the people in our groups.

In the past, some of us had either completely denied or otherwise discounted the usefulness of prayer. But *"Twelve and Twelve"* reminds us that "almost the only scoffers at prayer are those who never tried it enough" (p. 97). At first, some of us just assumed that we didn't know *how* to pray. The Eleventh Step gave us the guidance and assurance we needed by suggesting that we pray "for knowledge of God's will for us and the power to carry that out." Note that this Step does not in any way encourage us to ask for material things and/or power over other people. When we pray, we ask only for insight and guidance, and the courage and willingness we need to follow through.

Just as we exercise our bodies to maintain our physical fitness, we came to understand that we must exercise our spirituality in order to maintain our spiritual well-being. We learned that each day it is helpful to set aside some time to be alone with the God of our understanding. We sought out places and situations that would encourage us to be quiet and receptive. We allowed our troubled spirits to become calm and began to get some insights into the problems we were struggling with at the time. We subsequently found that we were free to hear and to learn. We have come to see meditation as the process of listening for God's will for us. *Twelve Steps and Twelve Traditions* suggests that meditation helps us to "envision our spiritual objective before we try to move toward it" (p. 100).

But given the "cunning, baffling, and powerful" nature of our addiction, we'd sometimes ignore God's will completely. Other times we'd desperately try to convince ourselves that we knew God's will for us, even when other recovering addicts in our groups warned us that we were only setting ourselves up to act out again. For example, some of us *chose* to remain in addictive relationships as we struggled with recovery. We refused to listen to others when they advised us either to end these relationships or do whatever we could to change them. *We felt that no one understood us*. To avoid the seductive trap of fooling ourselves in this way, we learned to "listen" to our feelings very carefully. We came to understand, for example, that if we had feelings of fear about being honest and letting other recovering addicts know of our plans to do something, we could be relatively sure that this was not the will of God speaking, but our addiction playing mind games with us. When we really began to pay attention to our pain and fear and thought about the ways we could maintain our sobriety, even those of us who had refused to listen to other recovering addicts took action: we willingly changed our destructive relationships or terminated them.

Our conscious contact with God really became a way of life for us when we began thinking spiritually *throughout the day*, not just at the beginning and/or the end of the day. When we began living our lives as *recovering* addicts, we found that we were able to face God and still be comfortable with ourselves and our plans. And at that point, life became a journey to be enjoyed rather than a tortuous experience to be endured.

The Twelve Steps*

Step One
We admitted we were powerless over our compulsive sexual behavior—that our lives had become unmanageable.

Step Two
Came to believe that a Power greater than ourselves could restore us to sanity.

Step Three
Made a decision to turn our will and our lives over to the care of God as we understood God.

Step Four
Made a searching and fearless moral inventory of ourselves.

Step Five
Admitted to God, to ourselves, and to another human being the exact nature of our wrongs.

Step Six
Were entirely ready to have God remove all these defects of character.

Step Seven
Humbly asked God to remove our shortcomings.

Step Eight
Made a list of all persons we had harmed and became willing to make amends to them all.

Step Nine
Made direct amends to such people wherever possible, except when to do so would injure them or others.

Step Ten
Continued to take personal inventory and when we were wrong promptly admitted it.

Step Eleven
Sought through prayer and meditation to improve our conscious contact with God, as we understood God, praying only for knowledge of God's will for us and the power to carry that out.

Step Twelve
Having had a spiritual awakening as the result of these Steps, we tried to carry this message to other sex addicts and to practice these principles in all of our activities.

* The Twelve Steps reprinted for adaptation with permission of AA World Services, Inc. © 1972.

12

Giving As Its Own Reward

The Twelfth Step begins with the promise that if we work the Program, we will have a spiritual awakening. As is true with most aspects of recovery, this awakening is a *process*, not an event. Working the Twelfth Step helped us move from an isolated abstract concept that there is a power greater than ourselves to an emotional and mental acceptance—a faith—that there is a God of our understanding. We found that the more we worked the Steps and really used them in our daily lives, the more spiritually awake and aware we became and the more ordered and meaningful our lives seemed to be. We also began to see an important connection between people and events that we had been completely unaware of in the past. *Twelve Steps and Twelve Traditions* describes the process of our spiritual awakening in this way: "When a man or a woman has a spiritual awakening, the most important meaning of it is that he (or she) now has become able to do, feel, and believe that which he (or she) could not do before on his (or her) unaided strength and resources alone"(pp. 106-7).

In the course of our recovery, most of us had spiritual *experiences*. We welcomed these experiences, particularly when we learned that they were signs that we were, indeed, beginning to awaken spiritually. These spiritual experiences occurred at different times and in different places for each of us. As we talked with other addicts, we could see similarities in the spiritual experiences we were having: feelings of safety, security, and community, and times when we could see ourselves so clearly as part of a whole yet not feel lost or insignificant in it. Many of us noticed that our spiritual awakening brought on a period of intense reflection that focused on the present. Most notable, perhaps, were the breakthroughs—we no longer had the need to control and even when we were alone, we were not lonely. Wherever and whenever we had these experiences, we found that instead of being plagued with doubt as we might have been in the past, we were reassured. Subsequently we began sharing our thoughts and feelings with others more openly and more frequently.

In working the Program, we came to know that it is filled with paradoxes: in order to stop acting out we must admit that we are unable to do so; help from others is essential to our recovery but we must recover on our own; in order to keep what the Program gives to us we must give it away to others; while the Twelfth Step promises us a spiritual awakening it also identifies our responsibility for "carrying this message" to other addicts. We carry the message to others not to benefit them, but for the sake of our own recovery. Note that the Twelfth Step does *not* say that we converted or saved other addicts, but that we "tried to carry this message." So many times we recalled how others had attempted to make us change when we were acting out and how defiant we were in response to them.

As recovering addicts, we came to understand that the best way to carry the message is to provide a *living example* of what the Program can do for an individual. We don't deny our problems or our past. We don't act as if we are saints. We don't allow ourselves to believe that we have found the only way to happiness. Instead we follow Tradition Eleven, which states that the Program is "based on attraction rather than promotion." We resist giving advice to others and focus instead on explaining to them how the Program works *for us*. We offer other addicts the same opportunities we had ourselves. We share our experience, strength, and hope with our fellow addicts *but we do not play God*. Instead, we regularly remind ourselves that others have Higher Powers of their own watching out for them.

At first most of us utilized a rather narrow interpretation of the second half of the Twelfth Step because we assumed that "carrying the message" referred exclusively to Twelve Step calls—two recovering addicts describe the Program to one addict who is still acting out. Although these Twelve Step calls are extremely important to recovery, we came to understand that there are many other kinds of Twelve Step work. For example, just our physical presence at a meeting communicates to other addicts that they are not alone. We came to understand that we are doing Twelve Step work and "carrying the message" when we sponsor others or discuss our views of the Steps with them, or share with them how we have used the Steps in specific situations, or just give our phone numbers to them. Eventually we came to see that we were working the Twelfth Step even as we carried out simple tasks like preparing coffee at meetings or cleaning up afterwards. We saw that even *newcomers* can engage in effective Twelve Step work and that no matter how long we've been in recovery, we can help other addicts. We also learned that it is important to avoid "two-stepping," wherein we admit our powerlessness then immediately set out to carry our message to others. *We simply cannot give away what we don't have*; for this reason, we need to work on all of the Steps, not just the First and Twelfth Steps.

We make our Twelve Step calls without having any particular expectations, but we are always prepared to follow through if the newcomer we talk to decides that he or she is ready and willing to recover. Chapter Seven in the Big Book ("Working with Others") helped us develop an understanding of the processes involved. We make a point of not going on Twelve Step calls alone because we don't want to place ourselves in situations that might set us up to act out again. Regardless of how long we have been in recovery, we frequently remind ourselves that we are still sex addicts and we must continue to be aware of the power of our addiction. We must guard against jeopardizing our own recovery or the recovery of another person. We always arrange to meet newcomers in safe, neutral places that will not in any way remind us of or actually trigger past acting-out behaviors. To help ensure that we won't slip back into addictive thinking or behaviors, we tell our stories to newcomers as we meet with them. We want newcomers to know from the start that we understand their pain, and we immediately give them permission to be open and honest with us.

Making Twelve Step calls in pairs as we do increases the likelihood that newcomers we visit will hear something in one of our stories that they can relate to. *We are always prepared to be judged by newcomers.* (When we look back, we can see how judgmental we were ourselves during the times we were acting out.) When they heard the details of our stories, some newcomers said things like, "*I'm not that bad!*" or "*I've never done anything like that!*" While working on the Twelve Steps, we are comforted to know that we have another recovering addict with us who supports us and accepts us just as we are. It is *not* our responsibility to convince the newcomer that he or she is an addict. Instead, we only tell these people what addiction had been like *for us*, what we were like when we were acting out, what recovery is like *for us*, and how we have changed. Instead of trying to "sell the Program," we allow the Program to speak for itself through our personal stories and our lives.

More often than not, we find that newcomers are grateful finally to have an opportunity to talk about what has been happening in their lives. At that point we answer their questions and give them some literature on the Twelve Steps. We find that some newcomers are very uncomfortable asking questions face to face; when this is the case, we make a point of exchanging phone numbers. Doing this helps keep the door open for maintaining contact with these people during the time that elapses between our conversation and their first meeting. Because we remember so well how difficult it was at first for *us* to make calls, we make a special point of contacting these people. Then if they express an interest in attending meetings, we ask them to make a commitment to attend meetings over a period of six weeks in order to get a good idea of how the Program really works.

Of course we always stress the confidential nature of the group and the importance of using first names only. In most situations, the two people who Twelve-Step the newcomer become that newcomer's sponsors for the first six weeks that he or she is in the Program. During that period of time, we call the newcomer regularly to offer our support and answer questions. *We encourage newcomers to call us and other addicts as well.*

We find that people don't necessarily come into the fellowship as soon as they are Twelve-Stepped but instead might come into the fellowship after trying several times to recover on their own. At that point many of them tell us that they remember our words and the fact that help *is* available. We never take credit for those who come into the Program or stay in the Program, nor do we accept blame when people reject the Program, fail to attend meetings consistently, or drop out of the Program entirely. *It is, after all, the Program that keeps people sober. And we learn through the Traditions that the Program is based on principles, not personalities.* We are responsible for carrying the message, not for creating or maintaining the willingness of any one person. We can only *help* people recover, we cannot force or otherwise manipulate their recovery. We frequently remind ourselves that other people (addicted or not) have their own Higher Powers and that their personal experiences and views may have led them to choose a path much different from ours.

Our adapted Twelfth Step suggests that we "practice these principles in all of our activities." Just as addiction affects all areas of a person's life, so does recovery. We cannot afford to be dishonest in any area of our lives. In recovery, honesty, openness, and willingness become fully integrated with our life-styles. The Twelfth Step is not a goal that, once attained, signifies that we are "recovered." We are fortunate in that our Program has no end and therefore establishes no limit on the amount of growth we can experience. We are not recovered addicts; we are *recovering* addicts. And if we choose, the Twelve Steps will be there for us—guiding us in hope and recovery for the rest of our lives.

13

Abstinence and Sobriety

"You mean I have to give up sex forever?" This was the first question many of us asked when we learned about our addiction and the Program. The concept of long-term abstention from sex is difficult enough for most people to consider, but it was *unthinkable* to us as practicing sex addicts. Most of us were people of extremes and many of us had been living our lives without placing any limitations whatsoever on our sexual behaviors. *"Anything goes!"* and *"Anything worth doing is worth over-doing!"* were mottoes that in some ways served to shape our lives.

When we first came to the Program, many of us decided that we should be celibate. Celibacy *did,* in fact, help some of us with our conscious efforts to slow down and consider carefully what we had been doing with our lives. Soon, however, we realized that celibacy was simply a means to an end, not an end in itself, and that the other extreme—compulsive abstinence from sexual activity—was not a realistic or healthy answer for us either. In fact, we found that compulsive abstinence from sex was just as unnatural to us as compulsive sexual behavior had been. In some ways, we sex addicts have much in common with our sisters and brothers in another Twelve Step group, Overeaters Anonymous (OA). We learned some important things from the people in OA about the difference between abstinence and sobriety. Recognizing the fact that it is not reasonable to abstain from eating for a significant period of time, recovering people in OA direct their energies toward learning to eat in healthy ways *without* eating compulsively.

When we began working on the First Step, we carefully considered the sexual behaviors that had harmed us and others in the past, then made lists of these behaviors. The lists we compiled helped us identify which of our behaviors were healthy and which of our behaviors were addictive and harmful. Despite the fact that each Twelve Step group develops its own working definition for addictive behavior, all groups acknowledge that addictive behavior is characterized by: feelings of being driven and preoccupied, a lack of control, and a tendency to place such a high priority on the behavior that it interferes with important tasks and relationships and is, in some way, abusive to the person himself or herself as well as to other people involved. Addictive sexual behavior—acting-out behavior we sometimes call it—leads to feelings of shame and depression; it has the effect of masking, covering up, or numbing feelings; and it also leads to isolation and a complete loss of control. Healthy sexual behavior, on the other hand, is characterized by mutual respect, a sense of clarity about feelings and communication, joyfulness, and genuine intimacy; it tends to make people feel emotionally and physically safe.

Once our obsessions were removed—through our Higher Power and a daily practice of the Twelve Steps—we found that we were free to begin enjoying healthy sex and all the pleasure it brought us. But having our obsessions removed and establishing healthy sex lives did not mean that we could resume doing everything we had done in the past. The key word here is *healthy*. Many of us didn't even know what healthy sexual behavior was because we had been sexually abused as children or had grown up in families that somehow communicated the idea that sex and sexual desires were inherently bad and shameful.

As we learned more about the characteristics of both addictive and healthy sexual behavior we also learned that the motivation for the behavior—not the behavior itself—is the most important element of our addiction. This insight helped us understand, for example, that even if a sex addict is involved in a committed and monogamous relationship with another person, the sexual behavior within that relationship is, nevertheless, likely to be addictive. Indeed, many of us never once had sex outside of our committed relationships, but still we acted out sexually. Some of us acted out by using sexual activity with our partners in order to escape our feelings; some of us acted out by threatening or otherwise manipulating our partners into being sexual with us; some of us pressured our partners to do things we knew they were uncomfortable doing. On the other hand, given the characteristics of addiction and the importance of motivation, we began to understand that behaviors such as having a sexual relationship with someone of the same sex, or having sex prior to marriage are not *necessarily* acting-out behaviors.

Early on, those of us who struggled with feelings of shame about being lesbian or gay had some difficulties determining what was acting-out behavior for us. At first some of us assumed that our sexual thoughts and behaviors involving people of the same sex constituted acting-out behavior, almost by definition. But we learned that our assumption was wrong and we needed help to see how we could be true to ourselves, maintain our same-sex preferences, and have healthy sexual relationships. Others of us had the mistaken belief that all of our behavior was healthy and we used our same-sex preference or bisexuality to defend our addiction. We were outraged when anyone would question our sexual behavior and ask us to look at it for signs of acting out. In the same way, also, we began to understand that whatever it is that motivates us to masturbate—not the act of masturbation itself—determines whether or not that activity should be considered acting-out behavior. Those of us who used masturbation to escape from feelings, isolate ourselves from others, and justify or reinforce our low self-esteem came to see that masturbation was, for us, acting-out behavior.

After spending some time in the Program, we realized that we were taking a narrow and simplistic point of view in assuming that we could actually "cure" ourselves of our sex addiction by simply eliminating all acting-out behaviors from our lives. Abstinence from acting-out behaviors did not resolve the *real problem*—obsessive thoughts that we struggled with every waking moment and sometimes even in our dreams. When we finally understood that we could not run and hide from our sexuality and that we are sexual beings whether or not we are engaging in sex, we found that we were ready to take steps to change our thinking and manage our lives.

After identifying the acting-out behaviors in our lives and making sincere efforts to eliminate them, we found that we were ready to set our boundaries and stay within them. But we needed the help of other addicts in order to do this because we were still so blind to our own addictions. So with help from our sponsors and other people in our groups, each of us set guidelines or boundaries governing our own sexual behavior—in other words, we discussed which behaviors we would allow ourselves to engage in and which behaviors we would not allow ourselves to engage in. Always, our goal was to work toward a healthy sexuality. As we began to establish specific boundaries, we found it extremely helpful to have support from those people—sponsors, for example—who knew our stories. Despite the importance of support from others, we came to understand that each of us had to live his or her own Program. At this stage in our recovery, we also learned the realistic application of the slogan "To Thine Own Self Be True"—that an appropriate boundary for one person is not necessarily an appropriate boundary for another person.

Since our addictions were, as the Big Book says, "cunning, baffling, and powerful!" (p. 58-9) we realized that we had to be alert to the ways we might set ourselves up for failure in establishing our boundaries. For instance, people who set boundaries that would not allow them to *purchase* pornographic material soon discovered that this boundary nevertheless allowed them to *use* pornography, as long as they got it from someone else or somehow gained access to it without purchasing it. In this case, *no use of pornographic material whatsoever* would have been a clearer and safer boundary to set. Most of us found that the mistakes and miscalculations we made as we set our boundaries manifested themselves almost immediately through a return of obsessive thinking.

When we first came to the Program, we not only assumed that eliminating sexual acting-out behavior from our lives would change our lives, we also assumed that all of our problems would be resolved if we maintained our abstinence. In time we found that it just wasn't enough to work on *not* doing something, we also needed to replace our acting-out behaviors with *positive action*. Active involvement in the Program represents one form of positive action we can take. Now we understand that *sobriety is abstinence combined with personal and spiritual growth which focuses on the removal of our character defects*. We achieve sobriety by working *all* the Steps, not just the first three of five Steps. The payoff for all this work— *serenity and feelings of contentment that would have been impossible to imagine during the times we were acting out*.

At first we were completely overwhelmed when we considered the tasks involved in attaining abstinence and sobriety. But we were able to relax somewhat when we realized that the attainment of abstinence and sobriety *is a process, not an isolated event*. At first many of us worked the Twelve Steps in order to avoid something—jail, being discovered, loss of a relationship, or despair; later on in recovery we worked the Steps in order to *gain* something—genuine intimacy, spiritual gifts, companionship, ongoing growth, and peace of mind. Miraculously, we were able to reclaim and place in proper perspective that which had been so long denied to us—a healthy sexuality.

When we worked the Steps and attended the meetings because we felt that we "had to," we knew very few moments of serenity. But once we began attending meetings and working the Steps because we *wanted* to, we also began to experience real serenity and real sobriety. One of the most important gifts of the Program is that it helps us care about ourselves enough to do things that are gentle and self-nurturing.

14

Sponsorship

We all felt so fortunate for the support and help of sponsors during the difficult early stages of recovery. As newcomers, we found that our sponsors were particularly helpful to us as we prepared to learn about the Twelve Steps and Twelve Traditions. Most of us had sponsors who had been working the Steps for a year or more and had already experienced sobriety. It was reassuring to know that because these people had been in the Program longer than we had been, they'd already faced and worked through many of the difficult times we faced.

Those of us who came to the Program after being Twelve-Stepped found that we actually began our work with the help of *two sponsors*—two recovering addicts who first told us about the Program. They met with us and told us part of their stories and also told us how they began the process of recovery themselves by working the Twelve Steps and Twelve Traditions. The information they shared helped clarify what the Program is and what the Program *is not*. From the time of our first meetings with them, our sponsors also emphasized the importance of confidentiality and anonymity.

After listening to our sponsors, we were able to let go of many of the myths and stereotypes we'd had for so long about sex addicts and sex addiction. Following these first meetings with our sponsors, they took us to our first group meetings. We realize now that it was a bit easier to enter those meetings already knowing two people in attendance.

These "temporary" sponsors continued to help us through our first six or eight weeks in the Program, a critical period of time when we worked to integrate the Twelve Steps into our daily lives and also began to establish ourselves within our Twelve Step groups. Our sponsors urged us to call them whenever we had questions or felt tense or uncertain. Following this initial period of time in the Program, many of us maintained sponsor-sponsee relationships with at least one of the two addicts who had Twelve-Stepped us. Some of us chose to maintain these relationships with our sponsors over time because they continued to be helpful and meaningful to our recovery. At this same point in time, however, some of us chose *new* sponsors who we felt could provide us with some special support or guidance. Whether we found new sponsors or stayed with the first sponsors we had in the Program, we all came to understand that it is not necessary that our sponsors be people similar to us or even people we would tend to choose as friends. In fact, many of us found that we actually learned more from sponsors whose backgrounds were very different from ours.

But no matter *who* our sponsors were, we sensed almost right away that they had special empathy and compassion for us because they knew our struggle so well and had firsthand knowledge of the life of a practicing sex addict; *they knew the pain and difficulty of recovery*. Our sponsors listened patiently to our stories and gave us permission and time to share our pent-up emotions with them. Our sponsors also gave us special encouragement and support as we explained addiction and recovery to other people in our lives.

Our sponsors were always straightforward with us when they didn't have answers to our questions or when they felt that we should seek help from a professional or from someone else in the group. They shared their weaknesses as well as their strengths with us and they treated us with *genuine respect*, even when we were convinced that we didn't *deserve* anyone's respect. Our sponsors were trustworthy and we knew they would always respect the confidentiality of our relationships and our conversations with them.

In time, we found that there was no need whatsoever to hide our struggles and pain from our sponsors, or from any other group members. We began to see that other people were not there with us to offer judgments or punishments as we struggled—sometimes unsuccessfully—to *not* act out. Instead we found that other people were there with us to provide us with support and help for the challenging journey of recovery. We found that our sponsors really meant it when they said things like this to us: "Call me before you go and act out or call me after you act out. In fact, you can call me *while* you're acting out! But please don't cut yourself off from others and isolate yourself because if you do that, you'll only be setting yourself up to act out again." Our sponsors reminded us that there were two primary reasons to call other people: when we felt that we needed to call them and when we felt that we *didn't* need to call them. By reminding us that *We* is the all-important first word of the First Step, our sponsors helped us understand a very important concept: that in order to maintain recovery, we need to stay in touch with other recovering addicts; *we cannot maintain recovery in isolation.*

If they sensed that we were reluctant to call other people in the group, our sponsors encouraged us to make "practice" calls. These practice calls involved phoning other addicts from our groups and saying something like this: "My sponsor told me to call five group members this week; you're the second one I've called. See you at the meeting. Bye!" After making these practice calls for a couple of weeks, the task of calling others in the group and having real conversations with them became less threatening to us. Our sponsors explained the importance of this special effort: if we were reluctant to call other addicts when things were going *well* for us, we almost certainly would be reluctant to call other addicts when things were *not* going well for us.

As we became more familiar with the Program and with the people in our groups, we developed new abilities to recognize and work toward the self-acceptance that recovering addicts have. Gaining self-acceptance in this way amazed most of us because we had come to the Program *filled* with self-hatred. Our sponsors talked freely of the gratitude they felt and continued to remind us that it was *the Program*—not merely their individual efforts, examples, and experience as individuals— that was helping us so much. To reinforce this concept, our sponsors pointed out this phrase in Tradition Twelve: "...place principles before personalities." Our sponsors did not attempt to play God; they taught us to rely on the Twelve Steps, the group, and our Higher power, rather than on any one or two individuals.

Some of us felt guilty because we were not accustomed to receiving genuine support without being required to give something in return. At first, we were still in too much turmoil to return that support in kind. But as our own recovery progressed and grew, we did give the love and compassion back—to those who looked to us to be their sponsors. In turn, we freely gave away to others the gifts of experience, strength, and hope that had been given to us. And we *did* help our sponsors by giving them opportunities to work the Twelfth Step in carrying the message to us. As our sponsors listened to us share our stories as newcomers, many of them heard themselves and what they had been speaking, thinking, and saying not long before us. They found they could strengthen and enhance their own recovery by explaining to us how the Program helped *them*. Our sponsors told us that whenever they reminded *us* of the importance of attending meetings, staying in touch with other recovering addicts, and working the Twelve Steps in their daily lives, they also reminded *themselves* of the importance of those elements of recovery.

During our first several months in the Program, most of us had intense relationships with our sponsors. But as we grew in the Program and learned more in recovery, we also sought out and received support from other people in our groups as well.

Nevertheless, we always worked to nurture the special relationships we had with our sponsors. We came to understand that it is not the job of the sponsor to monitor or police the actions of the newcomer. Nevertheless, we wanted to share news of our progress with our sponsors, so we checked in with them at least once a week and always tried to be honest with them. After our sponsors came to know us better, they were able to point out the old thinking and behaviors that they saw coming back into our lives from time to time as well as the growth and change they could see in us. *They celebrated our sobriety with us.* Here was a relationship with a person who cared for us and was willing to help us at any time of the day or night. In return, that person asked for nothing other than honesty and sincere effort. *Surely this was and is a relationship to cherish.*

15
Slips/Relapses

Not one of us would have come even *close* to succeeding in the Program had sobriety—abstinence from acting-out behaviors combined with personal growth and work within the Program— been a prerequisite for attendance at meetings. From the beginning of our work in the Program, we understood that the only requirement for attending Twelve Step meetings was a *willingness* to eliminate acting-out behaviors from our lives. Even though we tried our best to work the Program and live the Twelve Steps, sometimes we failed in that we had slips or relapses (resumption of obsessive thinking and compulsive behavior.) But we were told by our sponsors and other recovering addicts that slips and relapses could and probably *would* happen to almost everyone at one time or another and that even when these setbacks *did* occur we would, as always, be welcome at Twelve Step meetings. In time, we learned that we had to attend Twelve Step meetings and speak honestly with other recovering addicts in order to stop our acting-out behaviors.

When we *did* have slips or relapses, we were not punished— at least not by our fellow addicts. (Most of us agree that the *effects* of the addictive behavior are the *real* punishment.) Though our slips and relapses were very costly to us emotionally and spiritually, we did learn some valuable lessons from them. For example, some of us learned that we needed to listen better; some of us learned that we could not live the Program on a part-time basis; some of us learned that we needed to re-evaluate and/or change our boundaries; and others of us learned that other addicts really *do know* when we are setting ourselves up for failure. Most of us found that we had sponsors or fellow group members who could warn us that we were returning to old, self-destructive patterns of thinking and behavior, and therefore setting ourselves up for slips and re-lapses. Perhaps they could see that our priorities were becoming confused again and that we were putting other things ahead of recovery; or that we were neglecting our Maintenance Steps (Ten, Eleven, and Twelve); or that we were becoming compla-cent and actually believed that we had been "cured" of our addiction and were no longer powerless.

Many of us had mistakenly assumed that once we eliminated acting-out behaviors from our lives, we could go right back to spending time in the same places with the same people we had in the past, yet have no further problems with our addiction or addictive urges. Some of us were dishonest about our behaviors or emotions when we shared at Twelve Step meetings or with other addicts on the phone and intentionally "forgot" to mention something we'd had obsessive thoughts about or actually carried out. Some of us started feeling sorry for ourselves, then began losing the gratitude we had come to feel for the Program. These gaps in our recovery eventually led to argumentativeness and defensiveness, as well as feelings of frustration, depression, and loneliness. Most of us attempted to blame our setbacks on *everybody and everything* except the one factor that was affect-ing and perhaps even sabotaging our recovery: *we were no longer working the Twelve Steps*. But woe to anyone who dared to point out that reality to us—no matter how gently he or she tried to do so.

At first some of us found it very difficult to see how we were being self-destructive by acting out again just one time. Our thinking went something like this: I really didn't hurt *anyone* when I stopped at that porno shop. I certainly didn't get arrested or spend much money there, so what's the big deal? It was very difficult for some of us to see how even one incident of acting-out behavior could possibly affect our emotional well-being. Other recovering sex addicts could clearly see how we changed before and after we acted out, even though we were unable to identify these changes *ourselves*. Indeed, an important characteristic of addiction is the *inability* to see or feel the *effects* of the addiction. At first we were completely unable to see how, after acting out, we perpetuated the addictive cycle by playing mind games with ourselves: (Sure I drove fifty miles in order to buy some pornography, but I'm not powerless. This time I was in control and I knew exactly what I was doing.) In time, we found that we could not engage in self-destructive behavior even *once* without paying for it emotionally and spiritually. After acting out, we were always haunted by our own feelings of guilt; the consequences of our acting-out behaviors ultimately hurt us.

Before we came to the Program, many of us had *never* felt accepted by other people. Some of us had come to believe that in order to be liked by others, we had to be "perfect." Naturally, those of us who had experienced so much rejection in our lives fully expected to be rejected by the people in our groups when we told them of our slips and relapses. But sharing the things we feared would drive others away actually had the opposite effect—it brought us closer to others. When we discovered that these people understood, encouraged, respected, and liked us—despite our less than perfect behavior—we experienced a powerful, life-transforming change in our thinking. And, contrary to what we believed in the past, we learned that we were actually much *less* likely to act out again if we felt overall acceptance, respect, and responsiveness from other people. We came to understand that an addict who is isolated, shame-filled, and discouraged is much more likely to act out again than an addict who admits to a slip or a relapse yet is still understood, listened to, and encouraged. When we were sheltered and nurtured, we were much more likely to attain sobriety and maintain it as well. Not one of us was ever *shamed* into recovery.

When we first saw fellow addicts struggling with slips or relapses, we tended to be judgmental. Most of us vowed that

91

we would never allow these setbacks to mar our *own* recovery. But then we'd remember an important slogan that is used so often in conversations about the Program and how it works: "There But For The Grace Of God Go I." Saying these words actually helped us become more humble about ourselves and more understanding of others. Instead of judging our fellow addicts as they struggled and sometimes failed, we reached out to them with our support. We always tried to be there for these fellow addicts as they worked through their slips and relapses in the same way we would want and need them to be with us when we worked through our *own* slips and relapses.

16

Telling Others About Our Addiction

Some of us were almost *relieved* when we first heard the words "sex addict" used to describe us. At last we had some idea of what our problem was and we had a name for it as well. This new information helped us understand our thoughts and our behaviors. Finally we could let go of all the hateful names we had called ourselves through the years and learn to focus on identifying and working to eliminate the destructive patterns of thinking and behavior that had come to dominate our lives. But even with these new feelings of relief, it was still very difficult to say the words "sex addict" out loud. We listened to other people in our groups speak their first names loud and clear, then add "...and I'm a sex addict." Though the words were difficult to say at first, eventually we began introducing ourselves as sex addicts at group meetings for three reasons: to remind ourselves that we were still addicts; to work through the feelings of shame we continued to have about our addiction; and to help others see their own addictions.

Encouraged by new feelings of relief and freedom, many of us were eager to tell *everyone* in our lives that we were recovering sex addicts. In fact, some of us were rather impatient with oldtimers in our groups who cautioned us about sharing the details of our addiction with others by telling us that the slogan "Easy Does It" applies to all areas of our lives—including telling others about our addiction. At first we could see absolutely no reason to hold back; we *desperately* wanted to explain our past behaviors to our bosses, to our friends, and to members of our families. We also wanted to explain our new perspective in recovery by saying something like this to the people in our lives: "Hey! I acted the way I did because I'm a sex addict, not because I'm a bad person—I couldn't help myself." But being impulsive had gotten us into trouble before and we learned in recovery that we would need to *grow in the Program* before we could tell others about our addiction. Some of us were sure that we had found the ultimate excuse ("I'm sick!"), but until such time as significant change actually had been achieved, that's all it would have been—an excuse.

Recovery requires that we take responsibility for our addictive behavior. We learned that our *actions* really spoke much louder than any words we could say to explain our past behaviors or our present work in the Program. We came to understand that the *best way* to communicate to others that we were getting healthier was to do just that—*get healthier and demonstrate the change that had taken place in us with the example of our lives*. Similarly, rather than telling others how we planned to stop acting out and begin living within our values, we found it much more productive and positive to concentrate our energies on eliminating our acting-out behaviors, establishing our values, and learning to live with those values. We noted that the Amend Steps—Steps Eight and Nine—were more than halfway through the Twelve Steps. We learned that it takes a significant amount of work to prepare for the experience of actually telling people about our addiction and what we had done in the past. We found that we needed a longer period of sobriety in order to learn how to choose who to tell and also to deal effectively with the unpredictable responses that came from people when we told them about our addiction. Sobriety helped ensure that we wouldn't be so overwhelmed with negative responses that we'd act out again.

The Alcoholics Anonymous organization has been quite successful in lessening the stigma that was for so many years associated with alcohol addiction. Although great strides have been made in terms of reducing this stigma, many people still believe that any form of addiction automatically denotes immorality, weakness of character, or general lack of will power.

Previously we knew so well the incredible will power it took for us to get out of bed each morning, to go out into the world, and to act as if nothing terrible had happened to us the night before. We also knew the enormous personal effort that we'd had to make in order to recover. We learned that most nonaddicted people didn't really know what we had been through in order to recover and, therefore, many of these people were very judgmental and negative toward us when we told them about our addiction. But the fact of the matter is that the goal of the Program is to *help sex addicts recover*, not to educate society about sex addiction. The Twelfth Step says that we carry this message to "other sex addicts"—not to the world at large.

During the times we were acting out, many of us acted illegally. In recovery we learned that while we must take responsibility for our behavior, sharing our personal "horror stories" with others serves no real purpose other than perhaps further isolating us from them. We also began to understand that it was not fair to burden our loved ones with the details of our addictions and acting-out behaviors. Most of us discovered that our addiction had affected the people in our lives *enough* without subjecting them to further involvement and pain by telling them our stories. So we learned to share our stories with other people in the group and, of course, with our sponsors. These people were not likely to be as emotionally involved with us as our families and friends were. Also, our sponsors understood both addiction and the Twelve Step Program and could offer us help within the Program that our friends and families might *not* be able to offer us.

How did we actually tell others about our addiction once we'd discussed it with other group members, prayed about it, and felt it was the right time to do so? Some of us chose to remind people in our lives about a particular incident—an incident in which our acting-out behavior somehow affected them. Then we told them that this kind of acting-out behavior had become a pattern in our lives and we were getting help and support in a group setting so that we wouldn't act out in that way again. Many of us found that we had to be extremely careful regarding the details we shared when we told others about our addiction. In fact, some of us realized that we were acting out by telling others about our addiction because we shared intimate sexual details with them in order to shock and/or excite them. On the other hand, when some of us told others about our addiction we encountered people who did not understand the pain of addiction and insisted that we did not have a problem but were, instead, very fortunate to be sexually active to the extent that we were. In time we learned that we did not have a responsibility to educate these people, nor did we need to convince them of our pain and the destructive nature of our addiction.

Those of us who were involved in committed relationships eventually told our partners that we were sex addicts and that we were actively involved in a Twelve Step Program that was helping us to deal with our addiction. We shared the specifics of our stories with these people only if we believed that doing so would *enhance* rather than harm our relationships with them. When we talked to these key people in our lives, we were very careful not to shame ourselves or in any way abuse, blame, or shame *them*. We always tried to share this information with an emphasis on *recovery* rather than on the insanity of our past behavior. If the people we shared this information with indicated that they wanted to know more about sex addiction, we gave them copies of published material that had been helpful to us—material with a focus on real stories of real people who were recovering.

Because many of us had, in the past, broken promises we'd made to these people, we spoke of our addiction and recovery without making any promises or predictions with regard to the future. Now we understood that we would have to *show them through our actions* that we had changed, not just talk about the change. We waited until we had been sober for some time before we told these people about our addiction. We waited to tell others because we came to understand that if we had experienced sobriety, we were less likely to act out a self-fulfilling prophecy if and when someone happened to say something like this to us when we told them of our recovery: *"Sure, I've heard that before, but you'll be at it again in no time."* Some people were disrespectful and even abusive to us when we told them about our addiction. While we knew that we did not have to stay in abusive situations, we dealt with these reactions by reminding ourselves that we were telling others about our addiction not to help them, but to help ourselves. Some of us found that it was helpful to have our sponsors with us when we told our partners about our addiction. And if our partners also happened to be in recovery, it was helpful to have their sponsors present, too. Having a third party involved seemed to help *everyone* hear the messages more clearly. We wrote down exactly what we wanted to say to our partners and shared it with other addicts first. Preparing in this way helped us to be as clear as possible about what it was we wanted to say and how we wanted to say it.

Those of us who had children with at least some knowledge of our acting-out behaviors adapted our disclosures to their chronological ages and their emotional maturity. Those of us with very young children kept our messages as brief and simple as the following: "I was very sick and I did things that I don't want to do again. I am sorry for what I did and I am getting help so that I won't do those things again." When we told our children about our addiction—no matter what their ages—we always made sure they understood that we'd be willing to discuss our recovery with them whenever they had questions. We also told them the truth whenever we felt that we could not answer a particular question they asked or whenever we wanted to discuss a certain question or issue with other people in our groups before discussing it with them. We found that common sense and patience were the most valuable tools we had in talking with our children about our addiction.

Some of us chose not to tell other people about our addiction at all. We learned that the Program's strong emphasis on anonymity supported our choice to share the personal details of our addiction only with our Higher Power and our Twelve Step Fellowship. Instead we simply told others that we'd had some problems, that we had been acting inappropriately, and that we were in the process of getting the help we needed.

17

The Slogans

ONE DAY AT A TIME – EASY DOES IT – BE GENTLE WITH YOURSELF – H.A.L.T. – FIRST THINGS FIRST – ACT AS IF – IF IT WORKS, DON'T FIX IT – THIS TOO SHALL PASS – LET GO AND LET GOD – TO THINE OWN SELF BE TRUE – LIVE AND LET LIVE – KEEP IT SIMPLE – THERE BUT FOR THE GRACE OF GOD GO I

Many of us thought that the slogans were trite and simplistic when we first heard them at Twelve Step meetings. Some of us, in fact, resented it when recovering addicts reminded us of these slogans during our discussions about the struggles of addiction and recovery. As we worked the Program, however, we came to see the real value of these slogans: they represent important information and useful inspiration in a brief, memorable form. We came to see that these slogans are similar to the Twelve Steps in terms of their simplicity and substance. When we finally learned to stop just *saying* the slogans and start *hearing them* and *applying them to our lives*, we found them to be extremely useful tools for recovery.

• ONE DAY AT A TIME
Although an essential part of our Program involves writing a personal inventory and making amends for past behavior, we found that it was not necessary to spend time worrying about the past or punishing ourselves for it. Indeed, this slogan communicates the concept that we are responsible for our recovery *today and only today*, and that we need not be preoccupied with the past or the future. Contrary to what many of us had come to believe, we learned that we are not *prisoners* of the past. Furthermore, through our work in the Program, we learned that

no matter what we had done in the past, we were capable of changing. We came to understand that while we *cannot change* the past, we *can learn* from it so that we will not continue to make the same mistakes.

This slogan also freed us from spending time considering the "what ifs" of life. We came to believe that because we had turned our lives over to the care of God, as we understood God, things would ultimately work out as they should. This belief, in turn, helped us see that desiring a certain goal and working to achieve it is different from trying to *control* the outcome of everything in our lives.

When we first heard it said that ours is a twenty-four-hour Program, we assumed this was merely another way of saying that addiction and recovery never took a break. But we soon learned that this twenty-four-hour concept also refers to the fact that each day is broken into twenty-four hours. *Twenty-four hours of choice; twenty-four hours of potential recovery.* In fact, this was exactly the way we worked on our recovery at first—*one hour at a time.* When we found ourselves in particularly difficult situations, we'd promise ourselves that we wouldn't act out for the next hour or even the next minute. We learned not to take on any more than we could handle. *We began to see that whenever we focused our energies on the past or the future, we were losing at least part of ourselves to the here and now.* Learning to live in the present led to a more fulfilling life for us as individuals, yet made it possible for us to be more available to the people in our lives.

We knew that we were living both the First Step and this slogan when we stopped marking our calendars on the dates we expected to receive medallions. Because we had come to terms with our addiction, we knew that we could not *guarantee* to anyone—including ourselves—that we would be sober *any day but today.* We came to see our goal in terms of recovery, not in terms of medallions. During the period of our active addiction, we periodically swore off certain thoughts and behaviors, only to resume them soon thereafter. When we began to recover, we stopped swearing off thoughts or behaviors for any period of time longer than one day. We also came to understand that we would not get a *reprieve* from our addiction as a reward for the length of our abstinence or sobriety. We knew that any one of us could slip if we did not continue working the Twelve Steps, and we began to understand that no one is "slip-proof," because the addictive process is a factor in the addict's life whether he or she acts on it or not. We managed to arrest our acting-out behavior even though we knew we would never be "cured." *We continued to recover.* We discovered that while we would not get "extra credit" for not acting out during a certain period of time, we weren't trapped by the past either. Just because we had acted out yesterday did not mean that we would act out today. We learned that regardless of what we had done the day before, recovery could begin anew for us each and every day of our lives.

• EASY DOES IT

The numbering and the content of the Twelve Steps work together to tell us that we need to proceed slowly. In fact, everything we learned in the Program reinforces the concept that recovery is too important to be rushed. During the time of our active addiction, we were filled with despair, intolerance, rigidity, and impatience; we simply did not do things at a reasonable pace. We either tried to do things so fast that we tripped over ourselves in the process, or we never really got started at all.

At first some of us tried to use "Easy Does It" as a justification for avoiding our problems. For example, instead of seeing procrastination as a character defect to be removed by working Steps Six and Seven, we rationalized our tendencies to procrastinate by telling ourselves that we were going slowly and taking care of ourselves in a way that was compatible with the

Program. Our sponsors and other recovering addicts helped us find a pace that was most appropriate for us. This slogan serves as a reminder that in terms of our Program and recovery, it is dangerous for us to move ahead too quickly or too slowly. This slogan also helps us to be more tolerant of others. Early in recovery, many of us expected the people in our lives to change. It was useful to remind ourselves that "Easy Does It" is also a very helpful concept concerning our expectations of others.

• BE GENTLE WITH YOURSELF

During our active addiction, many of us set extremely high expectations for ourselves in order to attempt to control our acting-out behaviors. We pushed ourselves relentlessly in pursuit of the kind of achievement and perfection we assumed would prove our worth, *in spite of our addiction*. But the plans we made based on these unrealistic expectations backfired; even when we *did* manage to achieve our goals, we continued to think of ourselves in terms of failure and worthlessness and we continued to punish ourselves with abusive thoughts and behaviors.

In recovery, we found that we needed to make conscious efforts to bring gentleness into our lives as an antidote for the abuse and violence many of us had come to know so well. Other people in our groups taught us to be kind to ourselves through their nurturing and support. We found that as we reached out to others and spoke to them without harshness or judgment, we also began treating ourselves with respect and compassion. We stopped having negative and abusive thoughts about ourselves. Treating ourselves with gentleness certainly did not represent a way to avoid reality nor was it any kind of substitute for the "searching and fearless" honesty we needed to incorporate into our lives. This new gentleness did, however, represent a way that we could cast off the burden of shame that we carried and learn to be all that we could be. In time, we developed an attitude of acceptance and encouragement toward ourselves and others.

• H.A.L.T.

Hunger, Anger, Loneliness, and Tiredness—we learned that we needed to monitor and respond to these four conditions as we worked on our recovery. We could see that whenever we failed to get proper nourishment, we became physically weak and our energy was low. At these times, everything in our lives became more difficult, we became irritable and negative in our thinking, and we stopped having a sense of gratitude. We found that when we held on to our anger, we became resentful. Our feelings of resentment, in turn, led to self-pity. Actually, when we were angry at the whole world and feeling sorry for ourselves, we were setting ourselves up for a "reward"—acting out. Before we became part of the group, loneliness was a familiar condition for most of us. When we isolated ourselves from other group members, we became even *more* lonely. Then we started thinking that we ought to go back where people "really cared about us." When we began thinking this way, many of us ultimately returned to the same places where we had gotten into trouble in the past. When we became extremely tired, many of us told ourselves that we needed something to give us a lift and help us relax. Being addicts, of course, we tended to seek out other addictive acts. After working the Program for a time, we could see that when we allowed ourselves to get run down we actually set ourselves up for acting out, but that when we were alert and healthy we were much more likely to stay sober. Experience taught us that maintenance of good physical and emotional health is vitally important to recovery.

• FIRST THINGS FIRST

We found that this slogan actually functioned as a brake for our relentless perfectionism because it reminded us that we cannot do everything at once, nor are we *expected* to do everything at once. We learned that in recovery, life would continue to be a series of choices for us; we learned that our first priority in making these choices had to be recovery, for *without recovery we had nothing.* We came to see that we had to base each decision we made on how that decision would ultimately affect our recovery. We made a fundamental decision that subsequently affected every other decision we would make in our lives: we were not willing to risk the loss of sobriety for any short-term gains.

• ACT AS IF
At first we did not have complete faith in the Program, so we weren't absolutely sure that it would work for us. But our faith in the Program began to develop once we *experienced* the changes in our thoughts and behaviors that resulted from our work on the Twelve Steps. Until that time of transformation, we simply had to *act as if* we believed we could stay sober, *act as if* we weren't too sick to recover, *act as if* other addicts accepted us, and *act as if* we believed in a Higher Power. We tried our best to act as we thought recovering addicts would act. After some time in the Program, we realized that we didn't really need to *act as if* we were recovering anymore because *we actually were recovering.*

• IF IT WORKS, DON'T FIX IT
As newcomers, many of us decided that the Twelve Steps needed some rewriting so that they would be even "better" tools for recovery. Some of us objected to words or phrases here and there. In fact, when we talked with each other about our interest in "improving" the Twelve Steps, it turned out that each one of us, at a time early in the recovery process, felt that we just happened to be the one addict who could improve the Program "with just a few adjustments." But when we worked Steps Six and Seven, we were able to see and deal with our grandiosity. At that point we could begin to relax and accept the Twelve

Step Program without changes. The Program worked effectively for thousands of people just as it was written. It was *us*, not the Program, needing help in order to function properly. We also used this slogan to deal with our perfectionism. Some of us mistrusted ourselves even when our recovery was proceeding well. We'd analyze every aspect of our Program, and in spite of evidence that we were maintaining our sobriety and continuing to grow, we were convinced that we weren't doing enough. When we started getting critical of our own progress in the Program, this slogan helped us renew our trust in ourselves and our recovery.

• THIS TOO SHALL PASS
We came to see this slogan as a statement of faith that things would work out, that we would be taken care of, and that we would encounter only those challenges that we could handle on a given day. In time we discovered that there were no situations so terrible that they could *force* us to act out and there were no conditions in our lives that were so intolerable that acting out would help. But even in recovery, we found that our perceptions of time were grossly distorted when we were in moods or situations that we knew had led to acting-out behavior in the past— indeed, it seemed as if these moods or situations would last forever. Many times this slogan brought us the relief and help we needed...just in time. We found that there was no situation so bad that acting out wouldn't make it even worse.

• LET GO AND LET GOD
This slogan really addresses the use of the Second and Third Steps. Basically it tells us to stop fighting and allow ourselves to turn our concerns and problems over to God as we understand God. Those of us who saw the group as our Higher Power—or at least a part of our Higher Power—found that we were able to let go and let people in the group help us. Later we learned that when we were struggling with something, we could give it

to God and God would help us. We also learned that one way of *not* letting go was to spend time trying to explain God or second-guess God's will for us. No matter what our understanding of God was, we were able to make good use of this slogan and other spiritual tools as well.

• TO THINE OWN SELF BE TRUE
This slogan serves as a reminder that acting out when we're sure that no one will ever know about it is just as detrimental to our recovery as getting *caught* acting out. When recovery became the most important thing in our lives, we came to know our boundaries and specifically how, why, and when we had violated those boundaries. Not only did we come to know when we had overstepped boundaries, we also became keenly aware of the times we were being dishonest with ourselves and the people in our groups. We came to understand that our value systems are not imposed upon us by a person or a group of people, they develop within us. When we were away from our groups, we made conscious efforts to bring our value systems with us. We learned that we certainly did not have to be "caught" in order to be adversely affected by our acting-out behaviors and that to think otherwise was simply a seductive lie that our addiction was trying to tell us. Through experience, we learned that a three-month period of *honest sobriety* is much more meaningful and valuable to us than being awarded a pin marking three years of sobriety only because we didn't get caught acting out or being dishonest.

• LIVE AND LET LIVE
This slogan reminds us that each person must have his or her own Program. There were times when we did not agree with the boundaries other people in the Program established for themselves or the manner in which they were working—or not working—the Steps and Traditions. We found that it was always best for us to focus on our own Program and simply let

the example of our lives speak for us. (We know all too well how defiant we were when someone tried to tell us how to run our lives or work our Program.) We learned to treat others with the same respect, allowing them to follow their own process of recovery without interference from us. We remind ourselves that each recovering addict has his or her own Higher Power and that it is not our responsibility to decide how anyone else should work the Program.

• KEEP IT SIMPLE

As practicing sex addicts, many of us had become accustomed to crisis-driven lives. It seemed that we were always getting ourselves into situations that required immediate and complex solutions. When we came to the Program, most of us thought to ourselves that it looked far too simple to be practical or effective for us. Later on we realized that because the Program required only a few simple and straightforward tasks of us, we were much more likely to succeed. In fact we could see that only two primary tasks were required of us and that each of these tasks was relatively simple: to heal from our sex addiction and to help other sex addicts. We came to understand that it is far better to do a few things well in the Program than to try many different things and subsequently fail. The Twelve Steps and Twelve Traditions remind us of the value of simplicity in recovery.

• THERE BUT FOR THE GRACE OF GOD GO I

When we were still acting out and saw other addicts acting out we often thought to ourselves, *If I ever get that bad, I'll quit; I'm not so bad after all.* But once we got into recovery and realized how fortunate we were to know the Program and have some real choices in our lives, we began using this slogan in much the same way we would use a prayer. When we saw an addict struggling, we thought to ourselves, *It was like that for me before the Program and it could easily be like that for me again if I neglect the Twelve Steps. I am grateful for my recovery*. Each and every addict—recovering or not—teaches us some valuable lessons about ourselves and our recovery.

The Twelve Traditions*

TRADITION ONE
Our common welfare should come first; personal recovery depends upon unity.

TRADITION TWO
For our group purpose there is but one ultimate authority—a loving God as that God may express Himself/Herself in our group conscience. Our leaders are but trusted servants; they do not govern.

TRADITION THREE
The only requirement for membership in a Twelve Step group is a desire to stop compulsive behavior.

TRADITION FOUR
Each group should be autonomous except in matters affecting other groups or the fellowship as a whole.

TRADITION FIVE
Each group has but one primary purpose—to carry its message to those who still suffer.

TRADITION SIX
Our fellowship ought never endorse, finance, or lend its name to any related facility or outside enterprise, lest problems of money, propriety, and prestige divert us from our primary purpose.

TRADITION SEVEN
Each group ought to be fully self-supporting, declining outside contributions.

TRADITION EIGHT
Our fellowship should remain forever nonprofessional, but our service centers may employ special workers.

TRADITION NINE
Our fellowship, as such, ought never be organized; but we may create service boards or committees directly responsible to those they serve.

TRADITION TEN
Our fellowship has no opinion on outside issues; hence our name ought never be drawn into public controversy.

TRADITION ELEVEN
Our public relations policy is based on attraction rather than promotion; we need always maintain personal anonymity at the level of press, radio, and films.

TRADITION TWELVE
Anonymity is the spiritual foundation of all our traditions, ever reminding us to place principles before personalities.

* The Twelve Traditions reprinted for adaptation with permission of AA World Services, Inc. © 1981.

18

The Twelve Traditions

The Twelve Traditions provide us with valuable guidelines that keep us on the right course within the Twelve Step fellowship. The Traditions reflect the wisdom that was gained through experiences with group organization and group dynamics early in the life of the Program. If the addicts working the Program are to recover, the Program *itself* must be intact. Just as we used the Twelve Steps to guide our recovery as individuals, we used the Twelve Traditions to guide our groups in ways that are consistent with the principles of the Twelve Step fellowship. The Steps are suggestions, while the Traditions are *specific* organizational and procedural guidelines that pertain to individual groups as well as to the fellowship as a whole. The Twelve Traditions help to insure that the Program will be intact for us as well as for those who will follow us. The Traditions helped us establish and maintain organizational boundaries within our own groups as well as in our work and relationships with other groups. Observing and maintaining these boundaries prevents us from becoming enmeshed with other groups and/or organizations, thus allowing us to keep our focus on recovery.

In addition to guiding groups and the fellowship as a whole, the Twelve Traditions are also very helpful to us in terms of our *individual* recovery in that they give each of us twelve additional tools to work with. We know from experience that when all members of a group really understand the Traditions, the group itself becomes stronger and each individual in the group feels more grounded and secure in his or her own recovery.

1. Our common welfare should come first; personal recovery depends upon unity.

The Twelve Steps and Twelve Traditions work together to protect not only the individual rights of each addict, but also the group and the fellowship as a whole. The first word of the First Step is *We*; the first word of the First Tradition is *Our*. Although we came from many different backgrounds, it soon became clear to us that the differences among us were much less important than the similarities we shared. One significant aspect of our lives that brought us together and unified us was our need to recover from sex addiction. Because we all shared the need to recover, we agreed that we could not afford to have conflicts within or between our groups.

We learned that before taking any action as groups of addicts or as individual addicts *within* Twelve Step groups, we had to consider carefully how our behavior might affect our groups and the fellowship as a whole, as well as our individual recovery. We learned to be extremely careful so as not to allow the unity of our fellowship to be undermined by our egos in any way. We found that we could get so much more accomplished when we worked together in harmony, but that we didn't have to sacrifice our individuality in order to achieve that harmony. We did not allow our differences to *divide* us. Instead, we "agreed to disagree" and focused our energies on maintaining and strengthening the unity of the group and the fellowship. Because we knew that we were dealing with what the Big Book calls the "cunning, baffling, powerful!" characteristics of addiction, we agreed that we simply could not afford to argue over details and procedures. We knew that we would have to stand united because relapse was the ultimate price we'd pay if we allowed our egos to destroy our unity as a group.

2. For our group purpose there is but one ultimate authority—a loving God as that God may express Himself/Herself in our group conscience. Our leaders are but trusted servants; they do not govern.

This Tradition safeguards the fundamental right of the individual to believe as he or she chooses to believe, and it also identifies the ultimate authority for the group. We learned that "group conscience" really has nothing at all to do with majority rule or even the relative acceptability or popularity of certain ideas. "Benign anarchy"—this is how Bill W., co-founder of AA, characterized group conscience. We now understand this to mean that if we are true to the Program and listen to our hearts and to God as we understand God, eventually we will find the right answers *naturally*, and we will also make choices as a group that we would not be able to make as individuals burdened with personal agendas and vested interests. We came to see group conscience evolving from the choices all of us made based on the Twelve Steps and Twelve Traditions.

At the outset we were told that no one at the meetings is "in charge." In time, we learned that this "no-leader" guideline helps to ensure that groups will not be shaped by the needs, personality, and/or personal style of any one person. Regardless of how long a person has been in the Program and no matter what his or her age, employment, education, or training outside the group, that person never has more authority than any other person in the group. *Twelve Steps and Twelve Traditions* says this of oldtimers in AA, those people who the groups might naturally turn to for advice: "They do not drive by mandate; they lead by example" (p. 135). What this means is that, for instance, when an oldtimer in a group feels that there should be more talk within that group about spirituality or some other topic, that oldtimer simply *takes the responsibility for talking more about those topics himself or herself rather than attempting to force a change in other people.* Leading *by example* allows other people in the group to feel completely free to make their own choices, yet it gives them an opportunity to see what those who preceded them are doing with their lives.

Our groups have no "leaders"; trusted servants have no control whatsoever over anyone in the group. Being a trusted servant is a *responsibility*, not a status symbol, a reward for service, or even a title. Basically, a trusted servant is anyone who voluntarily uses his or her energy to help carry the message to other addicts. Trusted servants may be responsible for tasks such as picking up the mail, setting up for and/or convening meetings, cleaning up after meetings, and seeing to it that rent is paid to the organization that is providing the meeting facilities. After twelve weeks or some other prearranged period of time set by the group, responsibilities of the trusted servants are then passed on to other people in the group. We never force or otherwise require people to take on the tasks of a trusted servant for the group; instead we wait until they are ready and *ask* to serve in this way. Occasionally, newcomers to the Program are asked (or volunteer) to be trusted servants of the group. People seem to feel that they are part of the fellowship more quickly when they get involved in these ways. Each of us eventually took a turn as a trusted servant. Having these kinds of responsibilities in our groups for a period of time taught us so much about humility and our powerlessness over other people. Serving the group in this way was a form of Twelfth Step work.

3. The only requirement for membership in a Twelve Step group is a desire to stop compulsive behavior.

No one in our lives—not our lawyers, our therapists, our partners, or other people in our groups—decided *for us* that we were sex addicts. We learned that we had to make this decision *for ourselves*, but that we didn't have to make a public declaration of it. As newcomers, the very fact that we were *coming* to meetings was of much more interest to others than what we said or didn't say at those meetings. As always, our actions spoke louder than any words we could say. When we began attending meetings, we found that the only thing we really had to do was decide that we wanted to stop our compulsive behavior. We could no longer spend time and energy judging, using stereotypes, or moralizing regarding the thoughts and behaviors of other people. Instead of comparing ourselves to others in our groups, we looked for common bonds between us and we sought ways that we could work toward more effective communication.

At first many of us were concerned that the "wrong kind" of people might come to our meetings and subsequently destroy the Program. Some of us even thought it might be helpful to establish screening committees to meet with potential newcomers and determine whether or not they were *really* addicts, had a *genuine* willingness to recover, and should be *allowed* to attend meetings at all. We now know that these attempts to influence factors well beyond our control—namely, people and the composition of the group—were simply ways of trying to make sure that nothing terrible would *ever* happen to the fellowship. After all, our recovery was important to us, so of course we wanted to do whatever we *could* do to protect it and to protect the Program that made recovery possible for us in the first place.

Once we could see that sex addiction does not discriminate on the basis of age, race, religion, income, occupation, gender, sexual preference, or condition of health, we knew instinctively that our *recovery* Program could not discriminate on the basis of these things either. We finally got the help we needed when we sought advice from those who had worked in the Program before us. In studying the writings of AA, we learned that the people before us once had similar fears about the "quality" of other people in the Program. In reference to their attitudes toward people they felt uncomfortable with in the early days, the first people in the Program say this in *Twelve Steps and Twelve Traditions*: "Intolerant, you say? Well, we were frightened. Naturally, we began to act like most everybody does when afraid. After all, isn't fear the true basis of intolerance? Yes, we were intolerant" (p. 140).

But as they worked the Program, these first people in AA came to appreciate others in the group with different backgrounds—people they had perhaps even been afraid of—and they developed new ways of thinking about these other people that was actually part of their recovery: "How could we know that thousands of these sometimes frightening people were to make astonishing recoveries and become our greatest workers and intimate friends?... Could we then foresee that troublesome people were to become our principal teachers of patience and tolerance? Could any then imagine a society which would include every conceivable kind of character, and cut across every barrier of race, creed, politics, and language with ease?...At last experience taught us that to take away any(one's) full chance was sometimes to pronounce his (her) death sentence and often to condemn him (her) to endless misery? Who dared to be judge, jury, and executioner of his (her) own sick brother (sister)?" (p. 140-41). As we read these words, we could see that AA—the original Twelve Step fellowship—had certainly become stronger and more effective by adhering to the clear and uncomplicated path that is set forth in the Third Tradition. We trusted that our fellowship would be protected in the same way *and we were not disappointed.*

4. Each group should be autonomous except in matters affecting other groups or the fellowship as a whole.

Twelve Steps and Twelve Traditions offers this definition of a group: "Any two or three (addicts) gathered together for sobriety may call themselves a (Twelve Step) group, provided that as a group they have no other affiliation" (p. 146-47). At first some of our groups consisted of only two or three people. But eventually many of these groups became so large that additional groups were organized to accomodate the number of people attending meetings. When some of us felt that our groups were not meeting our needs, we got together with other addicts who had similar feelings; together we organized additional groups. We were pleased to discover that the fellowship as a whole was supportive of this kind of diversity; with suggestions and support, the fellowship actually offered assistance to these struggling new groups. After we had been in the Program for awhile, some of us also chose to start our own specialized groups (e.g. gay and lesbian groups). Some of us found that these special group meetings enhanced our recovery in ways that more general group meetings did not. Those of us who find these special interest groups helpful continue, nevertheless, to attend general meetings, for they are essential to our recovery.

During our time in the Program, we have attended meetings of many other Twelve Step groups. In the course of doing this, we have had opportunities to see a *variety* of meeting formats used effectively by a number of groups. Some meetings are open to anyone—family members, partners, friends, acquaintances; other meetings are closed and limited to sex addicts only. Some meetings have a drop-in policy meaning that there are no prerequisites for attendance; other meetings require that people be "Twelve-Stepped" before they attend. Some meetings consist of one large group of people sharing together; other meetings convene in a large group, then break into several smaller groups for discussion. Some meetings begin with each person in attendance saying his or her first name followed by the statement "...and I'm a sex addict"; other meetings begin with a moment of silence for the addicts who are still suffering. Some meetings focus on the sharing of personal stories; other meetings focus on one of the Twelve Steps.

After watching various groups support recovering people in a number of different ways, we understood that any meeting format is acceptable, just as long as it *works* and is within the Traditions. Regardless of the meeting format used, the groups all share two important elements: they are self-governing and they are completely free from any *outside* control or influence. We send representatives to Intergroup meetings to let other groups know of our existence and the choices we are making as a group, not to get directions for organizing and conducting meetings. We came to understand that while each group has the right to make mistakes, the group's autonomy cannot be used as an excuse to violate the Traditions or harm the fellowship in any way.

5. Each group has but one primary purpose—to carry its message to those who still suffer.

We learned a succinct but very important mission statement from Alcoholics Anonymous: "I am responsible. When anyone, anywhere, reaches out for help, I want the hand of (the fellowship) always to be there. And for that: I am responsible." The goal of each group is to help others who are suffering by working to ensure the continued existence of a group that is accessible and helpful to those who need it.

After we had attended meetings for a period of time, some of us found that we had concerns about the new people who came to our groups. For instance, some of us feared that these newcomers would take up too much time at meetings, or that they would not be appealing or trustworthy, or that their presence would adversely affect our *own* recovery. For a time, some of us actually lost sight of the positive influence newcomers have on *everyone's* recovery. We learned that we *needed* these newcomers. Not only did they remind us how serious our own addictions were, or how serious they might have become, they also reminded us of the primary reasons we attend meetings at all: to learn the Twelve Step Program and to learn to practice the Twelve Steps in all that we do. We also attend meetings to help others as well as to receive help and support from others as we work to arrest our obsessive thoughts and compulsive behaviors. We are grateful to newcomers for keeping us on the right track as well as for the many opportunities we have to watch them change and grow.

6. Our fellowship ought never endorse, finance, or lend its name to any related facility or outside enterprise, lest problems of money, propriety, and prestige divert us from our primary purpose.

Although we *cooperate* with other Twelve Step Programs as well as with therapists, treatment Programs, and institutions, we do not affiliate with these people and programs *as a group*. Organizations, groups, and individuals outside our groups often refer people to us for help, but we never refer people in our groups to other organizations, groups, or individuals.

We do not own property as a fellowship, so we hold our meetings in churches, schools, and other public and private facilities. Many of us meet in church basements or in spare rooms of other buildings in our communities. No matter *where* we meet, though, we *always* pay rent as a group. Doing this helps us to keep relationships with our "landlords" clear, straightforward, and free of obligations; we owe our "landlords" nothing because we regularly pay rent for the facilities we use. By paying rent, we feel that we are working to make sure no one person or group of people will ever expect or pressure us to support a particular organization, its issues or causes "in exchange" for the use of a meeting room.

We are a spiritual group and, as such, we seem to get by with a *minimum* of material possessions: a case for our literature, a post office box for mail, and a phone to receive the calls for help that come to us. The small amount of money that we collect goes only to pay our rent and to support the work of carrying the message; we do not invest this money nor do we purchase property with it. We never allow financial concerns to distract us from recovery.

7. Each group ought to be fully self-supporting, declining outside contributions.

During the time of our active addiction, many of us were very dependent upon other people; in recovery, we learned to be *responsible* to each other as well as to ourselves. *In this sense, each of us paid his or her own way in the Program.* Our groups have no established dues. The small amount of money per meeting that is requested is considered a *contribution* to help pay for rent and literature. No one is ever pressured in any way or asked to leave a meeting if he or she cannot afford to make a contribution or chooses not to do so. Instead of staging fund-raising events in an effort to support our Twelve Step work, we simply ask that each member do whatever he or she *can* do to make sure that the Program will continue to be there for us as well as for the addicts who still suffer and the addicts who will come to the Program in the future.

Despite our low-key approach to the issue of funding our Twelve Step work, "money problems" *did* develop in some of our groups. But our problems were very different from the money problems that most organizations face. Rather than having *too little money* to work with, some groups found that they actually had *too much money*. This surplus created problems in some groups when people disagreed about the most appropriate use for this extra money. In time we learned that in order to keep our focus on Twelve Step work and recovery, it is best to keep our financial reserves relatively low, thus avoiding trouble-some issues related to the use of extra funds. Following the example of AA, we set a two-hundred-dollar limit on the contributions that any one member in a group can make directly to the group or through a bequest during any given year. Because we cannot afford to be influenced by or obligated to anyone or anything, we do not accept contributions from other organizations.

When other people organize new groups in our areas, we always offer to help by sharing our Program literature with them and by offering suggestions based on our own group experiences. Some of our groups even help new groups with rent payments during the first few months of their existence. But after providing this initial help, we step back and allow these new groups to learn *for themselves* how satisfying it is to function autonomously. When we receive requests for help from people in locations where there are no other groups, we willingly send recovering addicts from our groups to do Twelve Step work with them. In these instances, both the established group and the newly organized group help pay expenses for those who travel to carry out Twelve Step work. Money remaining *after* the trip is returned to the contributing groups; those who do Twelve Step work never take money for their time.

8. Our fellowship should remain forever nonprofessional, but our service centers may employ special workers.

People in our groups who are employed in the helping professions tell us that they appreciate the opportunity to attend meetings without being pressured to assume roles of leadership. There are no addicts in our groups who receive more or less attention or help because of education, training, background, or vocation. *In our Twelve Step groups, we are all peers.* The recovering addicts in our groups who have careers in the helping professions understand that the counseling they do in the process of carrying out their jobs is not Twelve Step work and that in our groups, there is no such thing as a *professional* Twelve Step counselor or therapist.

As our groups became larger, we found that the tasks necessary to support our Twelve Step work (phone conversations, correspondence, meeting arrangements, and other work) grew to the extent that it was no longer reasonable to expect that everything could be taken care of by volunteers. Subsequently, we hired recovering addicts to do some of this work for the same wages we would pay nonaddicts to do the same work. *We never pay anyone to do Twelve Step work*; we only pay people for tasks that help facilitate Twelve Step calls. All of our workers—volunteer and paid staff—are guided by the Twelve Traditions. For instance, when addicts who are paid for doing support tasks make Twelve Step calls, they understand that they are doing so on their own time and without pay. When a recovering addict in one of our groups is interviewed (anonymously, of course) for an article on sex addiction, he or she accepts no pay for that interview either as an individual or on behalf of the group or the fellowship as a whole. In fact, *no money ever changes hands for the task of carrying the message*. The recovering person's reward for service and carrying the message is simple yet powerful and enduring: *sobriety*. And as recovering addicts, we know that maintaining sobriety is the only "payment" we ever really need.

9. Our fellowship, as such, ought never be organized; but we may create service boards or committees directly responsible to those they serve.

Despite the way our groups might appear to operate at times, the idea that we "ought never be organized" certainly doesn't mean that we should strive for, overlook, or encourage *disorganization*. On the contrary, this concept points us toward our Higher Power in much the same way that the Second Tradition does. We have no special members or central management positioned to control us, monitor our actions, or make decisions for us. Just as groups appoint trusted servants to help support

Twelve Step work, the fellowship facilitates gatherings of members from different groups to help support Twelve Step work. And neither the trusted servants nor those who participate in these gatherings have power or authority with respect to the group or the fellowship. In fact, these gatherings—service boards and Intergroups—were established to *serve* and support the membership in its work, not to manage the membership or tell the membership what to do.

Service boards and Intergroups were formed to allow groups to become aware of each other's existence so that they might help each other and learn from each other. Before any changes are made in the fellowship, all pertinent information is brought back to the groups for discussion by the Intergroup representative. This process ensures that any change in the fellowship will proceed slowly...and with great care. *There is no chain of command in the fellowship*. Since all of us are working to save our sanity *and our lives*, we find that we are able to work within and among our groups without having to rely on rigid structures to regulate our activities and processes as a fellowship. *We rely on group conscience to guide us*.

10. Our fellowship has no opinion on outside issues; hence our name ought never be drawn into public controversy.

This Tradition essentially frees us from concerns and tasks that are not related to the Program and recovery. Since our groups are made up of people from many different backgrounds, it is difficult to imagine *any one issue* that everyone in the fellowship would agree on completely. Even if we all *did* agree on something, it is unlikely that anyone would ever really know about it because we never give any one person the authority to represent the fellowship. As a fellowship, we do not lobby for or against *anything*. Individuals in our groups are free to be as outspoken and/or political as they would like to be, as long as they do not violate the Traditions or attempt to speak for the fellowship as a whole. The general guidelines set forth in this Tradition help us keep our public image clear and uncomplicated; this clarity makes it less likely that people will be afraid to refer addicts to us and that a variety of organizations will be willing to let us rent space from them for our meetings.

We have learned that our recovery is adversely affected when we become involved in controversies as a group or as a total fellowship. In one instance, those of us who were already attending meetings got so involved in fighting for our own interpretations of the issues that we actually scared newcomers away and shifted our focus away from recovery. Another lesson we learned came early on and gave us an opportunity to see quite clearly what can happen when we allow our focus to shift to issues that are not related to recovery and the welfare of the group: At one point, people in a certain group decided that it would be appropriate to reach out and offer some special help to a man in the fellowship who was facing criminal charges due to his sexual acting-out behaviors. In their genuine efforts to support this man in his struggle to recover, the people in this group wrote letters to the court verifying that he was, indeed, attending Twelve Step meetings and diligently working the Program. In fact, some of the people who wrote these letters of support requested leniency for this man. Word got out fast about this letter-writing effort and it wasn't long before other addicts with legal problems were asking groups to write letters requesting leniency for *them* too. Some of these addicts even asked those writing letters to the courts to make specific recommendations regarding sentencing. Eventually, people in this group—and other groups—were spending significant amounts of time and energy discussing and sometimes even arguing about whether or not individual addicts were doing well enough to "deserve" letters of support sent to the courts on their behalf.

Soon it became apparent that the groups were being used inappropriately by several addicts who were facing serious legal problems. Eventually the people who had allowed their energies to be diverted in this way learned that they were overlooking the primary purpose of the group—to ensure the continuation of the Program for themselves, for the addicts still suffering, and for the addicts who would come to the Program in the future. These people came to understand that by trying to influence the judicial process, they were actually violating the Traditions and losing their focus on recovery. Fortunately for everyone concerned, the people in this group soon became aware of what was happening. They got back on the track of recovery, let go, and left the issues involving legal procedures and sentencing where they always belong—within the legal system.

In response to this and other misuses of the supportive energy of the fellowship, a booklet was developed that briefly describes the Program and the fellowship. Addicts facing legal charges are now told that they are free to share this booklet with anyone, including attorneys and presiding judges. The people in this group—and other groups—came to see that as a total fellowship and as individual groups within that fellowship, we simply cannot afford to spend time dealing with legal matters or other controversial issues that take us away from our primary focus, *recovery*.

11. Our public relations policy is based on attraction rather than promotion; we need always maintain personal anonymity at the level of press, radio, and films.

Even though we maintain anonymity on an individual basis, the Program must be recognizable to others and accessible to them as well. *Ours is not a secret society.* In fact, we find that we must always be alert to the ways we can bring the promises of the Program and the hope of the fellowship to the attention of the public. We must do this so that people who have problems with sex addiction will know how and where they can get the help they need. The Program draws people through a natural attraction process; we know that we don't need to use hype or sensational tactics in order to attract people. While we do not advertise or recruit, we do whatever we *can* do to inform individuals and organizations about the fellowship in case they want to refer people to it. Every person who attends a meeting has the same status. We work to protect the anonymity and confidentiality of every person in the group, but we never reveal any information whatsoever about who is and isn't in our groups. We work to discourage situations in which people attend meetings only because someone famous is in a group; on the other hand, we work to discourage situations in which people stay away from meetings only because someone infamous is in a group.

The worth of the Program is so clear to us that we know in our hearts we don't have to sell it to others. When we go on Twelve Step calls, we know we don't have to *prove* to prospective newcomers that the Program and the meetings are helpful and inspirational. We know that when a person is ready, he or she will be able to hear *from our stories of addiction, hope, and recovery* how we have changed and how we were *naturally* attracted to the fellowship...without being *forced*.

Sometimes members of the media seek us out for stories on addiction. Cooperating with an interviewer who is seeking accurate information is generally regarded as an activity that is within the Traditions. But we never seek out interviewers or ask that stories on our addiction be written or otherwise made public; the interviewers come to us. And when we *do* talk about addiction with them, *we always make it a point to focus on recovery*. In the course of an interview, we never use our last names or any other identifying details about ourselves. When we are interviewed for video presentations, we always request nonidentifying camera shots (silhouette or from behind.) Anonymity helps to protect the fellowship as well as the individual addict. We cannot afford to spend time arguing with each other about who should have center stage. Anonymity also keeps us from becoming grandiose. We know that the *Program* is the *real miracle* in all of this.

12. Anonymity is the spiritual foundation of all our traditions, ever reminding us to place principles before personalities.

This Tradition—like the Third and Eleventh Traditions—serves to remind us that when we are in our groups, the only thing that really matters is the fact that we are sex addicts who want to recover. Who we are or what we do outside of the fellowship is not important. As we work the Program, we find the "*I*" so prevalent in active addiction gradually being replaced with the "*We*" referred to so often in recovery. Now this doesn't necessarily mean that we have friendships with everyone in our groups or that we even *like* everyone in our groups. What this *does* mean is that we have learned to give as well as receive from other addicts—without regard to personalities or personal feelings. We have learned that when wise words are spoken by someone in the Program, it just doesn't matter who speaks them. The purpose of attending meetings is not to socialize or to cultivate friendships, though most of us find that both are pleasant by-products of our work in the Program.

Many of us actually forgot about this Tradition, then suddenly remembered it when our groups became so large they split into two or more smaller groups and we lost regular contact with certain people who'd been important to our recovery. At first some of us were concerned that we would not be able to maintain our sobriety unless we stayed in the same group with a specific person—someone who had perhaps offered us special help and understanding along the way. Fortunately we came to see that no one recovering addict is essential to the recovery of any other addict. *The Program works because of the principles of the Steps and the Traditions and the support of the entire fellowship, not because of individual people in the Program.*

The Twelfth Tradition guided us to publish this book without using the names of any of the people who worked together to write it. We wrote this book on a completely anonymous basis in order to protect the fellowship as a whole, as well as the individual addicts who share their stories here. We wanted to make absolutely sure that no one would be treated differently just because he or she happened to be in the right place at the right time. *The Program made our recovery possible; without recovery, nothing would have been possible.*

Personal Stories of Addiction, Hope & Recovery

"Our stories disclose in a general way what we used to be like, what happened, and what we are like now."

Alcoholics Anonymous (p. 58)

Jim's Story

Even though my recovery record is not a perfect one, the past two years have given me more of a sense of belonging as well as more peace and serenity than I ever thought possible.

(After seven years in the Program; four years of sobriety.)

I believe that my sexual addiction actually began when I was a preschooler. My parents were divorced and often I was left alone. I can even recall being in my crib and fondling myself to relieve the pain of loneliness. The earliest sexual memories I have relate to the shame I felt about my genitals and having erections. I also remember that at a very young age, I was obsessed with girls and desperately wanted to see them undress; I began peeking in windows of houses in the neighborhood to watch girls and women undress. For years, voyeurism was my primary acting-out behavior. I'd watch women just to catch a brief glimpse of their breasts; I'd look into cars hoping to see women with their skirts pulled up; I'd stare at girls and women at the beach; I'd stare at women relatives during family visits. When I was a little older, I'd page through magazines looking only for pictures of women. Then, when I was an adolescent, I discovered pornography.

On several occasions during my early adolescence, I stood naked in front of the living room windows in my house, hoping that a neighbor girl would see me. (My feelings of shame never allowed me to remain there for a long enough period of time to be seen.) As a teenager, I was socially backward and I think this was due, at least in part, to the shame I felt about my preoccupation with sex. Actually, I knew very little about sex. When I was a teenager, I decided that I wanted to be a minister. I felt sure that I had experienced a spiritual calling, but now I realize that what I probably "experienced" back then was the

131

feeling that I was somehow *different* from other people. After two years in the seminary, I realized that I was spending more and more of my time masturbating, fantasizing, and using pornography. I was nineteen years old, confused, alone, and suicidal. I left the seminary and enrolled at a teacher's college. While I was a student there, I had sexual intercourse for the first time. After that first experience, I became *obsessed* with "how far I could go" with every date I had. Subsequently I met a woman; we dated for a year, then got married. Six months after the marriage, I began to withdraw from her and resumed my compulsive masturbation. Our intimacy was undermined; by the time we had been married for a year, I was having affairs with other women—mostly friends and coworkers.

At this same time, I was teaching high school and began fantasizing about my students. Sometimes I'd touch my students in ways that stimulated me but were so subtle I was sure they wouldn't notice. I romanticized many of these students, became overtly sexual with a few of them, and even had "an affair" with one. In time, my shame and fear about my behavior overwhelmed me, so I transferred to another school. But not long after the transfer, I started acting out with students in my new school. From that time on, I initiated sexual involvement with one or two female students each school year. I told myself I wasn't doing anything wrong because I refrained from having intercourse with these students; I was "only" fondling and kissing them. I also tried to rationalize my sexual relationships with students by telling myself that the girls involved were over the age of sixteen. But I was kidding myself on that point too, because I knew for a *fact* that one of the girls I was involved with was only fifteen. Finally one of the girls talked to her parents and they, in turn, told the school administration about my behavior with their daughter. I was forced to resign from my teaching position. At that time I still *believed* that my sexual relationships with students were based on choice—theirs and mine. Now I realize that I was deceiving myself. I was actually abusing these students by using my position as a teacher in a way that ultimately hurt them. Because of my sexual addiction, I was *harming* the very people I had made a professional commitment to *educate*.

I began healing from sex addiction in the fall of 1978. At that time, sex addiction was practically *unheard* of in the general population and there was very little acknowledgment of the problem among mental health professionals. Back then, I was filled with fear about my behavior and I was periodically meeting with five other people who were fearful about their sexual behaviors too. Together we were struggling to form a special recovery program based on the Twelve Steps of Alcoholics Anonymous. A friend of mine had told me about the group— that seemed to be the only way to get involved with the Program at that time. Our meetings took place in the back room of a restaurant very early in the morning. When our group began to grow in size, we talked to a clergyman about using his church for our meetings. We told him who we were and what we were trying to accomplish with this self-help Twelve Step group for sex addicts. Fortunately for us this clergyman understood compulsive behavior and addiction and he understood our need to share with each other as well; he was, himself, a recovering alcoholic. In an effort to learn how to facilitate our meetings, we talked with AA people whenever we had the opportunity.

At first, we found it very difficult to develop a definition of acting-out behavior that was acceptable to everyone in the group. Instead of debating this subject and trying to reach a consensus, we made a decision to give each individual in the group responsibility for determining what acting-out behavior was for him and what behavioral boundaries he would set for himself. For the first year and a half of its existence, our group was more or less limited to professional men. Because some of our group members were teachers, clergymen, and therapists, we initially had some concern that if the group expanded to include others, information about us would get out and our careers might be in jeopardy. As for the "men only" status of our group in the early days, that reflected a fear some of us had that we might act out with female members. There were homosexuals in our group as well as some heterosexuals who had acted out with men and other heterosexuals who had not acted out with men. Despite the fact that no one in our group had acted out with another group member, some of us were still fearful at that time that we might act out with women in the group. Confidentiality was another issue that our group had to confront in the very beginning. Some of the people in our group had acted out with children or had committed acts of violence. At first, some of us were uncertain about our responsibilities relative to people in the group who had actually broken the law or committed immoral acts. Did we have a *legal* or *moral* obligation to turn these people in? What did the Traditions (of AA) say about this? We were concerned that the confusion surrounding this issue might endanger all of us and undermine the openness, trust, and support we were trying so hard to build in this newly-formed group. Using the Twelve Steps as a guide, we decided that this issue could be resolved most effectively by the individuals involved; *we found that the Program worked when we let it work*. The sexual addicts in our group who had abused children or raped *turned themselves in* to get appropriate help for their addictive behaviors and also to complete the process of making amends.

My first few years in the Program were essentially a struggle with sobriety—defining it and achieving it. At times I even doubted that I was a sex addict. Early in my recovery, I remarried and while the "newness" was still in my marriage, I didn't feel like an addict anymore. I was so involved in this exciting marital relationship that I completely lost the urge to act out. *But this respite from my addiction was only temporary*. Before long, I was again obsessed with thoughts of masturbation, seduction, and extramarital affairs. I stopped going to Twelve Step meetings after two years of regular attendance because I felt that I no longer needed the group. But then, just as in my first marriage, I began having extramarital affairs again. I had felt hopeless after my first divorce and now I was feeling hopeless again—my compulsive behavior was about to ruin another family. The shame of another destroyed marriage was more than I could bear. When I saw that my obsession was becoming a very real and serious problem for me and the people I loved, I renewed my relationship with the Twelve Steps.

At the present time, my boundaries exclude pornography, sexual fantasies, and seductive behavior. The longer I was in the Program, the more clearly I could see how seductive and covertly sexual I had been through the years. During my first few years in the Program, I wasn't altogether clear whether or not I should consider masturbation a slip. (I knew for sure that masturbation with the use of pornography was *not* healthy for me.) Then after four years of work in the Program, I found that I could easily differentiate between compulsive masturbation and the healthy use of masturbation. To this day, however, the boundaries I have set exclude any use of pornography whatsoever.

Even though my recovery record is not a perfect one, the past two years have given me more of a sense of belonging as well as more peace and serenity than I ever thought possible. At the age of fifty-seven, I realize that I am still an addict. But now I have a Program, a support network of friends who know the Program, and intimate relationships in which trust is gradually building. My feelings of shame about the years of my life spent with inappropriate sexual behavior are lessening. Each time I listen to someone's First Step, I understand more clearly what sexual addiction is and how it has affected my life. *Listening to others helps me remember my acting-out behaviors and how really powerless I was; listening to others also enhances the gratitude I feel for having found the Program when I did.*

Ruth's Story

Living sanely means accepting where I've been and using that information to proceed to a new destination.

(After five years in the Program.)

I am a sex addict. More important, I am a sex addict in recovery. I came to the Program because of the emotional debris I had to live with as a result of my sexually compulsive behavior. I stay in the Program because the gifts I receive from it benefit me in every area of my life. I participate in a Program that accepts me as I am, sustains me with hope, and helps me to heal gently—layer by layer—and at my own pace.

I remember that one time in elementary school I was given an assignment, along with the rest of my class, to write an autobiography. Considering my life experience at the time, I concluded that the nun who was teaching our class certainly wouldn't want to know the truth about my life. So I created a positive autobiography filled with "Ozzie and Harriet" images and completely free of references to the abusive environment that was my reality. For decades to come, I continued to use that fantasy as my own. Sometimes I felt like a fugitive with false identification papers. But the traumatic childhood I disowned with my autobiography continued to haunt me in the form of chronic nightmares.

In high school, I played the role of class clown. But in spite of my comic mask, I was emotionally and spiritually shut down at that time in my life. I mistrusted girls and was afraid of boys. I was also needy, secretive, naive, and a people-pleaser. As a teenager, I somehow transmitted to others the message that I was a victim and that message was subsequently picked up by several adult men who sexually abused me during my adolescence. I used denial to protect my self-esteem and created new

137

stories about my life to add to my autobiography. I transformed traumatic episodes of rape and molestation into wonderful scenarios of love and romance and I numbed the pain I was feeling by retreating into sexual fantasies and obsessions. But all this time I was completely unable to deal with the self-hatred that was destroying my soul. As a teenager, I did not have the social and emotional experiences that most people have at this time of life. In fact, it wasn't until I was well into my thirties (and in recovery) that I began to deal with the life issues most people deal with during adolescence: personal identity, courtship, love, intimacy, and the dynamics of establishing and nurturing friendships. During my college years, I moved from almost complete social isolation to being sexual with almost any man who wanted me.

I figured that getting married and having children would be the best and most natural ways to stop my compulsive sexual activity. For a time, marriage and motherhood *did* put the brakes on my acting-out behaviors. But I brought to the marriage a variety of unresolved problems that would ultimately destroy it: emotional immaturity, chemical dependency, and a growing fear of intimacy. My husband and I were divorced after six years of marriage and then I experienced the hell of being a divorced woman who was also chemically dependent and sexually addicted. I began living a double life: I was a responsible parent and a conscientious employee by day, but at night and on weekends, I participated in self-destructive and indiscriminate sexual adventures.

During the years following my divorce, hundreds of men passed through my life. *I felt as if I lived in a house without doors.* I tried to control my compulsive sexual activity and sometimes I even abstained from sexual activity altogether—but my attempts to change never lasted for long. During the week, parenting and work controlled my acting-out behavior. But on weekends—with my children at their father's house and without the responsibility of work—insanity reigned in my life. Finally I decided that if I could just stay out of bars on weekends, I could finally end the horror of waking up with a stranger in my bed. The solution I devised ultimately jeopardized my life. I'd drug myself with barbiturates and stay at home each weekend because staying at home and losing touch with reality represented safety from bars and indiscriminate sex. Drugs kept me indoors and out of trouble from Friday evening until Sunday afternoon, when my children returned from their father's house. This pattern of using drugs in order to get myself through the weekend continued for months. Actually, flirting with death in this way held a certain appeal for me because it was consistent with my crisis-driven life.

Intense anxiety finally drove me to divulge some of my secrets to a therapist. I also told him that I was concerned about my drug use. A formal evaluation convinced both of us that I had good reason to be concerned, so I entered a chemical dependency treatment program. Unfortunately, no one on the treatment staff identified the sex addiction that coexisted with my addiction to chemicals. Instead, they told me that my compulsive sexual behavior was simply a manifestation of my chemical dependency and that once I recovered from that primary dependency, my life would improve in all areas. I listened to these professionals, then somewhat reluctantly considered the Twelve Steps of Alcoholics Anonymous. As I look back, I can see that even though I didn't receive help for my sex addiction through treatment for my chemical dependency, that treatment did give me some valuable gifts: the ability and willingness to open my mind to a spiritually-based Program.

Through this group and the Twelve Steps, I was able to remain chemically free. The fog lightened somewhat, but did not lift. I could not understand why peace of mind still eluded me, even after three years of abstinence from drugs and alcohol. I no longer picked up men in bars, but I continued to pick up men; I no longer exchanged sex for drugs, but I exchanged sex for money; I no longer woke up with strangers in my bed, but I did wake up with people whom I had no feelings for and even disliked; I no longer jeopardized my safety by picking up men in dangerous neighborhoods, but I was raped by people I knew. When I was drinking, I had almost no boundaries for my sexual behavior, but then I had almost no boundaries for my sexual behavior when I was sober, either. One man was too many; a dozen men were not enough. And the cast of characters in my life sometimes changed every week. In those days, if a person I liked left the scene, I "fixed" my pain by finding new partners to replace him. It was not unusual for me to be sexual with three or four men in one day. I realize now that I was driven not by a pursuit of sexual pleasure, but by my desperate need to escape the loneliness I felt. *To my way of thinking, my life was the problem and sex was the primary solution.*

Attendance at AA meetings helped me see the parallels that existed between my use of chemicals and my use of sex: preoccupation, euphoric recall, loss of control, delusion, obsessiveness, broken promises, and increased tolerance for pain. But this revelation was not enough. Overwhelmed by confusion and a need for secrecy, I didn't know how to change my behavior. I realized that my sexual acting-out behavior was beginning to pose a threat to my recovery from chemical dependency. I finally called for help after a horrible weekend in which I was completely out of control with my sexual behavior but still abstinent from drugs. I went through a long list of AA contacts until I found someone at home. Out of complete despair, I shared the details of my situation with this person. The real miracle in this contact was not that I opened up, but that out of a large metropolitan community, I had contacted an AA member who also happened to be involved in a Program for recovering sex addicts. My conversation with this man marked an important turning point for me. He told me that the Twelve

Step group he was involved with—the original group for sex addicts—had established a referral system within the therapeutic community. He said that I could start a group just as soon as I got some additional referrals. (This original group for sex addicts was, at that time, still limited to men.) I waited for four months to hear from other women. Then in December 1980, four of us women finally met together for the first time. Even though we were complete strangers to each other, we found that we had other things in common besides gender. All four of us had some background in the Twelve Step Program and acknowledged difficulty with our sexual behavior. We had a brief consultation with two men from the original Twelve Step group for sex addicts; they shared some information about meeting formats and encouraged us to form our own group.

The beginning of our group was hardly promising. After our first meeting (and after three years of sobriety in AA), I had a slip that lasted for three months; another member of the group dropped out after two meetings; the third member lived ninety miles away from our meeting site and frequently chose not to attend meetings on snowy winter nights; and the fourth member expressed doubts as to whether she was a sex addict. As we began meeting on a regular basis, the four of us had no real guidelines for dealing with our addiction, defining abstinence, or supporting each other in healthy and productive ways. What we *did* have were the Twelve Steps and the Twelve Traditions of AA and a commitment to each other that we would meet on a weekly basis. *As it turned out, those simple ingredients were enough.* Even so, some nights I was the only person to show up for a meeting and, oftentimes, only one other person was there with me. Sometimes our group seemed to function much like a toddler functions—teetering, falling, getting up again and again—and then, thank God, finally heading somewhere. A few months later, we began getting some additional referrals.

My first months in the Program underscored some parallels between my addiction to alcohol and my addiction to sex. Back when I was drinking, I was not at all selective about the men I invited to come home with me. In a similar way, when I was compulsive in my sexual activities, I experienced the shame that triggered my urge for alcohol. With love and care, both of my Twelve Step groups helped me understand that it would be impossible for me to be "mostly straight" regarding one of my addictions or the other—either I was on the road to recovery or I was in a ditch. Once I got back on the road to recovery in both of my Programs, my life really began to change for the better. I knew that I had a lot of work ahead of me, particularly in the area of honesty, but I was determined to stay with the Program.

As our group struggled for its own life, boundaries, and identity, I struggled with those same issues as an individual. I finally realized that, unlike alcohol, I needed to integrate sex into my life in a healthy way rather than eliminate it from my life altogether. Because sex represents a very basic need, I would have to determine what was appropriate sexual behavior for me and what was addictive sexual behavior—no small task. I discovered that my negative attitudes about both men and women were continuing to feed my self-destructive behavior. With the group's help, I discovered that I had given men the highest priority in my life, at the expense of myself and my relationships with women. Men were gods to me and sex was my ritual of appeasement. I had subconciously placed all women in one of two categories: competitors to be avoided or judges to be feared. And I felt that I would be humiliated should any woman discover my secrets. I had two particular blind spots I needed to acknowledge and address: I could not see the possibility of women as friends, nor could I see men as potential threats to my peace of mind. *All of this changed as I worked the Program.*

I had to learn several important lessons during my first years in the Program, but I quickly found that I had come to the right place to learn them. First of all, I wanted to find the intimacy which had eluded me for so long. I told my story and then the people in my group expressed their concern for me. I found that they gave me the support I asked for without asking anything of me in return. Instead, the people in the group stayed with me and kept loving me. I reciprocated by listening to their stories and offering my support to others. I expected nothing of them in return; nevertheless, I chose to remain for our mutual benefit. I loved these women. Surprisingly to me, it was in the process of sharing within a group of women that I first discovered my capacity for intimacy.

Ideally, parents provide the trust, support, nurturance, and safety that help the child develop a capacity to be intimate. These skills are then tested in adolescence and further refined in adult relationships. My own family was neither safe nor supportive. The "Ozzie and Harriet" autobiography I had created in grade school, added to, and carried with me on to adulthood had masked different truths that I was now willing to face and work through. My reality was that from early childhood on, I had been subjected to violent and continuous abuse. Later on in my life, I perpetuated that abuse myself through indiscriminate sexual pursuits and chemical use. But finally, with the help of the group, I gave myself a chance to learn new ways of thinking about myself. When I learned to experience and value nonsexual intimacy, I also developed my own guidelines for determining what, for me, is appropriate sexual behavior and what is destructive and addictive sexual behavior. I came to understand that a sexual relationship was appropriate for me only if I could see in it a real potential for the honesty, safety, sharing, reciprocity, and commitment that make up intimacy. The group encouraged me to adopt a "wait and see" attitude whenever I felt unsure about the potential of a relationship. When I did get involved with unsuitable partners,

I acknowledged that I was relapsing and perhaps even testing my own ability to conduct my life as I had conducted it in the past. Most important, I discovered that the old high I had experienced was gone. This high was based on a lie that I believed: that sex—regardless of the situation, condition, or motivations involved—was the best thing life had to offer. *But I came to know better*. I developed a tolerance for living without men in my life, and I carefully cultivated a growing sense of myself as a deserving and worthy person.

After three years in the Program, I realized that I had a new stability in my life and felt that I was ready to leave the Program and move ahead with my life. But then my best friend, also a recovering sex addict, confronted me about some areas of my life in which I continued to be stuck: I still failed to ask for the help I needed; I still isolated myself from others at times; and I still spoke only in generalities about the problems with my current sexual involvements. My friend helped me see something very clearly: I could leave the Program feeling relatively stable, or I could enrich my life and deepen my healing and my new sense of self-worth by staying in the group and working the Twelve Steps. *I chose to stay.*

The Twelve Steps (especially the First, Fourth, Fifth, Eighth, Ninth, and Twelfth) helped me integrate my sexual history with the rest of my life. *Living sanely means accepting where I've been and using that information to proceed to a new destination.* In dislodging the shame and fear I had about my past behavior, I have used the past in much the same way a person uses the rearview mirror of a car—neither dwelling on the flash of images there, nor refusing to look back. The Twelve Step Program guides me as I set goals for my recovery and it provides valuable assistance on the road to achieving those goals.

There is a part of me that is older than my addiction, part of me that predates all of the violence and all of the abuse I have experienced. I recognize that part of me in a photo I have of myself as a toddler. Recovery allows me to recognize, recapture, and pursue the healthy goals of the wise child in me. In reclaiming the child I once was, I am free to choose to live and love.

About eighteen months ago, I met *Ray. Shortly after we met, we chose to have an exclusive relationship. This potential for love frightened me. (Good fortune falls hard on the unsuspecting addict.) While my Program had prepared me to recognize and avoid destructive relationships, I still had no skills or experience in building and maintaining healthy relationships. With Ray, I would begin to learn many things.

Along with commitment came panic, and often I expressed the panic I felt during sexual activity. While making love, I would fantasize about violence and focus on vivid memories of being raped. At first I tried to withhold this information from Ray. But my friends in the Program encouraged me to be open with him about the problem. One person in my group told me to pay close attention to the feelings I had *preceding* these fantasies and recollections. Another person in the group suggested that I examine how these internal scenarios— "movies," as I called them—worked for me and/or what purpose I thought they served. These suggestions helped. Moreover, I realized that I had an option in that I could share with Ray what I was experiencing. Fortunately, he was open to this. I discovered that I was fearful of losing control and being hurt as I had been as a child. Before I met Ray, I had been abused by every other man I'd been close to emotionally.

Gradually, my long-held secrets lost the power they once had in my life. The terror abated, neither Ray nor I ran from each other, and I found that I was at a positive new place in my relationship with him as well as with my recovery. Ray has been a man unlike any man I have known. From the start, I loved him for his intelligence, humor, integrity, and passion. I was ready to work hard for our love and even allowed myself a dream that our relationship would last for a long time. I amazed myself with my optimistic vulnerability. I desperately wanted Ray to be the last in a long line of lovers. Yet, despite our best efforts, Ray and I did not live happily ever after. So far, our relationship has been trying, rich, volatile, tender, rageful, proud, perplexing, and momentous...but not smooth. We may not stay together.

Sometimes my "conscious contact" with my Higher Power comes to me through daydreams and imagery. In an effort to understand the ways I have contributed to the shakiness of my relationship with Ray, I often drift off in reverie. In my mind's eye, I frequently see the two of us setting up an obstacle course on an open field. Ray arranges some of the barriers and I set up the others. The two of us work together to move the more imposing barriers into place. We finally suit up for the race and face the obstacles of our own design.

The close and harmonious times Ray and I have together seem to alternate with our destructive contests. Sadly, I believe we use the instability in our relationship to justify distancing ourselves from one another even further; this distance makes peaceful times less likely. In Ray, I have chosen a person much like myself—a person who seeks intimacy yet resists it.

Intimate relationships are difficult for everyone. But intimate relationships have extra challenges for me as a sex addict. I have an enormous capacity for creating pain for others and expecting pain in my own life. I still struggle with self-delusion, denial of reality, and a deep fear of trusting other people. I recognize that each of these continuing struggles has a profound effect on all of my involvements. I benefit from a group and a Program that keeps me honest and helps me counteract my addictive tendencies.

In a recent Fifth Step, I discovered that resentment is still a central issue for me. I see that my feelings of resentment create a need for me to work *against* others rather than *with* them.

Resentment puffs me up with self-importance and actually functions as a cheap substitute for self-esteem. It serves to frighten others off and it robs me of lasting and loving companionship. I can see that throughout my life, I have been enslaved by my resentfulness in much the same way I was enslaved by my addiction. Forgiveness frees me to lead a richer life. Forgiveness is incompatible with resentment and, therefore, it represents the best path out of my self-imposed isolation. Forgiveness of myself and others helps keep me away from the path of addiction and on the road to true intimacy.

* Name has been changed to ensure anonymity.

Joe's Story

I grew up and started admitting how I felt.

(After three years in the Program; sixteen months of sobriety.)

I was very shy and indecisive as a child. Somehow, I also got the message that physical pleasure and sex were sinful and wrong—certainly not subjects to be talked about with other people. I remember one time when I was very young, my mother fell asleep with her dress pulled up and I crawled between her legs and cuddled up close to her. I felt safe and warm there until she woke up and angrily said that she'd spank me if I ever did anything like that again.

When I was eight years old, my dad left my mom. What I remember most about him before he left permanently is that he was away from home a lot and never seemed to have much time for me and my brothers. I hated doing any kind of work for him because he never was satisfied with my efforts. No matter how hard I tried or how productive I was, he always told me I could try even harder and do an even *better* job. I felt that he mistreated my mother; he often belittled her in front of my brothers and me. Strangely enough, even though I was afraid of my dad and could see his weaknesses, I always held out hope that someday he would return to our home permanently. After he moved out, I *hated* seeing him with other women when we'd visit him; I thought of the other women in his life as "hussies."

I started window-peeping when I was eight years old. Even though I knew that sneaking around and looking in other people's windows was "weird," I found it so very exciting. Window-peeping gave me feelings of power and control. Underwear was also very exciting to me when I was a young child. I found that I could really escape from life and forget about my problems by simply paging through catalogs and looking at underwear. As a youngster, I always chose to play with younger children so that I would be looked up to and could feel like a "big shot." It was very difficult for me to carry on conversations with people. I found it easier to make up lies, brag, and show off. But whenever someone confronted me in the course of a conversation, I'd back off immediately. School was confusing and frightening for me because there was always something new to learn there and that just meant that there was also potential for making mistakes. I invariably chose the easier way to do things, even if that easier way was sloppy and less effective. Girls my age or older always seemed so smart and I felt so dumb. I never knew what to say to these girls, so I tried to avoid having any contact with them whatsoever. I soon discovered that I could feel like an all-knowing important person if I dated girls who were younger than me, small in stature, and intimidated by my age and my size. Even though I enjoyed dating younger girls, I felt self-conscious about spending all of my time with people who were so much younger. Sometimes I felt like an insect living completely outside its environment.

When I was fifteen, window-peeping was still the biggest excitement in my life. As I looked in windows, I'd think about adventure, exploration, and being a tough guy. I took great pride in being a man. When I was with boys my own age, though, I'd never admit that I wanted to do the sexual things they talked about wanting to do. In fact, when other boys my age talked about sex, I'd pretend not to hear them or I'd refuse to participate in the conversation by saying "I don't lower myself to that level." I still had a deep feeling that sex was dirty, sinful, and wrong, yet I really wanted to know about it, at least as much as other boys my age did.

During much of my adolescence, I still believed that masturbation caused blindness and insanity. Then when I was seventeen, a friend of mine who was two years older taught me about masturbation. He touched me and it felt good; I trusted him, so I thought everything was okay. But part of me still felt that I had sinned and that God would be angry with me. I really liked this friend until he touched me; after that he seemed to be obsessed with the idea. One time he jumped on me while we were watching television in his bedroom and after that incident, I decided I no longer could trust him. I had a lot of guilt and shame about this experience and wondered if somehow I was responsible for his behavior toward me. Despite the fact that I felt hurt and betrayed by this friend, I was very sad the day I learned that he had been killed in military service.

When I was nineteen, I got married. Neither my wife nor I was sexually experienced at the time and she was really more interested in sexual activity than I was. I didn't know much at all about sex, but I certainly didn't want *her* to know how uninformed and inexperienced I was. I decided that I hated sex when I discovered that I was unable to sustain an erection. I felt dumb and humiliated, but I covered my feelings by acting all-knowing and superior and by following women on the street. My mother died only three days after I got married. I missed her terribly, but I was angry at her too. In fact, when I'd follow a woman on the street, I'd think about my mother and say to myself, This will show you. I wasn't only angry at my mother, I was angry at most women, most men, and *everything about the world*. Sex scared the hell out of me, but following women on the street seemed to fulfill an urgent need.

When I was a little older, I realized that I had feelings of lust and guilt every time I looked at a woman. Here I am a married man, I thought, and I'm obsessed with the idea of following strange women on the street. Whenever I was cruising the streets, I was ready to hurt, destroy, or otherwise remove from my path anything I thought of as an obstacle. I was sure that nobody cared, so I didn't care either. I began living two separate lives: during the day I was mild and easygoing, but at night I was filled with rage and hate and *I desperately wanted to be anyone but me*. In the dark, I felt unafraid and powerful; this

151

power was a source of release and satisfaction for me. Later, I'd feel guilty about my thoughts and behavior and I'd try to stop myself from acting out again that night. *A normal life seemed totally out of my reach*. After a lot of obsessive thinking one day, I followed a woman as she left a store, then grabbed her. Almost immediately, I felt terribly guilty and shameful about my behavior and vowed never to do *anything* like that again. But I just couldn't forget the excitement and power I felt at the moment I grabbed this woman: I felt so manly and in complete control of the situation. I became more and more compulsive about following women and, in the process, I spent an enormous amount of money and told so many lies to cover myself that I frequently tripped myself up in conversations. One night, my "cruising" almost cost me my life: I was driving around looking at women, lost control of the car, and had an accident that resulted in broken eyeglasses, a concussion, and higher insurance rates.

In time, my compulsive cruising affected my education, my career, and my family life. I missed classes, my grades dropped, and I finally quit school. I turned down promotion opportunities at work out of concern that new and different responsibilities might interfere with my cruising. By this time, I was a father and I felt tremendous guilt knowing that I was leaving my young sons home alone at night so that I could cruise the streets. When I'd return home after a night of cruising, I'd always make a special effort to treat my wife and sons and to assure them that everything in our lives was just fine. Shame and guilt completely controlled me once I returned. I'd agree with everything my wife said just to avoid being questioned. I wanted to have sex with her, but I felt undeserving. When I was cruising, I hated everyone and thought about how *useless* my life was. I judged and condemned other people and told myself that *I was a better person*. I really hated women for "making" me feel so inadequate about myself. My acting-out behaviors got even bolder and eventually I raped a woman. I enjoyed the moment of conquest but was unable to sustain an erection. This enraged me and I became even more violent and abusive in subsequent assaults. Every night, I'd go to a church and pray for God's help so that I could stop assaulting women. But every new day, my addiction seemed to intensify. I just didn't care about anything anymore except acting out.

Finally I was arrested, and for the next three years I was in treatment at a state hospital for my addiction. The treatment wasn't at all like I expected it would be. I had assumed that I'd be subjected to brain surgery, shock treatments, or whatever else it took to "make me right." Instead, and to my surprise, my treatment focused on learning to *own* what I had done, learning to acknowledge and confront my feelings, and learning to be responsible for my behavior. What actually "happened" to me in treatment? *I grew up and started admitting how I felt.* For the first time in my life, I learned to be honest. I also learned to stop blaming everyone else for the problems in my life—*now that was hard!* While I was in treatment for my addiction, I also realized that I needed to have people in my life I could talk to about things that bothered me.

When I was first out of treatment, I had no guarantee that I wouldn't rape again or go back to my crazy ways. The only thing I knew for sure was this: I would keep talking about the things that troubled me and I would admit my addictive urges to others. As it turned out, doing these things helped me get on with my life by relieving some of my guilt. Now I find that I have healthier relationships with all women because I have learned to see them as people and I finally have learned to treat them as human beings rather than sex objects. My wife has become more assertive and now she *tells* me what she is feeling and she lets me know when she is uncomfortable with me. We are equals now and each of us is more independent and self-assured than in the past. Our sexual relationship has grown more compassionate and tender and we've learned to talk through the tough times. I now see my wife as my friend, not my property.

The Program saved my life and without it I'd be lost. I continue to struggle with my recovery and I know that I could have a slip at any time. But because of my experience in treatment, my group meetings, and my phone conversations with other sex addicts, I'm sober and I'm thankful to God.

Rick's Story

Finding the Program was like having a ton of bricks lifted off my chest.

(After twenty months in the Program; twenty months of sobriety.)

I often felt unhappy and lonely as a child. When I was seven years old, I discovered that masturbation not only made me feel better, it also helped me relax and escape from sadness and loneliness. As far as I was concerned, there was only one drawback to masturbation—the good feelings it brought didn't last. Sometimes I'd masturbate two or three times before going to bed at night and again the first thing in the morning. Before long, I also discovered that I could masturbate in the bathtub as well as in bed. I'd masturbate against the rough surface of the cast-iron tub until my penis was raw and sore.

Then one day my mother caught me masturbating in the bathtub and became very upset with me about this; she told me that what I was doing was "naughty" and I should never do it again. I felt so embarrassed about my behavior. After that incident, I unsuccessfully tried to stop masturbating. When my mother caught me masturbating for the third time, I was desperately ashamed and told her through my tears that I just couldn't stop. This time her response was different: she held me close and told me that what I was doing was okay. As I buried my head in her chest, I first became aware of the softness of her breasts and told her they felt like pillows. She let me rest my head against each of her breasts for several minutes. Cuddling with my mother in this way was pleasurable but confusing in the same way that her conflicting messages about masturbation confused me: I had never been allowed to do this before and somehow I just knew I'd never be allowed to do anything like it again.

I began masturbating in places other than my bed and the bathtub. I'd masturbate as I sat in a chair looking at magazines and while I was lying on the living room floor in front of the television. Sometimes I'd masturbate so much that it was even painful for me to walk afterwards; I can still remember the excruciating pain of rug burns on my penis. Several times I made unsuccessful attempts to stop masturbating just long enough to allow my penis to heal.

One day I found a sex-oriented joke book in my brother's dresser drawer and started reading it as I masturbated. But I quickly set this book aside the day I found a pornographic magazine in his drawer. At first I struggled with my decision about whether or not I should open the magazine at all. I had once promised myself that I'd never read a "dirty" book, so I felt sure that God would not want me to look at this magazine. But as I held the magazine in my hand, I realized that I was shaking with anticipation. Finally I decided to open it—just to see what naked women really looked like. The minute I saw the pictures, I started masturbating. I immediately felt guilty, but the experience was so arousing that I knew I'd want to look at magazines like this whenever I could. I decided that it was okay to masturbate and look at pornography—as long as I didn't *buy* pornography.

My commitment to never buy pornography lasted until I got married and moved out of my parents' house. When I realized that I no longer had access to my brother's pornographic material, I began buying my own; I even started a collection of pornographic books and magazines. I justified my purchase of this kind of material by telling myself it was "classy, not trashy." I soon modified my earlier commitment not to buy pornography and instead promised myself that I'd never buy what I considered "hard-core" porn. Masturbation was taking more and more of my time before I got married. I assumed that once I was in a marriage relationship, I wouldn't be so preoccupied with masturbation. *I was wrong*. When my wife was unwilling to have sex with me two or three times a night, I'd go downstairs and masturbate for hours while she slept. I'd return to bed only when I was completely exhausted.

After three years of marriage, my wife and I went to a counselor. Our relationship had never been on really solid ground and we argued *constantly*. I pressured her for more and more sexual activity and told her that she was not to talk to certain people at work because I felt they were putting "crazy" ideas in her head. Whenever I felt she was beginning to assert herself, I'd scream and yell at her until she backed down. After three years of counseling, only one thing had changed in our relationship: my wife was convinced that I had an extraordinary need for sexual activity. She decided that she could help me by understanding me and accepting the fact that I had a need to masturbate frequently. So with my wife's understanding and approval, I masturbated in front of her when she didn't want to have sex with me and sometimes just after we'd had sex. I also took her to R-rated drive-in movies and masturbated as she sat beside me; this seemed to bring a more intense high than the pornographic magazines did. When my wife complained about these drive-in movies, I started going to them by myself.

Thoughts of sex began to fill every waking moment of my day. I had always enjoyed looking at women and thinking about them sexually, but now whenever I was driving, I'd slow down at the first sight of an attractive woman. In fact, whenever I'd see a woman I thought was particularly attractive walking down the street, I'd quickly turn my car around and drive by her again in order to get another look at her. My compulsion progressed to the point that I'd even stop women on the street and ask for directions to fictitious locations just to get a better look at their bodies and have more time to fantasize about them sexually. I'd approach these women, establish eye contact with them, and try to get them to maintain eye contact with me. I fantasized that these women *wanted* to have sex with me. At first most of my fantasies focused on having a loving relationship with a woman who loved me and satisfied me sexually. But as time went on, my fantasies changed dramatically. In the privacy of my car, I'd call women names and think about various ways I could exploit them. My fantasies became more and more violent; I even fantasized about assaulting women and forcing them to be sexual with me.

So many times, I made up my mind that I was going to stop this "sinful" behavior and free myself at last from my tremendous guilt. When I felt that way, I'd throw out my collection of pornography and promise myself and God that I'd never again buy or even *look* at this kind of material. But, as always, I started collecting pornography again almost right away. Then I'd hunt for used copies of the very same pornographic books and magazines I'd thrown away the last time I was overcome by guilt. One day I decided to visit an adult bookstore—just to see what it was like. While I was there, I remember feeling intense anger that *anyone* would operate such a business, but I also experienced an intense sexual high. As I masturbated on the floor of this bookstore I kept thinking to myself that the owner *deserved* to clean up the mess. I continued masturbating at home, desperately seeking different ways to do what I'd been doing for years. Eventually my addiction was so uncontrollable that I even forced foreign objects—a pop bottle, for example— up my anus. Of course I considered the possibility that the bottle might break, but getting high seemed to be worth any risk or danger involved.

I began fantasizing about prostitutes. Out of curiosity one night, I called a sauna that was generally known to be a front for prostitution. I inquired about rates and asked several leading questions about the women who were working there that night. This phone call excited me, so I masturbated in order to stay aroused and made call after call to other saunas in town. A pattern developed in these phone calls: my conversations became more and more direct and, eventually, I was verbally abusive. I justified my behavior by telling myself that the people I was calling *deserved* my verbal abuse because, after all, they were working at saunas.

Then one night a friend of mine and I decided to go to a topless bar—just to see what it was like. Actually, I was afraid to go because the bar was located in a section of town that I considered unsafe. *I went anyway*. The friend with me at the bar that night was embarrassed to be with me because I kept touching myself through my pants. I told him my underwear was uncomfortable but, in truth, the intense high I experienced that night seemed well worth any embarrassment. Despite my experience, I did not return to a topless bar for more than a year. I felt I wasn't that "low." During that time I went to lingerie shows instead. I told myself that these shows were different, not at all like the sleazy topless bars I had visited. The lingerie shows were really just topless bars, but that didn't matter to me. When I was at these shows, I was higher than ever. I'd put my hand in my pocket and fondle myself; I didn't care who saw me.

Eventually I started going to topless bars again. Then one day when I was in one of these bars, I discovered that there was a hole in the pocket of my pants. I punched my hand through the hole and began to masturbate. After that I even began planning my trips to these bars so that I'd be sure to have old pants on. Then during a very busy work day, I happened to drive by a topless bar. I was wearing a brand new pair of pants and didn't have any cash with me. I knew for a fact that I didn't have the time or the money I needed to go into that bar on that day. But before I knew it, I was shaking with anticipation about the prospects of masturbating in the bar. I cut out the pockets of my pants and begged a service station attendant to let me write a check for more than the cost of a bottle of windshield washer fluid (which I didn't need anyway) so that I'd have enough cash to be served in the bar. Through the years, I had broken so many promises to myself. Along the way, I also had promised myself that I'd never pay a stripper to dance for me—somehow this kind of activity seemed like prostitution and I felt that I was "above" that sort of thing. But soon I had broken this promise to myself also, and was totally out of control. I began talking to the strippers I encountered in bars and even considered approaching some of them for sex. I blamed the stress of my failing marriage for this newest broken promise.

After going to four marriage counselors, I finally decided to get a divorce. During consultations with my attorney regarding my divorce plans, I was referred to a therapist. I was angry about being asked to go to yet another counselor but felt that if I went through with this one last effort, I'd be able to divorce my wife and still have a clear conscience. Instead of giving me courage to go through with a divorce, this psychiatrist confronted me with the reality of my sexual problems. Relieved to hear his explanation of my behavior, I even was willing to accept the label of "sex addict." Finally I understood why I always had this overwhelming desire to have sex. The psychiatrist told me about a Twelve Step group for sex addicts and soon after that I began attending Twelve Step meetings. The group's encouragement helped me set limits on my sexual behavior and for the first time in my life, I got in touch with my feelings. Gradually, I began to feel better about myself and my marriage began to improve. My wife and I argued less and the arguments we *did* have were not as violent and unproductive; some of our arguments were *constructive* and I found that I was actually *learning* from them. Through all of this, I found out that it's *okay* for my wife and I to disagree with each other.

My first three months in recovery were hell. I'm sure I would have given up completely had it not been for the oldtimers in the group—the continuing hope I could see in them and their many reassurances that things would get better. As I began my fourth month in recovery, I felt some serenity and peace of mind. Each month that goes by now, I feel more comfortable with my Program and my progress. For me, the best thing about recovery is that I don't have to do everything by myself. I really don't *need* to have all the answers. *Finding the Program was like having a ton of bricks lifted off my chest.* Each day that goes by now, I feel better about my relationships with my family, with other people in my life, and with God. Now after twenty months of sobriety, I feel that life is worth living. For the first time in years, I feel happy. I'm thankful to the members of my group for their unconditional love and for their acceptance of me "just as I am." Most of all, I am thankful to my Higher Power (God) for allowing me to hear and to have the willingness to change. Sometimes I wonder how I can make amends to all the people I have exploited and abused through the years. I am truly sorry for the wrong I have done to each person. Time and circumstances will not allow me to *personally* apologize to all the people I have harmed, but I am willing to make amends and change for the better. And if I change for the better, the world around me will change for the better.

(Postscript: after twenty-eight months in the Program; one day of sobriety.)

Today my biggest struggle is with masturbation. For twenty-two months I was abstinent from all of my compulsive sexual behaviors, including masturbation. But then six months ago, I masturbated during the middle of the night. From that time on, my acting-out behavior has progressed from masturbation in a half-awake state in the middle of the night to a conscious act in the light of day. But I've come to realize that masturbation is not the *problem* as much as it is a *symptom* of the problem. I believe that the real problem lies in the fact that my relationship with my Twelve Step group changed within the last six months and I did not seek productive ways to deal with the effects of that change.

Our group had become too large and we subsequently split to form two separate groups. It just so happened that many of the people who had helped me early in my recovery began attending the other group meeting because it was held in a location that was more convenient for them. Suddenly I was an oldtimer in my Twelve Step group. Looking back, I now realize that my thinking—and therefore my behavior and my relationship to the group—changed about this time. I was afraid that I would be thought of as the "leader" of this reconstituted group, but that didn't happen. Previously, I had been very aggressive when interacting with other group members. I had a reputation for being very blunt and for "telling it like it is." When the original group split into two separate groups, I felt abandoned and alone. Looking back, I feel I made an unconscious decision to avoid conflict in this instance. I wasn't willing to take risks because I no longer felt that the strongest members of the group were there to support me. I became passive and less vocal.

I now realize that thinking of myself as the group "leader" had a negative effect on me and on the group as a whole. This mind-set made it almost impossible for me to turn to newer people in the group for the help and support I needed. When my life became stressful because of work and family pressures, I turned to masturbation rather than to my group as a way of dealing with my situation. My first slip became the "reason" for my second slip; my second slip became the "reason" for my third slip, and so on. I felt that if I could not stay sober in the middle of the night, it didn't really matter whether or not I stayed sober during the day. I convinced myself that as soon as the stress in my life abated, I'd be sober again. I realize that I have been using these excuses for six months now. *Enough! Now, back to the Program.* My choice today is clear: I can grow closer to my Program and therefore closer to peace and serenity, or I can move further away from my Program, peace, and serenity. I know that just as I worked the Program at the beginning of my recovery, I can work the Program through the issues that are in my life today.

Jerome's Story

*What a relief it was not to be alone anymore and
to finally turn my will over to my Higher Power.*

(After thirty months in the Program; twenty-five months of
sobriety.)

"You've got it made." People said that to me so often when I
was growing up. My father was a charming university profes-
sor, my mother came from a very prominent family, and we
were wealthy. But even though we acted as if our lives were
great and people always told us how fortunate we were, I sensed
that something was wrong. I always felt so distant and numb;
sometimes I even felt as though I was living in a time warp or
on a completely different dimension from other people.

Later on, when I was an adult, a woman I was going with
commented that there was a distance between us and asked me
to go to couple's therapy with her. I agreed to the therapy as a
favor to her. I knew, of course, that *I certainly didn't need any
help.* But after just a few sessions of therapy, I could see that
my parents had really *ignored* me when I was a child. I had
never learned to reach out to others; I had never learned to give
or receive love. *Even within a supposedly secure family unit, I
felt all alone.* Now that I had these insights about myself and
my background, I decided to improve my relationships with
people by sharing my feelings with them. But when I began
expressing my feelings to the woman in my life, she became
distant. After a short time in therapy together, we split up and
went separate ways.

Following the breakup of that relationship, I started individual therapy and very reluctantly began to look at my sexual
behavior. Even with the new understanding I had of myself,
my childhood, and my family background, I still felt distant—
not just from my family, from *everyone*. In time, I came to

understand how I had violated my own moral standards by treating women as sex objects. For years I bought pornography with money I needed for other things and I spent so much of my time with sexual fantasies and activities that I had no time left for friendships. Every day, I spent hours thinking about sex, masturbating, looking into windows with a telescope or binoculars, and gawking at women. (By "gawking," I mean looking at someone only as a sex object.) Every night I resolved to stop doing these things, but as soon as I woke up the next morning, I'd start thinking again about exciting new ways I could act out that day. Before long, my life was totally *consumed* by my sexual acting-out behaviors and I had no time or energy left for communication, feelings, *real* friendships, or intimacy. When I realized that I was completely alone, I was overwhelmed with sadness and I actually grieved for my life. Nevertheless, I was ambivalent about my acting-out behaviors: I wanted to stop, but I didn't want to stop.

I attended my first Twelve Step meeting for sex addicts reluctantly but also with a small sense of hope. I expected to find a group of sleazy looking men in trench coats hanging around darkened corners, so I was surprised and relieved when I got to the meeting and saw normal looking people who were sitting in a well-lighted room, talking and laughing. At first, I found the group meetings meaningless, even corny. I just couldn't believe that the people in this group would be willing to help me. No one had ever helped me before, so why would anything change now? I also found it very difficult to believe that simple things like prayers and Twelve Steps could change my life. The prayers, readings, and format of the group meeting reminded me of church and I *hated* church. For years, I had vacillated between agnosticism and atheism. Also, I was fearful about sharing details of my sexual acting-out behaviors with people in the group. I was afraid that if they knew me and knew what I had done, they wouldn't like me and then I'd be *completely alone*. But in spite of my fears, I kept going to meetings. I decided that I really had nothing to lose because my life was so lonely, empty, and out of control. And when I found out that other people in the group had some of the same fears I had, I was relieved. *I wasn't alone after all.*

At first, I had no use whatsoever for the concept of God, and the thought of phoning someone in the group for help *terrified* me. But as I worked the Steps, I found some meaning in the Program that led me to *try* praying to God. I actually began to see God as a nurturing father figure who takes care of the earth. And the more I prayed to God, the more trusting I became of other people. Gradually, I began to feel better about the prayers, the reading, the group, and myself. I felt less lonely. I began to have some real hope that my life could improve. When I finally *did* call other people in the group, I was pleasantly surprised: they helped me and I was able to help them.

With the support of my sponsor, I decided to present my First Step in the group. When I finally shared the nature of my sexual addiction within the fellowship of the group, I understood for the first time how powerless and unmanageable my life had become...*but I also felt much less lonely*. I could see more clearly than ever before that I could not fight my addiction alone. I *knew* I would need help from others, including God. Just praying to Him, I felt more comfort and serenity than I had ever felt before. Through the First Step and with the guidance of other people in the group, I also could see how my addiction was manifesting itself in my life: in compulsive, self-destructive masturbation; in loveless "lovemaking"; and in countless hours spent avoiding life by engaging in voyeuristic activities. I felt shameful and powerless about these acting-out behaviors. I knew that I had to set boundaries for myself, so with the help of my sponsor I did just that.

My boundaries then and now exclude the following acting-out behaviors: voyeurism, masturbation, use of pornography, pornographic fantasies, sexual activity with another person when it is not an expression of love, and thinking of women as sex objects. This last boundary—thinking of women as sex objects—was particularly difficult for me because just glancing at a woman out of the corner of my eye could trigger a powerful addictive urge. At first, I was very upset about the fact that this behavior was so difficult to stop, but then I realized that I could not *control* my addictive urges with will power. Instead, I learned to *recognize* my addictive urges for what they were; with the help of God and the Twelve Steps, I realized that these urges would pass without my feeling compelled to act out.

Following much prayer, meditation, and supportive group encouragement, I finally made a decision to let go of the paraphernalia I had acquired through the years in order to support my voyeuristic activities. During the ten years of my acting-out behavior, I had amassed an enormous collection of telescopes, binoculars, and other equipment. One day, I tossed every one of those items into the trunk of my car, brought them to my Twelve Step group meeting, and asked my sponsor to get rid of everything for me. It was quite a sight for the group to see as they watched me lug my "optical" equipment across the parking lot. Despite our best efforts to remain serious about this important Third Step activity, we couldn't help but see some humor in it. The moment turned into a celebration! *What a relief it was not to be alone anymore and to finally turn my will over to my Higher Power.*

Later on in my recovery, I realized that contact with my family often triggered my addictive urges. After reflecting on this, I decided that it would be advisable to stop communicating with my family for awhile. As difficult as this decision was to make and carry out, not seeing my family for a time actually helped me let go of a powerful but erroneous perception that I had carried with me for years: that the world is a terrifying place and no one can really be trusted. Prior to my recovery, I thought of people as sources of pain. Now, I'm much more likely to think of people as loving and worthy of trust. Now I also think of *myself* as a loving and trustworthy person rather than an empty and unworthy one. Now, after more than two years of recovery, I have good, healthy relationships with people. I am very much in love with a woman and we plan to marry soon. I am also close to several men and I love them as friends. The relationships I have with people today fill a void that I unsuccessfully struggled with for years. I have never felt so whole and full of love. I feel joy and gratitude just to be alive and recovering, and I trust in God that the rest of my life will be rewarding and fulfilling.

Barbara's Story

At last I was able to let go of the burden of resentment, one person at a time.

(After three years in the Program.)

It was my birthday and my brother and I were at a small party with friends. I had invited my brother to be my escort for the party and had offered to give him a ride home afterwards. (Having my evening planned in this way, I felt reasonably sure that I would be able to get through the night without a stranger in my bed.) As cake was being served, everyone shared personal thoughts about the year that had just ended and hopes for the year ahead. I rarely reflected in this way because it was just too painful for me to see all the events in my life as a composite. What I said to my friends that night and what I really thought were *two completely different things*. In fact, what I thought allowed a truth to hit home: if I continued to live my life as I had been living it, I wouldn't make it through the next year. Murder or suicide would get me first. As I celebrated my birthday that night, I knew I needed help. *I had been trying to change by myself, but it wasn't working.*

The next day I made an appointment with a therapist. During my first session with her, I explained my situation: I was involved in a very destructive relationship with a man but couldn't seem to get out of that relationship and move on. I also mentioned to her that two days earlier, I almost had been raped by a man I'd just met, but had managed to talk my way out of it.

At the therapist's suggestion, and with her support, I developed a plan for ending the relationship I was in. After I had accomplished that, I returned to see the therapist with a realization that I still felt empty and desperate. In fact, I was suicidal. I simply did not know how to live on my own. The therapist asked me questions about past relationships and I explained to

171

her that prior to the relationship I had just ended, I'd been sexually involved with several people during the same period of time. Some of these involvements had been brief; others were ongoing. The therapist gave me a brochure that outlined a Twelve Step Program for people dealing with sex addiction. Though it was very difficult for me to associate myself with the concept of "sex addiction," and the label of "sex addict," I was surprisingly relieved when the therapist recommended the Program to me. Of course, I felt that I was different from other addicted people because I was "in control" of my behavior. But even as I sat there listening to the therapist describe the Program, I was exhausted from acting out the night before. I had spent the night being sexual with a new acquaintance, a man I wasn't even sure I *liked*.

Later my therapist asked more questions about the "near rape" incident I'd mentioned in my first session with her. I explained that, even though I supposedly had a committed relationship with my boy friend at the time, I had talked on the phone for three hours one night with a man I'd met only once and our conversation was sexually explicit. The man I talked to on the phone finally convinced me to come over to his house. It was then two A.M. in the morning and I could tell by the way he was talking that he was hallucinating. I had no idea what was causing his hallucinations but I told myself, "Maybe this man is *crazy*, but I'm sure he's harmless." I told the therapist that as soon as I arrived at this man's house and saw him, I knew from his appearance that I could not have sex with him. He was furious when I refused to continue the fantasy we had started with our phone conversation.

Before I finished relating this story to my therapist, it was clear to *both* of us that I had willingly placed myself in an extremely dangerous situation that night: I was almost raped and I could have been murdered. When I realized this, I first began to understand that I was *not* in control of my sexual behavior. I also realized that I'd been keeping secrets from myself, from my lovers, and from my friends. On many occasions I had betrayed my commitment to a person I had a relationship with by acting out sexually with another person. But I always managed to convince myself that if I didn't actually engage in *intercourse*, I hadn't broken the "rules." I rarely enjoyed sexual activity when I acted out. Instead, it was the attention, the touching, the excitement of pursuit, and the *danger* that drew me to sexual encounters and generated a "high" for me. When I'd act out sexually, I often associated with people I knew I wouldn't even choose as *friends*. Though I had no history of drug use, I started taking drugs to help me through encounters with multiple sex partners.

I began to see that my addiction went beyond my sexual actions; I realized that I was also addicted to "love" and romance. Through the years I had come to see romantic relationships as the perfect antidote to my pain and helplessness. A predictable pattern developed in my relationships with men: I would become very dependent on the man I was currently "in love" with; essentially I'd make him my higher power. Then, I'd switch from romantic preoccupation with the relationship to angry sexual obsession and acting out. All the time I knew that I wanted to be married and have a family; I really didn't *want* to be indiscriminately sexual or get myself into dangerous situations. But I also knew from experience that whenever I felt enough despair or pain or helplessness, I would act out sexually.

When I attended my first Twelve Step meeting, I was relieved to hear other women express some of the same ideas I had only thought to myself. Finally I had a chance to meet other people who really *understood* the double life I had been leading. Underneath my professional, well-educated, "I've got it all under control" exterior, I was living a life of chaos and despair. As I listened to these women share their stories, I began to feel a measure of hope. *These women were living without acting out!*

Through the examples of their lives, they taught me something so valuable: *that even though I couldn't control my compulsive behavior through will power, "a power greater than myself" could show me a way back to a manageable life.*

In my early days in the Program, I understood Step Two to mean *came to believe a power greater than myself would get me out of this one.* I used the group as my higher power then. The group helped me make healthy new choices in the midst of chaotic situations. For example, one time I called a member of my group from a bar after I "automatically" offered to give a man there a ride home. (I had acted out with this man in the past.) The group member I phoned that night helped me find the courage and the words to withdraw my offer. Another time I was visiting a friend at his home and he began to take his clothes off, assuming from past experience that we were going to be sexual. Instead of just accepting the inevitability of having sex with him that night, I focused on my commitment to the group and found that I had within me the power to say good-night to this man, then drive home and call a Twelve Step group member for support.

As I continued to work on my recovery, I learned to gauge how safe I felt in certain situations and I learned to make choices and set limits according to the new power I had within myself. By this time I had identified my compulsive behaviors and I was able to make some rational decisions about what situations I should avoid. As a practicing sex addict, I'd had no personal boundaries. In recovery, *safety* was—and continues to be—the key word I use to evaluate and set my boundaries. When I first came to the Program, I was not capable of having sexual contact and remaining safe. After I came to the Program, I chose to be celebate for a time because I knew that I needed to find new ways of caring for *myself* before I could have a healthy sexual relationship with another person. I realized that for years I had communicated ambiguous messages to men about my sexual intentions and that I needed to stop flirting in order to feel safe and communicate clearly. When I was acting out, I would tell *any* man sexually explicit information about myself—regardless of the context in which I knew him. I began to realize that this was one of the ways I had set myself up to be victimized. In recovery, I set boundaries for myself by intentionally speaking to people in a very conservative way until I learned to judge the appropriateness of my words. I based my behavior on two things: my perception of the degree of safety in the situation and whether or not I really wanted a closer relationship with someone. My sponsor suggested that I use this rule of thumb: *when in doubt—don't!* These words were a useful guide for me.

As the fog that had obscured my sexuality cleared, I once again had access to memories of the physical and sexual abuse that had occurred earlier in my life. The support and understanding of my "sisters" in the program helped me through this difficult time and helped me realize that no one is "too damaged" to recover. I came to believe that I *deserved* a healthy life and that my higher power was showing me a path to this life one day at a time. I also discovered that I had learned to speak to myself in an abusive way. This ongoing self-punishment set me up to feel shameful. I actually came to believe that I *deserved* abuse from others. To counteract this pervasive belief, I began to make a conscious effort to speak to myself with respect and gentleness. I also realized at this point in my recovery that pornography was a part of my acting out, so I disposed of my pornographic magazines and literature.

Early in my recovery, I continued to masturbate compulsively. I convinced myself that this form of sexual expression was *completely safe* because it had no negative consequences, especially when compared to my acting-out behavior with other people. As I spent more time in recovery, I continued to masturbate. Over time, though, I was able to change my personal attitudes and practices regarding masturbation. In the past, I

175

used a vibrator to stimulate myself in what I now consider a compulsive manner. (The only way I could stop using the vibrator was to have a friend keep it for me.) After ten months in recovery, I found that instead of using a vibrator compulsively, I could *choose* when to use a vibrator to stimulate myself. Now when I masturbate, I make use of fantasies that are gentle, nurturing, and self-affirming, not fantasies that activate the "love" or sex addict reaction. Now when fantasies emerge that are incongruent with the boundaries I set for myself, I gently redirect my thoughts. I also ask myself, What am I feeling right now? What emotions am I dealing with? At these times I usually find that I am afraid and that I need to slow down and find a way to feel safe.

When I started dating again, I felt as though I was starting over: I had to learn how to be with another person, how to take risks, and how to allow intimacy to develop naturally. *All of these things were difficult for me.* When I finally allowed myself to be vulnerable again, I experienced fear, caring, joy, love, and confusion. By sharing their own experiences with me, my sisters in the Program reassured me that I needn't feel ashamed about starting over and feeling ill at ease in certain situations. Even in recovery I continued to battle my former obsession with romance because I still had a tendency to see romance as the perfect solution for all of my problems. When I began to have obsessive thoughts, I found it helpful to call a Program member and/or work on Step Three instead of calling the current man in my life. By doing this, I found I could restore God as my guide and affirm the fact that I was on equal terms with my partner.

Each of the Twelve Steps is crucial, but the Fourth and Fifth Steps have special importance for me and for my recovery. As I look back at my healing from sexual addiction, I attribute as much significance to the three times I worked the Fourth and Fifth Steps as I do to my daily commitment and willingness to recover. The first Fourth Step I wrote came from my feelings of intense anxiety and grief. At that time in my life, I could hardly sit still for fifteen minutes; my grief was profound and I cried endlessly. After writing about both the defects and assets of my character, I made a list of the exact nature of my wrongs. As I prepared this list, I made an entry on a page I titled "Shame" each time I had feelings of shame in recalling a certain event. I was very gentle with myself when I dealt with these memories and I asked my sponsor for some special support. I wanted one person to *hear* me and one person to *support* me in my grief, so I arranged to do a Fifth Step with both my sponsor and a strong and trusted Program acquaintance. With the three of us together, I found it much easier to experience the profound healing forgiveness from my higher power. I had unprecedented feelings of relief when at last I was able to let go of the grief, guilt, and self-hatred I had carried with me throughout my life.

I worked the Fourth and Fifth Steps a second time when I hit an impasse in my Program at Steps Eight and Nine. At that time, I was feeling very resentful that I'd been victimized by other people in so many ways. I wondered why in the world I should be willing to make amends to others when I felt so hurt by them. In order to work through this resentment, I designed a pseudo-step for myself—*I made a list of all the people I resented and became willing to forgive each one of them*. My higher power guided me through this process. When I started the list, I was completely unwilling to forgive *anyone* and, furthermore, I felt *justified* in my unwillingness. By the time I got to the Fifth Step, however, I was willing to discuss my involvement in each event, but I was still blind to so many things. Again, my sponsor and my trusted Program acquaintance gently but honestly confronted me about portions of my past I had neglected to bring out or hadn't really looked at. A major and very painful transformation was underway as I admitted that their insights had merit. Again, tremendous healing took place, healing more powerful than I had ever experienced. *At last I was able to let go of the burden of resentment, one person at a time.* My self-righteous "victim" gave way to acceptance of others and acceptance of myself.

Later on, I worked the Fourth and Fifth Steps in response to the shame I continued to feel when I was in the company of nonaddicted people. As long as I looked for love and support *within* the Program, I could accept it and believe it. But I held on to the belief that people *outside* the Program would judge me harshly and perhaps even condemn me. As I continued to search my past, I finally realized that as a child I connected the commemorations of torture I heard about in worship services to the violence I was subjected to at home. I developed a belief that violence, torture, and pain actually helped people feel closer to God. Through reading, meetings, writing in my journal, and prayer, I could see that the concept of God I now had in recovery was in conflict with the concept of God based on my religious upbringing. In an effort to resolve this conflict, I arranged to do a Fifth Step with a member of the clergy within that faith. I trusted her, so I told her my story and asked for a blessing to move ahead with the new concept and understanding of God that had evolved for me in recovery. She granted her blessing without hesitation and offered understanding and compassion for the pain I had endured. Since that time, I have had no doubts about the validity of my spiritual path and I am healed of the shame I once experienced outside of my Twelve Step group.

I am most grateful to God and the Program that I have my recovery today. My sisters in the Program have taught me so much through the examples of their lives. Now I know that I don't have to live in the chaos and preoccupation of an active addiction, yet I don't have to lead a perfect storybook life either. Instead, I work my Program with whatever feelings and circumstances are in my life *today*. I don't know what the future holds for me in terms of relationships. I leave the future to the care of God. But an important milestone in my recovery occurred six months ago when the relationship I had been in for a year ended. I was able to grieve the loss without feeling hopeless and despairing, and without visiting the obsession or compulsion of my addiction.

After three years in the Program, I feel healed from the wounds of my childhood and my addiction. I continue to call myself a sex addict because I realize I will always be capable of falling into the delusions and compulsions of my past. But I no longer feel like shameful, damaged goods. I know that I am lovable and I am capable of loving others in a significant and healthy way. The task of my recovery is to broaden and deepen my spirituality. In this process, I am finding ways to broaden and deepen my sense of a healthy sexuality as well. I now introduce myself at meetings in two interchangeable ways: "Hi, I'm Barbara; I'm a sex addict. I am Barbara; I am dedicated to a healthy sexuality."

Charles's Story

...I would never exchange the honest imperfections of my life today with my old life of lies and delusions.

(After four years in the Program; two years of sobriety.)

I was born into a wealthy family. Looking back, I think we had almost every material possession a family could possibly want in order to lead a comfortable and affluent lifestyle. When I refer to my "family," I'm referring to my mother, my father, my two older sisters, myself, a laundress, a cook, and my maternal grandmother. With the exception of the cook, I believe that every adult in my family was a practicing alcoholic. During my parents' frequent absences, I was cared for by my grandmother. She was an angry alcoholic who frequently took her rage out on me. Once when I was very young and accidentally had a bowel movement in my pants, my grandmother threatened to make me eat it as punishment. She taught me that I was inferior to her and inferior to everyone else as well. I learned this lesson about my basic inferiority *so well* that I continue to struggle with it even now in my middle years.

Life with my parents was not much different from life with my grandmother. My father was frequently unavailable because of work, physical illness, or the effects of alcohol consumption. I have almost no memories of spending quality time with him; in fact, I could only *guess* what it might be like to have a father really involved in my life. My mother was intoxicated almost every day and when I'd wake up feeling fearful in the middle of the night, I'd often climb into her bed, crawl under the covers, and caress her body. She never stopped me from doing this, nor did she even *acknowledge* my behavior. I had always assumed that my mother was asleep when I crawled into bed with her. I now believe that she was aware of what was happening, but chose not to do anything about it. For this reason and other reasons as well, I consider myself an incest victim.

By the time I was twelve years old, I knew three things: that I was a failure, that adults frequently got drunk, and that being sexual with someone could make me feel safe. The winter of my twelfth year, my father died of an alcohol-related illness and my mother was admitted to a hospital with tuberculosis. As disruptive as these events would be to most children, they really didn't bring much change into my life because my parents had been there for me so seldom. Nevertheless, I was concerned and frightened about my lack of emotional response to these traumatic events in my life—I felt something must be terribly wrong with me. Whenever I spoke with other members of my family, we completely avoided dealing with our problems and concerns by saying things like, "Well, life goes on; we'll just have to play it by ear." After my father's death and my mother's hospitalization, I was sent to live with my godfather and his wife because my father's side of the family didn't want to bear the responsibility for me. During the six months I lived with them on their farm, I experienced the first and only real parenting I have ever known. Years later, I would also realize that the time I spent with these people may have saved my life.

Despite the fact that I was happy living with my godfather and his wife, members of my family decided to send me to a quasi-military boarding school in an effort to "straighten" me out. I was upset by my family's decision to send me away to school and I knew that my godfather and his wife would suffer great emotional pain when I left. But even though I didn't want to go to boarding school and wanted to stay with my godfather on his farm, I felt powerless to protest my family's decision in any way. By this time, my powerlessness was so profound that I didn't even know I *was* powerless. Looking back, it seems as if I was sleepwalking through life. Somehow, I had learned that the key to survival was doing whatever I was told to do. So when my family said "boarding school," I agreed. I was so out of touch with myself I wasn't even aware that deep inside me a little boy was screaming "No! I don't *want* to go; I hate the idea!" All the time my life *appeared* calm, but I was actually *filled* with rage. This conflict between my outer calm and inner rage would manifest itself in my sex addiction as well.

The boarding school I was sent to was very strict; in fact, corporal punishment was freely used in dealing with students who broke school rules. One of the few social outlets available to us was dating the girls who lived in town. I was delighted to know that the girls I met thought I was appealing. I quickly discovered that when I was with a girl, I felt much less lonely, frightened, and strange. I had finally discovered a wonderful new escape from the realities of my life—involvement with the opposite sex. At last, I had found a way to overcome the powerful negative feelings that I had carried with me for so long, feelings of inferiority, shame, and worthlessness. I wanted any girl at any time and in any place. As long as I was being embraced by a girl, nothing really mattered to me because then I felt really safe and all right with my world.

After I had attended this boarding school for three years, my family sent me to another boarding school, again with my compliance, but against my wishes. This school was different from the other boarding school I had attended in that we were not allowed to date at all. I found I was *miserable* without the companionship of girls. I began masturbating frequently because doing so gave me at least some momentary relief from my loneliness and those old feelings of being worthless and inferior. I also began drinking, often with the *intention* of getting as drunk as possible. Not even the memories of miserable hangovers or vomiting deterred me from drinking night after night. In fact, I thought of these unpleasant consequences as the "badges of honor" I earned on the road to becoming an experienced drinker. When I was a little older, I chose to use a variety of drugs that seemed even more powerful than alcohol. In a desperate effort to feel good about myself again, I became compulsive about using pornography, making out with girls, attending strip shows, and masturbating. But despite all of my efforts, I remained frightened of life and tormented by feelings of inferiority. Those feelings of fear and inferiority seemed to subside only when I was intoxicated or when I was being sexual with a woman.

After I got to college, my chemical use expanded to include pot, speed, downers, and psychedelics. I convinced myself that as long as I wasn't using heroin, I wasn't in any real danger of becoming addicted to drugs. It seemed to me that all of my friends used drugs in much the same way I did; people who *didn't* use drugs were no friends of mine! At this time in my life, I was terribly ashamed of the fact that I was still a virgin. So at the first possible opportunity, I had intercourse with a woman—in spite of the fact that I hardly knew her and had no real interest in her. Even though I was not at all attracted to this woman, intercourse with her seemed like the greatest thing in the world. After that first experience, being sexual with women became the focus of my life. Hugging and kissing were no longer satisfying or powerful enough for me; intercourse was the only activity that I felt was really worth my time. I decided that I wanted lots of sex from *lots of different women* and I wanted it on *my* terms.

Even when I had a steady girl friend and was engaging in regular sexual activity, I still arranged to have additional sexual encounters "on the side." I knew that society expected me to be monogamous, but I regarded that expectation as a stupid rule that simply didn't apply to me. And I did have a double standard in that I always insisted that my girl friend be faithful to me. In time, my addiction almost cost me my life: one day I was at the beach getting drunk and trying to find someone to be sexual with when I suddenly remembered that I had a date back in town for the spring prom. With a supply of beer and bourbon in the back seat of my car, I ran a red light, hit another car, "totaled" my own car, and ended up in the hospital along with the driver of the other car. I was arrested for drunk driving while I was being treated in the hospital emergency room. I used family money to hire a lawyer to get me out of the mess I was in and that is exactly what he did. I felt smug about the fact that I had enough money to hire the best attorney in town. He subsequently found a loophole that reduced my DWI charge to reckless driving. I never admitted how guilty I felt; instead, I bragged to all my friends about how *smart* I was.

During the time I was a notorious drunk and womanizer, I happened to meet a woman who thought I was wonderful. We were so strongly and addictively attracted to each another that we thought we were deeply in love; we got married. I became so intoxicated at my wedding that I threw up and passed out during the reception. Soon after we got married, the two of us decided it might be a good idea to move to Europe—at least in part because I'd been thrown out of college for poor grades and chemical use. It was while my wife and I were living in Europe that I discovered a filthy street lined with bars and prostitutes. Even though I was afraid of being robbed, contracting venereal disease, destroying my marriage, or just being discovered on this infamous street, I couldn't *resist* returning to it again and again. The fear and disgust I felt about this street only added to my feelings of excitement about it; this street represented a way I could get all the sex I wanted! Money was no object, so I began *paying* for sex.

By the time I was thirty years old, I was acting out my addictive behaviors practically every day of the week. At that time in my life, my wife and I moved back to the United States and had a child. Before long, we had a home of our own and I was established in a successful career. My life probably looked just fine to the casual observer but, in truth, both of us were profoundly unhappy and our marriage was dysfunctional. There was no honesty between us, both of us drank too much, and each of us was involved in an extramarital affair. In those days I referred to our marriage as "Victorian"—to me that meant that while we *appeared* to be a respectable and loving couple, we were actually living irrational lives characterized by intoxication and unfaithfulness. But instead of trying to deal with my feelings of self-doubt and unhappiness, I chose to continue on in my patterns of drinking, lying, and unfaithfulness. I was completely preoccupied with getting drunk and having sex. I constantly dreamed of sex and began buying sexual stimulation from prostitutes and pornographers on a regular basis. In fact, sex became like a chemical "fix" for me. I was dealing with powerful sexual urges every hour of every day. I was always trying to get high, yet always wanting and *needing* more. In the process of trying to fulfill these urges, I broke every rule of morality I had ever believed in; I just didn't care about *anything*. I felt as though I was dying in a cage and didn't have a key for the lock that kept me trapped inside. Actually I became a slave to both of my addictions—sexual and chemical. I no longer had any choice about my behavior. Some days I'd go out, ostensibly just to get something at the store, then end up spending *hours* in a pornographic theater. Whenever I had some extra money, I'd go to a sauna parlor for sex. Sometimes I'd go to a sauna because I was turned on after watching a pornographic movie; sometimes I'd go to a sauna because my wife had refused to have sex with me; still other times, I'd go to a sauna for no real reason other than this: *I couldn't stop myself.*

Sometimes I felt so terribly out of control that I was afraid I might rape a stranger. The thought *sickened* me, yet the powerful urge to do this kept coming back to haunt me. Some mornings, I'd wake up after a long night of drinking and have absolutely no recall of what I had done the night before. When I heard or read in the newspaper that a rape had occurred the previous night, I always had a sick feeling that *I* might have been the rapist. I don't think I'll ever know for sure. Despite the fact that the thought of rape horrified me, I continued to fantasize about it. And even though I knew rape was wrong, I constantly struggled with an intense anger toward women and a desperate urge to harm them. So many times I went to a sauna parlor hoping that if I paid to have sex with a stranger, I'd be better able to control my urge to rape an innocent stranger on the street. In its own abusive and irrational way, this "lesser of two evils" strategy *did help*. As I recount my experience, I am both saddened and angered when I realize how lonely and painful it was to know only *destructive options*.

I was frightened whenever I went to a sauna, but somehow I always managed to convince myself that the fear I felt was really excitement. I always used an alias when I patronized saunas because I was so terribly afraid that I might be photographed and/or recorded on tape while I was there. When the woman I had hired to be sexual with me actually entered the room, I always felt so anxious—not only because I was there paying for sex, but because I was worried she might refuse to do what I asked of her. I always found it very difficult to ask these women to give me what I wanted. I'd drink in order to get the courage I needed to talk with them about what it was I wanted from them. I also hoped that the alcohol in my system would delay my ejaculation. The real moment of truth for me always came *after* I had negotiated with the woman regarding the specific sexual activity I wanted her to perform and the price I was willing to pay for it. My goal in all of this was to get a stranger to be sexual with me *on my terms*. Almost always, my requests of the women who worked in the saunas were the same: I'd ask her to remove her clothing, massage me, let me massage her, and then perform oral sex on me. I loved everything about this kind of sexual encounter—everything, that is, until the moment just after my ejaculation when the woman

187

would routinely say "that's it," put her clothing on again, and walk out the door. I always wanted the woman—this complete stranger—to hold me in her arms after we had been sexual rather than to just walk away from me; I was so lonely. But I never *asked* one of these women to hold me because I didn't want to risk looking dumb or emotionally needy.

This pattern of acting-out behavior continued on for four years. During that time, I was convinced that there were two kinds of sex: the kind of sex that exists in good marriages and in literature—the kind of sex I seldom experienced—and the kind of sex I found in pornography, extramarital affairs, and saunas. It was this second kind of sex that I felt I needed so desperately, yet was completely trapped by. Life at home became so crazy that my wife finally demanded that I give her a divorce. The thought of losing my wife and my son absolutely *terrified* me because a family—even a *crazy* family—was so important to my sense of self. Feeling trapped, I seriously considered suicide every day for a week. I could get myself to the bridge, but I just couldn't make myself jump. I wondered whether or not I was a completely worthless person. My mother and her friends had always told me what a fine boy I was, but because they always treated me as if I was somehow strange or inferior, I never really believed what they said. I finally discovered that I was unable to just throw my life away, mostly because of all the love and care I had received from my godfather and his wife after my father died. They had always told me the truth about myself and my family, even when the news was bad. One of the reasons I'm alive today is because these people treated me with genuine respect. At that time in my life, they were the only people who told me over and over again that I was a fine and worthwhile person and that the serious problems in my family were not my fault. This affirming message from them served to sustain me during some of the darkest and most self-destructive days I have ever known.

I decided that I *could* go on living. But after a time, sex and alcohol were no longer effective painkillers for me. Again my thoughts turned to suicide. Sometimes I felt as if I were in a bomb crater, completely isolated from all of humanity. Then for some reason one day, I prayed for the first time in my life. I actually *prayed for death*, but got an opportunity for new life instead. This opportunity for new life came in the form of an Alcoholics Anonymous meeting my friends invited me to attend with them. At that meeting, I finally realized that I was an alcoholic. I subsequently stopped drinking and using other drugs, and I also swore off *all* sex. During all those days and weeks that I felt I was in a void, I started seeking answers that might help explain how I had come to this utter desolation in my life. Slowly, I began to see the reality of who I was and where I had come from. I knew that I was still powerfully drawn to saunas and pornography, despite the fact that I was chemically free, fully aware of my destructive acting-out be- haviors, and involved with a woman I thought I might really be in love with. I was afraid that I might never be able to build a healthy, romantic, loving relationship with a woman. More than anything, I wanted to be loved by a woman in a healthy way. But no matter how hard I tried, I couldn't stop acting out. Just thinking about the possibility of leading a double life was *intolerable*. There *had* to be a way to stop acting out.

I tried to work my problems out in therapy, but my feelings of shame interfered with my efforts to be honest. Also, my therapists told me that they believed my compulsive sexual be- havior was an integral part of my alcoholism. No one I con- sulted with at that time even mentioned the possibility that I might have an additional and *separate* addiction relating to my sexual behavior. I continued to search for a way out of the trap I was in. Finally one day I told my story to a friend and he asked me if I had ever heard of sex addiction. He told me that he had problems with his own sexual behavior and that there was a Twelve Step Program that was helpful to him and other people he knew. When he invited me to join him at the group's next meeting, I almost cried with relief. For the first time in my life, I knew I had a place where I could safely share all of my sexual secrets and self-doubts. *That was the beginning of my new life.*

In the four and a half years since I accepted my alcoholism and my sex addiction, I have attended Twelve Step meetings dedicated to sobriety and spiritual growth. To me, recovery means that I will no longer try to deal with the pain of life through compulsive sexual behavior or compulsive use of chemicals. My first wife and I finally divorced and I survived that ordeal; then I lost my job and survived that; I even survived the painful experience of going back and exploring all of the abuses in my childhood—abuses I had spent more than thirty years trying to deny or undo.

My life in recovery is not perfect. *But I would never exchange the honest imperfections of my life today with my old life of lies and delusions.* When I am afraid and feeling pain, my initial reaction still is an almost irresistible urge to get intoxicated in any way possible. But now I have *support* for staying sober. I have since remarried and I am establishing a healthy relationship with my children. Life, for me, will always be a struggle to overcome the voices that tell me how inferior, dumb, or crazy I am. On bad days now, I still sometimes find that I am listening to those negative "voices." But on good days I choose to call other recovering addicts and get the support I need so that I won't abuse myself by retreating back into addictive behaviors. Now I have *choices* about the way I live my life— choices I've never really had before. If I choose to stay in recovery, I will continue to have choices for the rest of my time on this earth. Now my life is so much different and so much better than I ever expected it could be—or thought I deserved—back when I was a child growing up lonely and unhappy in the midst of affluence.

(Postscript: After five and a half years in the Program; three and a half years of sobriety)

It has now been one year since I wrote my story. For me, being a recovering sex addict is living a life of honesty and being respectful to myself and others. Now when I'm in emotional pain, I *talk* to other people about it; when I'm frightened and want to act out, I get help. I continue to have flashes of addictive thinking. For instance, when I see an attractive woman, I still sometimes catch myself thinking, *She's beautiful; I've got to have sex with her!* But then I'll quickly counter that reaction by saying to myself, I don't even know her and besides I'm married now and I love my wife. My values have changed dramatically. During my active addiction, I never *dreamed* I'd have the high standards and values that I have today.

This was the year I told my children about my addiction and my recovery for the first time. One day I said to my children, "Do you want to know about those meetings I go to?" The response was affirmative. I tried my best to keep it simple by just saying, "You know, when I was married to your mother, I used to have affairs with other women. I'm unhappy that I did that and I don't want to behave like that ever again. So I get together with a group of men at least once a week, and we encourage each other to be honest and faithful in our relationships." As the years pass, I will continue to share the truth about my addiction and recovery and then, one day, my children can read this story and know that I wrote it.

My prayer for the future is that I will continue to use those tools of the Program that work best for me: the phone calls to members of my group, the Twelve Steps, the meetings, the shared meals, and all the contacts I have with my fellow recovering sex addicts.

191

Allen's Story

Slowly, I'm learning that I don't need to be alone and I don't need to reject intimacy in an effort to protect myself.

(After twenty-nine months in the Program; twenty-seven months of sobriety.)

As a young child, I tried to get love and attention from my parents in many different ways. But the pain I felt from their rejection and abandonment was overwhelming and I learned to stuff all of my fears, anger, and sadness. I also learned to reject other people before they could have a chance to reject me. After a few years of self-imposed isolation, the pain and energy it took to stuff my feelings began to affect me physically: I had migraine headaches when I was in junior high school and stomach problems when I was in senior high school. I turned to girls in an effort to numb my emotional pain. But the very thing I was seeking to relieve the pain—a relationship with a girl—brought even *more* pain. Time after time, I'd fall madly in love with a girl, only to drive her away with my compulsiveness. And each time a girl left me, I'd again live through the intense feelings of rejection and abandonment that were so much a part of my childhood. I looked for other forms of relief, other "painkillers" and in doing so, I discovered masturbation and pornography. I knew I had a powerful new antidote for my pain when I found that I could lose myself in sexual fantasies for hours at a time.

When I was in high school, I began dating the girl I would later marry. At that time in my life, sex was the only form of love I could recognize and this girl soon learned that she could get anything she wanted from me by engaging in sexual activity with me. I felt trapped. *I knew something was terribly wrong, but I didn't know what to do about it.* When she began talking about marriage and I procrastinated, she entered into a sexual relationship with one of the campus "studs." Sometimes she'd call me and tell me about their sexual activities. I was absolutely torn apart when she did this: on one hand, I desperately wanted to hear the explicit details of their sexual encounters; on the other hand, it was very painful for me to think about her being sexual with another man. I was sexually aroused by the stories she'd tell, probably more aroused than ever before. But the pain I felt was as strong as the arousal. I had such an enormous fear of being abandoned and rejected by this woman that I put myself through hell just to avoid feelings of loneliness. *I couldn't let go of her.* If her goal in all of this was to make me jealous, she succeeded. I *was* jealous of the relationship she had with another man and I married her.

By the time we got married, I was totally shut down emotionally. In order to cope with my situation, I began doing things I'd never done before: I'd sneak into the women's locker room at school and watch women as they showered; I'd sit in empty classrooms masturbating as I watched women walk by; I'd steal porno magazines from bookstores; I'd spend hours masturbating while my wife was at work; I'd drive around campus without any clothes on and masturbate; and I'd expose myself in ways that *looked* innocent—I'd hang drapes in my window with no clothing on, or wear loose shorts in the summer and let my genitals hang out when young women were around. All of these activities were *extremely risky,* but I never was caught. On the campus commons, I'd stand naked on a secluded balcony at the top of the stairs and masturbate. As I stood there one time, I heard two women talking to each other as they walked up the stairs. One woman was telling the other about the "pervert" she'd seen in the area the day before. Right after she said that, both women looked up and saw me, naked and frantically trying to hide. They ran, and I quickly dressed and left. I was scared to death about what might happen after this incident. For days, I expected the police to come and apprehend me, but they never did.

During my last year of college, most of my waking hours were spent thinking of different ways to "get my rocks off." The shame, guilt, and fear I felt about not being able to control my behavior was driving me away from everyone in my life. I had no friends, and my wife and I never went out. Instead, the two of us stayed home every night and watched television. As I look back on it, the pain of the isolation and loneliness we felt was *staggering*. After each incident of acting out, I could see how "perverted" and uncontrollable my actions were. Yet *while* I was acting out, I felt like an athlete in competition: I'd feel a surge of adrenaline in my body, I'd sweat, and my heart would pound wildly. Whenever my schedule permitted, I'd masturbate for hours at a time. Now it's difficult to remember *exactly* what I was feeling during the times I was acting out. I do remember feelings of anger and extreme rage; sometimes my jaw *ached* from clenching it so tightly in anger. But eventually, my acting-out behaviors took a toll on my grades and my finances.

Just before graduation, the local sheriff came to our apartment and, with my wife watching, he arrested me for exposing myself at the beach. I was hauled away in handcuffs and spent the night in jail. I was so emotionally upset that I was physically ill throughout the night. My parents and my wife were waiting for me when I was released the next day. After a long and uncomfortable silence, I finally explained my arrest with an enormous lie: I told them that some girls at the beach just happened to walk by my car while I was changing into my swimsuit. No one in my family ever questioned or challenged this explanation and I was astounded when the case was dropped by the district attorney. *I had gotten away with my acting-out behavior again!*

After college graduation, we moved to my wife's parents' farm. I wanted to try farming, even though I didn't have any experience, so I took some courses in agriculture at the area vocational-technical school. Every night on the way home from class, I'd stop off at the college campus and window-peep. Soon, I discovered where R-rated movies were showing in the area; I'd sit for hours and watch these movies while I masturbated. Our neighbors at the time had a young daughter. On several occasions, this young girl and I would let our dogs out at the same time in the morning. I'd always stand at the back door without clothes on, just watching for her reaction. Seeing the momentary fear and hurt on her face when she saw me was like looking into my own soul. I always wondered if she stuffed her feelings about this violation in the same way I had stuffed my feelings when I was a child.

Obviously, my marriage was not thriving at this time. One day—in fact it was the day after Christmas—my wife told me that she was involved with another man and wanted a divorce so that she could marry him. Almost before I knew what had happened, I was divorced, living in a large city, and doing the kind of work I was trained for in college. *And I was alone*. I was scared and I was filled with rage and pain. I tried window-peeping again, but the excitement I was looking for just wasn't there for me anymore. I tried walking around outside at night with nothing on except a long football jersey and lifting it up when girls walked by, but that "adventure" wasn't enough to numb my pain anymore, either. Then I heard about some outcall massage and modeling agencies that were fronts for prostitution. I began spending all of my money on prostitutes. Having prostitutes come to my apartment whenever I wanted them to seemed to numb my pain, at least for awhile.

After about three months of frantic acting-out behavior, I was invited to dinner by a woman from work who was going through a divorce. I accepted her invitation and we enjoyed each other's company. One weekend soon after we started dating, I helped this woman and her children move to another apartment. During the move, her boss showed up to help. I immediately assumed she had an intimate relationship with him. I left her apartment, but returned there the next morning. She couldn't let me in because her boss had spent the night with her, so I invited her to come over to my apartment later that morning. When she arrived, we talked and cried together. I cried about the pain I felt knowing that she was sexually involved with another man. She cried about the pain she felt for many different reasons. *I was completely hooked on this woman from the moment I knew she was sexually involved with another man.* After our talk, we were sexual with each other. All the while, I thought about the fact that she had been sexual with another man just a few hours before. I promised this woman the "stars" if she would marry me.

We got married four months later and then, suddenly, I had financial responsibility for three stepchildren and a pregnant wife—all on my entry-level salary. I started borrowing money in order to maintain my new family in the lifestyle they were accustomed to. It wasn't long before I felt enormous pressure from my changing life situation. I began arriving home late almost every night because after work I'd spent time watching movies and masturbating in an adult bookstore or because I'd spent time parked in a supermarket lot, masturbating as I watched women walk by. Soon these adventures were no longer enough for me, so I started driving around town and exposing myself whenever possible.

For the next three years, I was involved with acting out at least once each day. And all the time, I was desperately trying to hold on to my job and convince my new wife that nothing was wrong. I told some outlandish lies during that time. When my wife asked me why I was late, I'd tell elaborate tales about shopping trips, breakdowns of machinery at work, flat tires, and other car problems. She never really believed me; she was sure I was having an affair. When she seemed skeptical about my stories, I'd scream and holler about her lack of trust in me, then feel like dirt. In a desperate effort to deal with my pain, I began exposing myself to women almost every day, either on the way to work or on the way home. Eventually, I was caught exposing myself in a department store. I was told to seek counseling but, once again, I didn't have to face any *real* consequences—I didn't even have to go through the process of pleading guilty. Instead, I went into therapy and told my therapist everything. Then, after six months of treatment, he wrote a letter telling the court how hard I had been working. Throughout this ordeal, I never told my wife what was happening. I was not yet ready to deal with the terrible pain of trying to balance my secret life with my family life.

Things went from bad to worse at home and I continued acting out in the same ways I had acted out before my arrest. I felt shameful and dirty, and often wondered how it was that I had such a wonderful family when I was such a "worthless pervert." Finally, my wife decided that she couldn't stand it any longer and gave me an ultimatum: either we would have counseling as a couple or she would file for divorce. We started seeing a counselor and soon after that, I was arrested again for indecent exposure. I hired an attorney to represent me this time and also opened up and told my therapist about my compulsive behavior. But I still didn't tell my wife anything. Both my therapist and my attorney told me that I was a sex addict and that there was help available in a self-help Twelve Step group for sexually compulsive people. From that time on, my life started to turn around.

The court put me on probation with the provision that I attend weekly Twelve Step meetings and that I continue on with my therapy. My therapist really pressured me to tell my wife about my problem. I knew I had to choose between the isolated life of a practicing sex addict and a life of intimacy and honesty. I finally told my wife about my addiction during a therapy session. After her initial shock, rage, and questions, we began the process of attempting to heal from the pain and destruction of the past. Despite our genuine efforts to keep our marriage intact, we decided to separate and eventually we divorced. This was a very painful decision to make, but the way my life is going now somehow tells me that I did the right thing back then.

When my wife and I first separated, I felt so depressed and worthless that I didn't even care what happened to me. One winter night, I was racing down a slippery highway when I lost control of my car and wrapped it around a utility pole. I suffered thirteen pelvic fractures and spent four weeks in the hospital and two months out of work. But during that time, the outpouring of love and care from people in my Twelve Step group gave me the additional strength I needed to recover—physically and mentally—from the accident.

My injuries and my divorce represented the lowest points in my life. I finally had acted out my suicidal thoughts. I had reached "bottom," and I saw it as the only way to completely let go of *all* my unhealthy ways. I entered a treatment program to help me live without my compulsive sexual behavior and I used the Twelve Steps and the members of my group as resources. Up to this time, I had struggled through almost two years while attending a Twelve Step group, but I hadn't really worked the Steps in my daily life. My abstinence was nothing more than "white-knuckling it" through the obsessive urges and pain I continued to struggle with. When I first came to the Program twenty-nine months ago, I was scared to death of the men in the group. They immediately saw through all the mental manipulations I'd throw at them; *they were so honest.* I was angry at them—and frightened by them—because they were urging me to give up *all* of my addictive behaviors. For years, my addiction had been like a real friend to me because it was always there to help me ease the pain of living. Now the men in this group were telling me that my addiction was an integral part of the pain I felt. I didn't like what I heard, so I fought these men and their suggestions with every manipulative tool I had. All this time, I continued going back to meetings though, because somewhere deep inside I knew these men were right.

As I look back over the last twenty-nine months, I am grateful that the Twelve Step Program gradually has become a way of life for me. The Program first helped me see what is right for me and it *continues* to help me make decisions about what is right for me. The Program helped me develop boundaries concerning my behavior. These are the boundaries I set for myself: no pornography, no sexual behavior outside of intimate emotional relationships, and no masturbation. I now understand that for *me*, masturbation is self-abuse because I use it to mask and/or deny my feelings. My boundaries in no way limit the quality of my life; on the contrary, my boundaries have freed me in many ways. But quite honestly, sometimes I'm angry as hell for the presence of the Program in my life—because it allows me to experience some very painful feelings *as facts. In saner moments, though, I realize that I'd probably be dead by my own hand had I not found the Program when I did.*

I no longer try to stuff feelings. In fact, I'm hopeful now for a life that is *filled* with feelings. Now, for the first time in my life, I'm learning to experience and share my feelings. God, as I understand God, is now an affirming presence in my life. For me, the Twelve Step Program is not a religious program, but a spiritual one. At first, I found the concept of "a power greater than ourselves" a very difficult one to accept. But, slowly, I'm beginning to realize that this power helps me connect with others; this power helps me make choices about my behavior; this power helps me reach out and risk rejection. My boundaries do not in any way limit the quality of my life.

Slowly, I'm learning that I don't need to be alone and I don't need to reject intimacy in an effort to protect myself.

It's not easy to recover. *In fact, recovery is painful.* But recovery is also full of life, laughter, intimacy, hope, love, togetherness, and serenity. I find that I must put as much energy into recovering from my addiction as I used to put into acting out. At any one moment in time, I can choose between addictive isolating thoughts and experiencing the feelings of finally growing up at the age of thirty-one.

Jenny's Story

*...forgiveness begins with ourselves, then grows
to include those who have hurt us.*

(After four years and four months in the Program; three years
and three months of sobriety.)

This addiction hurts so much. I didn't just wake up one day and
decide I was going to be addicted to sex. In fact, I was *terrified*
of sex and any kind of close relationship. As a child, I was
subjected to severe physical and emotional abuse and I learned
to be afraid of people. Most of the time, I just wanted to be left
alone; but even when I *was* alone, I was miserable. In a desperate attempt to free myself from the emotional pain that tormented me, I attempted suicide when I was thirteen years old.
What began as an escape from the abuse and emotional pain I
had experienced eventually led to an addictive lifestyle: I didn't
trust anyone and spent most of my time fantasizing about ways
I could hurt myself, then acting out those fantasies until I had
an orgasm. I withdrew more and more from life and after a
time, I actually had to inflict physical pain on myself in order
to experience the sexual highs I wanted so desperately.

During my years of self-imposed aloneness, I occasionally
tried to reach out to people; I'd allow one person at a time into
my life. Between people, I spent years in my own secret world
of addiction. Because I had very few social skills, I was re-
strained and cautious with others. I succeeded in keeping most
people away with my shyness, my inappropriate behavior, or
by ignoring them altogether. I was a virgin when I was raped
at the age of eighteen by the fifty-seven-year-old caretaker of
the building where I lived.

I saw this man as an authority figure, so when he asked me
to go for a ride with him, I went without hesitating. I never
questioned people in power. This man raped me while I was in

his car and from that time on, I was available to him whenever he wanted me. He assumed total power over my body, my finances, and my life for the next three years. During this time, my coworkers saw me as a loner who couldn't be trusted. I told everyone at work that I lived with my aunt and uncle, when all the time I was really living with this man and his wife and he was continuing to abuse me sexually. Not only did I lie to my coworkers about my living arrangements, I lied to them about every other aspect of my life as well. *I was totally alone and isolated.* At times, my deceptiveness and the intensity of the sexual abuse overwhelmed me and I'd make obscene phone calls in a desperate attempt to relieve the pressure I was feeling. But my lies grew more complicated and I continued to deceive myself. Somehow I managed to convince myself that I was loved and cared for by the man who was abusing me. As I became more and more dependent on him, his moods began to shift without warning. I never knew when or how he would abuse me. But the violence this man subjected me to was so much like the violence I had experienced as a child that *it all felt strangely comforting to me.* I found I didn't have the courage to leave this man; *I felt that I had nowhere else to go.*

Again, suicide seemed to be the only way out for me. I took an overdose of pills, only to face long-term hospitalization when I regained consciousness. The man I was trying to escape from had rescued me. *Now I felt that I owed him my life.* I felt sure that following this crisis, our relationship would change and at last I'd be safe with him. The relationship *did* change, but it only got worse. He became even more obsessed with violating me; he demanded sex in public places and added guns to our sexual activity. Soon I was living in an almost constant state of terror, but I discovered that my feelings of terror led to an uncontrollable thrill that intensified my sexual highs.

Concerned that his wife might discover he was being sexual with me, this man moved me to another apartment. At first, this move actually helped me to distance myself from him some-what. But his anger intensified when he discovered that I was available to him much less often. Finally he said he'd leave me alone only if I'd give him money. When I agreed to do that and opened my door to hand him the money, he burst in, grabbed the money, and raped me. My three years with this man ended just as they began—with terror and rape. After he left, I knew I was still in danger, but I also felt lucky to be alive. I didn't trust *anyone* at this point and I decided that the only way I'd be safe would be to isolate myself from everyone. I lived in fear that he would come after me; I was sure he'd try to kill me if he did. As the months passed, my feelings of loneliness became more intense. I began to miss the terror, the thrill, and the sexual highs I had experienced; I could feel my compulsive-ness returning.

I assumed I'd be okay if I could just go out and meet men and be sexual with them. But I was much too frightened to be with anyone. Now my isolation was *complete,* so I decided I'd just have to take care of my sexual needs by myself. I became so compulsive about masturbating that I'd inflict pain on myself in order to have an orgasm. My addiction was worse than ever, but I felt that I had no real reason to change my behavior. I believed that I had done such horrible things in the past that *I didn't matter* and I certainly didn't deserve to be in a relation-ship with anyone ever again. I now see that my addiction was actually *fed* by the shame I felt about my sexual behavior. Sometimes, though, I worried that my compulsive masturbation would end in accidental death. Over a period of time, I had been hospitalized for various "accidents," but no one had ever questioned me about them. Eventually I found that I needed even more physical pain in order to achieve an orgasm, and I resorted to self-flagellation, electric shock, and burning myself while I masturbated. I told myself that I wasn't harming anyone but myself when I did these things. I felt that I was innocent of any wrongdoing, just as long as I didn't go out and get someone else involved in my violent sexual practices.

I decided that living with someone might be one way out of my violent self-abuse. I felt sure that marriage would take me away from my shameful secret life and my compulsive need to inflict pain on myself in order to experience sexual highs. The man I married didn't know about my past. I soon discovered that he didn't even *care* to know about my past; he was totally wrapped up in his own life. Though I held on to the illusion that ours was a loving partnership, I soon realized that even in marriage, I was isolated. My solution to this isolation was to include my husband in my compulsive sexual behavior. Finally, I violated my last rule and got someone else involved in my sexual self-abuse. The relationship I initially saw as my salvation was now adding to my feelings of shame. I decided to see a therapist. When I described my sexual behavior to him, he jumped up from his chair, screamed at me that I was lying, and ordered me out of his office. My worst fears were realized: I had no one to turn to and nowhere to go. I felt certain that taking my life was the only way out of all the shame and pain I was feeling. Again I attempted suicide and again I was hospitalized. After I was discharged from the hospital, I attempted to abstain from sexual activity *completely* in an effort to control my behavior. But the more I tried to abstain, the more control I lost.

My compulsive behavior intensified and eventually forced me to begin living two separate lives. My competent, polite, cheerful, responsible self performed appropriately on the job and in public. I had enough money to live alone and no one at work or in public knew anything about my secret sexual life. During the week I was fine, but from Friday evening until Monday morning, sexual self-abuse completely dominated my life. *I lost whole weekends to acting out.* During those times, nothing seemed to matter but my addiction. My life pattern was set: my shameful self was in control when I inflicted pain on myself to satisfy my sexual needs. After my divorce, I had no hope of ever being sexual with another person again, so I felt justified in being sexual with my animals. So many times I promised myself that I would learn to control my acting-out behaviors or stop them completely, but *my feelings of shame continued to feed my compulsion.* I felt that I didn't even *deserve* to be safe.

In my isolation, I turned to food for comfort and consequently gained a lot of weight. I decided there was really no reason to maintain my appearance because I was too ashamed and fearful to become involved with other people. But I did have some concern that my weight gain would adversely affect my health, so I decided to try therapy again in order to lose weight. Over a period of time, I began to trust the therapist and willingly shared with her more and more information about my life. It was only after years of therapy that I trusted this therapist enough to share information with her about my sexual behavior. When I told her about my efforts to stop masturbating and my concern that I might die while inflicting pain on myself, *she actually believed me!* This therapist I had come to trust made it clear that she felt my situation was serious; she recommended that I get involved with a Twelve Step Program.

I went to my first Twelve Step meeting feeling that I was in a double-bind: I was *terrified* I would "belong" to this group of sexually addicted people, yet fearful that I wouldn't be accepted. I assumed that, by definition, sex addicts had long histories of being sexual with many people. And here *I* was, a loner and totally self-consumed; I was sure I would never fit the criteria for group "membership." I attended a meeting, got a sponsor, and continued to struggle with intense urges to inflict pain on myself. For me, the recovery process involved attending meetings where we'd concentrate on one of the Twelve Steps, then discuss and share possible applications of that particular

Step to our daily lives. Over and over again, the women at these meetings told me that I had dignity and that the only thing required of me was a willingness to be honest and a sincere desire to change my behavior. As I shared the details of my addiction with others, the walls I had built around myself began to crumble. Slowly, I learned to trust the other women in the group. *I finally realized I was not alone anymore.* The women in this group were really *there* with me and no one left the meeting in disgust when I shared the painful details of my story. Instead, each woman there had her own story of pain and shame. As we shared our stories, we also shared tears, humor, gentleness, and huge doses of hope. Finally, I was with other people who understood me; I understood them, too. *My feelings of complete isolation finally began to lift.*

My road to recovery was not a smooth one. At first I tried to hold on to certain parts of my addiction. There was a time when I was in so much emotional pain that I was sure I wouldn't be able to survive without the "anesthetic" of my sexual self-abuse. I felt that my addiction was just too powerful to give up altogether. Then I decided that the group didn't matter that much and all I *really* needed was my therapist. When I told her this, she immediately put our client/therapist relationship on the line: she told me that if I chose my addiction instead of the group, she would *not* be willing to see me anymore. I was frightened when she said this because I truly believed I could get along without the Program, but *not* without my therapist. When she leveled with me in this way, *I finally realized I had to choose between acting out and recovery; it was clear I couldn't have both.* I knew that if I resumed my old ways, I'd eventually destroy myself. At this point, I had been abstinent for several months, but when I began acting out again, it seemed as if I had never stopped at all. I knew then that I'd have to "go to any lengths" to recover from my addiction. My therapist really forced the issue for me: she told me she couldn't bear to watch me destroy myself with my addiction. *I chose recovery.* For the first time in my life, I allowed myself to be totally helpless; *I surrendered.* I no longer allowed myself to think that I had quick solutions or perfect answers to my pain and addiction.

In response to my surrender, my fellow addicts offered me hope and support and they taught me about the power of love through the example of their lives. They also encouraged me to be honest and gentle with myself. I applied the Twelve Steps to my life with soft but consistent guidance and an unfailing belief that serenity *is* attainable. People in the group gave me positive support for the changes I made in my behavior and they suggested ways I could release my pain without returning to my addiction. As I continued to share my story with others, my feelings of shame gave way to a sense of serenity. *I learned that forgiveness begins with ourselves, then grows to include those who have hurt us.* I began to move ahead with my life by exercising the freedom of living in the present. For the first time, I felt some relief from the pain that had haunted me for so long.

Realizing that violence and gentleness cannot coexist, I have looked to gentleness as a guideline for my recovery. I find that as long as I am gentle with myself and have a *willingness* to be honest, I continue to receive the gifts of spiritual recovery and freedom from acting out. During my first year in recovery, I began to speak in specific terms about how I had inflicted pain on myself. During that time, I also learned to acknowledge, understand, and honor my sexual preference. As a lesbian, I discovered that I had some real concerns about what aspects of my sexuality were related to my addiction and what aspects of my sexuality were natural, healthy, and nurturing. As I did my Fourth Step inventory, I learned more about the personal strengths that helped me survive—creativity, intelligence, and a belief that part of my sexuality was completely untouched and untainted by my addiction. The group affirmed my strengths and helped me apply them in my recovery. During my second year in the Program, my empathy grew, I learned to be supportive of others, and I learned how to live within boundaries I set for myself. As much as those of us in the group cared about each other, we chose not to be sexual with each other. But instead of hiding or denying our feelings of caring and love, we talked to each other with respect and compassion. Gradually, I developed new guidelines for my interactions with other people.

When I began to accept myself as a whole, worthwhile person, capable of loving and being loved, I also began to integrate into my daily life the personal strengths that were so helpful to me early in recovery. Time and time again, I confronted the fact that I *do* have the ability to care about others. I began to really communicate with others when I finally became willing to be honest. I was gentle with myself, but worked hard to have honesty in all my actions. With abstinence, I am now able to explore healthy, intimate relationships. I no longer need to objectify another person or set myself apart from others with my feelings of shame. I now have real choices in my expression of love and these choices may or may not include being sexual. In recovery, I have found a peace of spirit that helps me through difficult times and allows me to express my feelings honestly and respectfully. Other major gifts in recovery are the deep, loving friendships I continue to have with the wonderful, creative, intelligent women who are in my Twelve Step group. The miracle of the Program humbles me over and over again. I am grateful that my addiction gave me an opportunity to know a Higher Power in my life. I believe my Higher Power led me to this Program and wants me to find peace from my addiction. I find that I really *can* live the Serenity Prayer a day at a time. Each day, I have the choice to accept what I cannot change, courage to change what I can, and wisdom to know the difference.

I maintain my recovery one day at a time through prayer, meditation, and service. Prayer and meditation keep me centered with my Higher Power. I have found that when I am not centered with my Higher Power on a daily basis, I lose my awareness of where I belong and I tend to withdraw from others. *I now understand that isolation feeds my sex addiction.* I have also learned that in order to really have the Program in my life, I must give it away to others. Giving the Program away requires honesty, humility, openness, willingness, and service to others. When I use my personal strengths to help others, my Higher Power reveals Herself to me. As I work my daily Program, I find that each difficulty I encounter offers me another opportunity for growth and self-revelation. *As I come to know myself better, I move closer to my Higher Power.*

Without this Program, I never would have come to understand gentleness as the only path away from violence. Now in recovery, I finally am able to comprehend and practice being gentle with myself. I am so grateful that I was offered the gift of choosing between addiction and recovery. Each day that I affirm my recovery, I receive other gifts as well: clarity, joy, love, a real sense of belonging to this world, relief from my compulsions, and peace of mind. Most of all, I have come to believe that I am not alone and unworthy of love, but that I am a person of value who deserves to give and receive love and gentleness.

Frank's Story

Even my worst day in recovery is better than the best day I had while I was acting out.

(After two years in the Program; twenty-one months of sobriety.)

I believe that my addiction started when I was eleven years old. I remember that there was always a great deal of pain in our family. My father traveled frequently and my mother hated the town we lived in. I remember being told that I was different from other kids in town and that I'd have to be the man of the house whenever my father was gone. When my father *was* home, he was always fighting with my mother. In a desperate attempt to avoid the fighting, I finally worked out an escape plan: I'd go into the bathroom, lock the door, and take a bath. I spent *hours* locked in that tiny room, hiding from the world outside. And it was there in the bathroom that I first discovered masturbation. My discovery seemed like the greatest thing that could ever be because it helped me to forget the pain and loneliness I felt outside that room.

I quickly developed an addictive behavior pattern around masturbation: I'd set my alarm clock so that I'd have some extra time to masturbate before school in the morning; I'd even go to bed early at night so that I'd have plenty of time to masturbate before I fell asleep. At that time in my life, I didn't know how to obtain pornographic magazines, so I spent hours looking at photographs of underwear in catalogs. Almost right away, I set some arbitrary rules to control my sexual behavior. For example, I'd tell myself that I could masturbate to only one photograph per page. Even then, I sensed that if I *didn't* set some rules, I'd lose control and masturbate at the sight of every picture on every page. Early on, I decided that masturbating and looking at photographs for sexual pleasure *must* be wrong,

213

because no one else talked about doing such things. I continued to enjoy this little diversion of mine anyway. By the time I was thirteen, I was masturbating five times a day and desperately wanting to be sexual with girls. I didn't have a certain girl in mind, I just wanted to have sexual experiences with someone, *anyone*. I went out with girls my own age when I first started dating, but I soon discovered that these girls didn't respond to the pressure I put on them to be sexual with me. While other young people my age were giggling about holding hands, I was fantasizing about oral sex. Now when I look back on those years, I realize that I missed out on so much innocent discovery and joy because of my obsession with sex.

Because I matured early and looked much older than my chronological age, I started seeking out older girls when I was only fourteen years old. At that time, in fact, I looked and acted old enough so that I could buy liquor. I intentionally started hanging around with older boys who had cars so that I'd be able to expand my search for girls. When I was unable to get a ride from someone, I'd just hitchhike to other towns and look for girls. Soon I had a sex partner in each town I visited. I had always assumed that masturbation and pornography would lose their appeal for me as soon as I had my first sexual experience with a girl, but when I lost my virginity at the age of fourteen, my obsessions became even more powerful. In addition to masturbating every day, I would have sex with one or more girls every day. By the time I was in my early teens, I was already using sex to deal with my feelings and my problems. I'd masturbate when I was lonely, anxious, happy, sad, scared, and/or tired. Whatever the problem, I truly believed that masturbation could make it better. As soon as I turned sixteen, I bought a car of my own so that I'd be able to search for sexual partners in an even larger geographic area.

I didn't have many male friends when I was a teenager. I discovered that most boys my age were not particularly interested in spending all day talking about sex and all night *looking* for it. And, of course, other boys were often angry with me because I had tried to have sex with their girl friends. When I was fifteen years old, a male schoolteacher started to be sexual with me. This man would give me "gifts" whenever I visited him at his home. I was not attracted to him sexually, but I did like the attention and gifts he gave me; actually, I felt powerless to refuse his requests. I kept telling myself that I really had no reason to be intimidated by this man and that it was sophisticated and hip to be sexual with women *and* men. Nevertheless, I was always terribly afraid that someone would find out about my sexual behavior with this man.

During my teenage years, my mother's friends often commented about how cute I was and how sexy I looked in my tight blue jeans. I enjoyed all the attention I got from these adult women. It somehow seemed like an affirmation of my manhood to get this kind of attention from married women, yet I felt sick to my stomach each time one of them hugged me, rubbed up against me, or even touched me.

I got a job when I was a teenager in order to pay for car expenses and all of the condoms I was using. It just so happened that I went to work in a store that employed a number of women. Subsequently, I had sex with as many of my female coworkers as possible. Most of these women had more money than I had and some of them bought me liquor or gave me "gifts" of money after I had sex with them. In the course of having dozens of sexual encounters with married women, I began putting myself in potentially dangerous situations. Oftentimes, I'd arrange to go to womens' homes and have sex with them while their husbands were away at work. When I visited a woman whose husband had a long history of drinking and violence, I'd tell myself that my sweaty palms, rapid heartbeat, and shallow breathing were just signs of sexual excitement, not terror at the thought that I might be discovered and maybe even *killed*. (This was not the first or last time during my acting out days that I would confuse fear with excitement.)

I began to suspect that other people didn't live the way I did. But when I talked about my obsessions and behaviors with the few friends I had, they assured me that I didn't have a problem. In fact, some people told me that I was living out every man's dream. *But these people didn't hear the loneliness in my voice.* I concluded that my life would settle down when I found the right woman. I wasn't sure how I'd find her because I was spending almost all of my time with older married women. And when I *did* spend time with women my own age, I had sex not only with them, but with their sisters, their cousins, and sometimes even their mothers. During this time, I frequently was sexual with people I didn't respect or even *like*. But none of this mattered as long as I could have sex; *any sacrifice was worth it*.

I started picking up women in bars and ultimately contracted venereal disease. I was so completely out of control by this time that I actually tried to pick up a woman while both of us waited in line to get shots at a V.D. clinic. I was relatively isolated at school because almost everyone knew of my obsession with sex. I was also filled with rage, and this rage seemed to manifest itself when I was being sexual with women. In fact, one time I was so violent with a woman when she refused to have sex with me that I broke her leg. I also raped a woman I knew when she refused to have sex with me—I really don't know what I might have done had this woman put up more resistance than she did. I was terrified about my behavior and completely out of control. I finally turned to drugs in a desperate effort to "mellow" out. But I used drugs in the same compulsive way I had used sex—everywhere, all the time. I'd get high on drugs before school, in school, and after school as well. The drugs "worked" in that they slowed me down for awhile, but I realized that I always made a fool of myself when I was high. I knew

I'd have to choose between sex and drugs. This choice was really quite easy for me because I knew that no woman wanted to have sex with a fool.

Somehow I managed to establish a relationship with a woman I had admired for a long time. When we started dating, I promised myself I wouldn't be sexual with her; I wasn't going to let sex interfere with this promising new relationship. At first, I did abstain from having sex with this woman and I even reduced the number of other sex partners in my life. (I lied to her and told her I was not sexually involved with anyone.) But it didn't take me long to realize that the theory I'd had for so long was wrong: finding the right woman was *not* the solution to my problems with compulsive sexual behavior.

Thinking that I needed a fresh start, I chose to go away to college; my girlfriend went away to college in another town. By the time we went our separate ways to school, we were engaged and planned to get married when we graduated. Because of my new start in college and my plans for marriage, I promised myself that I would not be sexual with anyone while I was away at school *and I really meant it.* But even though I fully intended to honor this promise, I lost control immediately. When I felt lonely on my *first night away,* I dealt with those feelings of loneliness by being sexual with someone. Just a couple weeks later, I had resumed my compulsive behavior pattern: I'd have sex with five different women during the week, then spend weekends with my fiancée.

I was so afraid of getting someone pregnant that I had a vasectomy when I was only eighteen years old. My fiancée wanted us to be sexual, but because of my experiences with other women, I was fearful that a sexual encounter between us would *destroy* our relationship. I also feared that I'd completely lose control of my behavior once I started being sexual with her. In fact, I was so afraid of being sexual with her that the first time we made love, I completely blanked out and had no real sense of what was going on. Once I had sex with her, I lost the last excuse I had for my compulsive behavior. No longer could I say, "I'll stop messing around when I finally have the opportunity to be sexual with my fiancée." Realizing that I had no more excuses for my compulsive behavior and wanting to spare her any additional pain, I ended our relationship. I was too ashamed to tell her the *real* reason I was ending it, so I just lied to her and said I didn't love her anymore. Severing this relationship was very painful for me. And the best, most reliable way I could think of to numb that pain was to be sexual with women as often as possible. Now that I was a "free man" again, I was somewhat relieved to know that I would no longer have to feel guilty about being unfaithful to my fiancée.

One of the women I was sexual with while I was engaged seemed to me the "perfect woman," perhaps the woman I'd been searching for in all of my sexual encounters. She appeared to enjoy sex as much as I did and, furthermore, she was willing to do anything of a sexual nature that I suggested. I couldn't *imagine* having a better relationship. I was sure that the pain I still felt would go away as our commitment to each other grew stronger. This woman and I had sex whenever we could. For example, instead of studying at the library, we'd find a private room and fondle one another as we read. Looking back, I can see so clearly that whenever I was confused or frustrated about my studies, I'd immediately want to be sexual. Rather than working through my feelings, I avoided them *completely* by engaging in sex. This woman and I engaged in sexual activities so often that I didn't even have time to be sexual with other women. Together, we tried something new and invited other women to be sexual with us. We subsequently lost many friends who would not tolerate our constant references to sex and our propositioning of other friends and strangers.

Our frenetic sexual activity with other people continued until we both graduated from college and moved into an apartment.

We found it much more difficult to locate sex partners after we moved off campus, so we began advertising for them in news-papers. Ultimately, these advertisements resulted in my having sexual encounters with men. Now *everyone* was a potential sex partner for me. My girlfriend and I would go to bars, pick up women, take them home, and then photograph them in the underwear we collected. I'd tell myself that this life I was lead-ing was the *good life*—not every man was lucky enough to have a woman in his life who'd help him pick up sex partners and apply makeup to the nude models he photographed. In addition to the group sex my fiancée and I participated in, our sexual activity with each other changed: we began engaging in bondage and sadomasochism and we also began acting out our violent fantasies. For example, I'd hold a gun on her and "rape" her while calling her abusive names. Once I started doing these things, I was afraid *not* to continue for fear that this woman might decide I was boring and leave me. At the same time, I was afraid that I might begin to *enjoy* the new things we were doing. I didn't discuss my fears and confusion with *anyone*. People often told me that I had it made, but I knew the truth: I was completely out of control and abusing myself and others as well. I blamed myself for corrupting my lover. As much as I cared about her, I hoped that she'd realize what was happen-ing, end the relationship, and just leave me to my masturbation and pornography.

When I finished graduate school and got a job as a social worker, my double life really began to take hold. I spent my days helping other people break their addiction to drugs and I spent my nights acting out my own addiction. *I hated myself for being such a hypocrite.* When I began to notice the similarities between my clients' drug use and my own sexual behavior, I began to see that I had an addiction to sex. In an attempt to stop acting out sexually, I attended meetings of Al-coholics Anonymous. But I quickly discovered that I could not *lie* my way into a Program that is built on a foundation of honesty and truth. I left the AA meetings I attended feeling worse than I had when I arrived. The people in the AA group I attended accepted me and welcomed me, but I found that I was unable to accept myself or their fellowship because of my fear of opening up and telling my sexual secrets. I decided that I was, indeed, addicted to sex, but that *no one else had an addiction quite like mine*. At that point, I resigned myself to a long and miserable life because it seemed that my energies were tied up either in acting out or in struggling not to act out. When I no longer had the energy to even go *out* anymore, my lover began going out alone. One night she came home and told me that she had spent some time with another man and really enjoyed herself. Finally, I could see the end of our relationship coming. I knew that no one else would want me in the emotional, mental, and spiritual condition I was in at that time. I decided to take care of the mess that was my life by killing myself. For some reason, though, I felt I owed it to my profession to at least call a suicide hot line before I took my life. This call, I felt, would constitute the perfect end to my life. The man who answered my hot line call was evidently inexperienced and/or improperly trained, because he put me on "hold" after I told him of my desperation. I flew into a rage and smashed the window of the phone booth I was calling from. I vowed to overcome my addiction just to spite this insensitive person on the phone and whatever kind of God would allow my life to disintegrate in this way.

I stopped being sexual with almost everyone but my lover, but the passion was gone from our sex. Both of us were there for each other *physically*, but absent emotionally. I began to masturbate more often, making regular promises to myself that I quickly broke: I'll only masturbate ten times today; I'll never masturbate at work; I'll never sink so low as to use that kind of pornography. My penis ached and my ejaculations no longer gave me any sense of pleasure or release. Again *I was driven and out of control*. Time was the only real limitation I could see. What would it take for me to stop? I often wondered if losing my lover or my job would make me quit acting out. I was already losing my sanity, but *that* realization didn't seem to be enough to motivate me to change. Then one day, as if by accident, another sex addict told me that I was not alone in my sex addiction. He said that there were other men and women who had known firsthand the hell I was living in. But even more miraculous, he said, *these people had recovered; they had healed*. He told me incredible stories about people who were no longer driven, people who could be faithful to their lovers, live sane and healthy lives, *and still be happy*. I told this man that I would settle for not being driven; happiness seemed too much to hope for.

Before I went to my first Twelve Step meeting for sex addicts, I vacillated between thinking I'd be the only person at the meeting with any intelligence or class, and thinking that they may not even allow me into the group because I was so sick. In either case, I knew the people in this group wouldn't be like me because I was different. As it turned out, the other sex addicts at the meeting were more *like* me than *unlike* me. The one thing we all had in common was the one thing that really mattered: we were sex addicts. But still I was afraid—afraid that the Twelve Steps might not work for me and that I'd *never* recover. At the same time, I was afraid that The Twelve Steps *would* work for me and I'd have to give up my acting-out behaviors forever. Neither option seemed very pleasant. I wondered who I'd be if I stopped acting out. I had worked hard to establish and keep the reputation I had. In fact, being a sex addict was my identity, my personality. My whole life revolved around sex and I was convinced that I'd be nothing at all without it. The way I dressed, my humor, my priorities—everything in my life revolved around my being a sex addict. *How could I possibly let go of all that?*

With the help of the group, I set my boundaries and called my sponsor every week, just as I was supposed to do. And I didn't act out. *At least I didn't act out until I got really lonely.* Rather than calling my sponsor one time, I acted out instead. I told myself it wasn't such a big deal because I couldn't possibly get caught. It wasn't as if I'd broken the law, or been arrested, or lost my job. I had merely broken a commitment to myself one time and one time only. I had absolutely no intention of telling the group about my slip; I'd *never* get a medallion that way. I just knew I wouldn't be able to live the rest of my life without acting out. I told myself that I was much better than I *had* been and that I had at least *some* control over my behavior. But for some reason these things I told myself *just didn't ring true*. I sat through the whole first half of a meeting before I told the other group members about my slip. They immediately reassured me that it was okay—that slips happen to almost everyone at one time or another and that I was welcome to continue coming to meetings. But then one person in the group spoke directly to me and said, "I still accept you, Frank, but if you're ever going to get better *you'll have to be true to yourself.*" His words echoed in my head and I hated him for what he said. Who did he think he was to tell me what to do?

Before long, the stresses of life got to me and I sought out an old friend—pornography. It happened that my supply of pornographic material was there in the closet, right where I had put it, *just in case*. I decided to look at it and *not* masturbate. But once I got back into the addictive cycle, I was completely powerless. As I unsuccessfully tried to ejaculate, the words I'd heard at my last group meeting were still ringing in my head. Finally I burned the pornography, just as I had done so many times in the past. But this time I did something different after burning it: I called another sex addict on the phone. This time

I told him what was really going on with me, how lonely and afraid I was, and that I desperately wanted to continue acting out. This man told me to pray. I didn't know what to pray *for* or who to pray *to,* so I simply said the First Step aloud over and over again. I was so angry about being an addict. Tears streamed down my cheeks as I pounded the walls and screamed out each word of the First Step. "Help me!" I cried. Then I said the Second and Third Steps aloud. I prayed for a bolt of lightning or the voice of God to come into the room, but nothing happened—nothing except for the fact that *I did not act out that day.* After this incident, I suddenly had several new opportunities to act out: my first sponsor left the Program and started acting out again himself; my girl friend moved out; people I'd had sexual encounters with in the past showed up at my door; and publishers of pornographic magazines continued to send their materials to me even after I wrote and told them to take my name off their mailing lists. But through all these circumstances and changes, I managed to stay true to myself and stayed sober.

During my acting out, I had always "sexualized" my emotions. This is to say I had always assumed that whatever I was feeling, that feeling meant that I had a need to be sexual; I continued to have problems with this even in recovery. Then I developed a close relationship with another member of the Twelve Step group I attended. I respected this man for his ability to use the Twelve Steps, as well as for his wisdom, his humor, and the fact that he seemed to genuinely *like* himself. I often thought about him sexually, even during meetings. I'd drop hints as we spoke and I'd try to establish eye contact with him while he was sharing with the group. One evening, after our regular meeting had ended and some of us were getting ready to go out for a meal together, I saw my opportunity to have some time alone with him. I asked him if I could ride to the restaurant with him and he agreed. When we were in the car, I started talking about how I wasn't really sure if I was homosexual or heterosexual. I told him that even though most of my acting-out behaviors had been with women, I considered the possibility that I might be gay and perhaps needed to learn to be comfortable with that fact. He pointed out to me that sex addiction is not about *who* a person acts out with but *why* that person acts out at all. *This man just wouldn't take the hint I was giving him.* I tried again: I told him that what I thought I *really* needed was a loving, gentle relationship with a man—a relationship that would help me decide, once and for all, if I was homosexual or not. He said, "I agree that you need loving and gentle relationships with men, Frank, and I would be honored to be one of those men." I was overjoyed when he said this and fully expected that we'd skip dinner and go straight to his apartment for sex. But as he began speaking again, I realized that wasn't what he had in mind at all. "Right now," he said, "it really doesn't matter if you're gay or not. All that matters is your recovery. You don't have to consider your sexual preference until you're sober and can *stay sober*. I care about you and I won't endanger your recovery or mine by being sexual with you. You need to learn to love and be loved by other men without having those relationships involve sex. I can care about you and want to be with you without wanting to have sex with you."

I didn't know what to do. The concept of caring deeply for someone *without* sexual involvement seemed so radical, so completely *unnatural* to me. I decided that this man must have said what he did because he really didn't like me and didn't *want* to be sexual with me. *He was putting me off.* For most of my life, I assumed that I had to give my body to someone for him or her to be willing to spend time with me. After spending more time in recovery, I would come to understand that this man had gently taught me a very important lesson about real intimacy.

When I finally told my girl friend that I was a sex addict, she was furious with me. I expected that she'd break off our relationship immediately, but she didn't. What surprised me most, though, was that she was angrier about my masturbation than she was about my sexual encounters with other women. Later on she explained her reaction: she figured that if she satisfied me sexually and was willing to engage in sex with me whenever I wanted, she'd actually be able to *control* my addiction. It seemed that the healthier I got, the more confused she became about my addiction and our relationship. Now, I was the one who considered ending the relationship. Thankfully, she got into a Twelve Step Program of her own—one designed especially for co-dependent people. But our relationship continued to be a struggle, even when both of us were getting help. There were so many changes in the ways we interacted with each other: we were fighting a lot and we often abstained from sexual activity with each other. During these times of change, we often wondered if there was more to our relationship than sex and sickness, and whether or not recovery was worth losing each other. After more than a year of struggling together, we decided to make a statement to ourselves and the world regarding the important changes in our relationship: we got married. People from our respective Twelve Step groups came to the wedding, supported us, and celebrated with us as we made a commitment to each other.

As my wife and I struggled with the challenges of a new marriage, I was still struggling with my addiction. I continued to play games with the boundaries I had set. For example, I'd qualify masturbation in an effort to make it something other than acting out. ("...only once a week"; "...only if I don't think about anyone but my wife"; "...only if I don't think about sex at all"; and on and on.) I finally realized that anything I had to have so many rules around *must* be addictive. I finally admitted to myself, my group, and my God that masturbation was addictive behavior for me. My acting-out behavior had actually *numbed* my emotions and I had mistaken every feeling I had for a sexual urge.

I recall that at one meeting a man who had been very important to my early recovery announced that he was leaving our group to meet with another group because the meetings were more convenient for him. One by one, each person in our group said good-bye to this man and thanked him for his help. When my turn came, *I had no words* and I began to weep. I went to him and he held me as I cried. My tears actually said more than any words because this man knew how hard it was for me to cry and to trust other men. Another milestone in my recovery occurred at a group meeting when I was telling my First Step story: I actually *experienced* my emotions for the first time. I had told the facts many times before, but felt nothing. There was nothing special about this particular meeting—as always, our group consisted of five men sitting in a church basement, trying to help each other. But when I told my story on this particular night, I didn't just talk about my pain; *I really felt the pain*. For the first time, I realized how lonely, hurt, and shame-filled I had been and still was. I had always considered only the anger, never the sadness, the fear, and other emotions. I *hated* what I was feeling that night and was concerned that others in the group might think that I was weak. Feeling as low and worthless as I did, it was so hard to trust that they still cared about me.

Not all of the emotions I have discovered are painful ones. For example, I have discovered my laugh—not the little smile and chuckle I had when I was acting out, but a noisy, fun, belly laugh! Sometimes newcomers to meetings wonder how we can laugh and joke with each other, but they soon learn that a certain amount of levity is an essential part of the process of learning to be comfortable with other people and learning to care about them.

Now I realize that in recovery, I have everything I was trying to achieve by acting out: friends, acceptance, affection, and spirituality. I still don't know how to adequately explain spirituality; I do know what it is *not*. For me, spirituality is not becoming a fanatic and it is not standing back from life or refusing to enjoy it. Now I know how and what to pray about at night and during the day as well. I pray for the willingness to continue to work the Twelve Steps and the knowledge of which spiritual path to take. I end each day with a prayer of gratitude for my recovery—even at the end of a day when things didn't go my way. *Even my worst day in recovery is better than the best day I had while I was acting out.*

(Postscript: After three years in the Program; six months of sobriety.

Just a few months after writing my story, I had a slip that proved to be a very valuable lesson for me. When I first became involved in my Twelve Step group, I was there for *me*. I hurt so much at that time and I wanted to recover more than I wanted anything else. I was willing to give up whatever I *had* to give up for recovery. I figured that I would lose my girl friend and maybe my job, but I knew that any sacrifice would be worth it if I could just stop acting out and stop hating myself so much. After my first full year of not acting out, I figured that this recovery process wasn't so difficult after all. I had been trusted servant of my group and was liked and respected by others. In the meantime, my girl friend and I had gotten married and I had established my career.

Suddenly the pain of my early days in recovery seemed very distant to me. I was much less concerned about missing meetings or forgetting my reading and my prayers than I had been early in my recovery. I decided that I didn't need to continue calling another addict each day. In fact, by the time I got my two-year medallion, I wasn't working a *personal* recovery

227

program at all. I wasn't acting out, but I wasn't sober either. I was fantasizing in many of the same ways I had fantasized *before* I came to the Program. I still attended meetings, but I didn't talk about *myself* very much. I was far too busy helping others and trying to look good. I made phone calls to other sex addicts, but only to see how *they* were doing. I never mentioned the continuing struggle I was having with my *own* addictive urges; I felt sure I could handle things by myself after the two good years I'd had in recovery. After all, I hadn't acted out during that time. If things got bad then, I'd just call someone. *I knew I couldn't act out anymore.* What would my group say if they found out? What would my wife do if she found out? I was sure that these questions alone, and the fears they represented, would keep me sober.

Then one day, I acted out. But before I did, I considered the option of calling someone from my group and *not* acting out. I decided not to do that. After my slip, I gave myself a *hundred* reasons why I would not have to call my behavior "acting out"—even though my behavior was clearly outside my boundaries. *I didn't call anyone from the group.* I was afraid I'd lose control and continue acting out. I didn't lose control, so I thought to myself, Well, this proves I can do what I want to do now because I've got everything under control.

After my slip, I went to my group meeting as usual and told my squad how well my recovery was proceeding. I even comforted another addict and offered him some suggestions when he told me about a recent slip *he'd* had. I found that as the meeting continued on, I struggled more and more with my own reality. I invented more reasons why I wouldn't have to call what I had done acting-out behavior. I was so anxious I was afraid that I might throw up right there at the meeting. Suddenly I realized that I couldn't sit still any longer; I burst out with my admission: "I had a slip last week!" I fully expected the men I sponsored to gasp in shock or move away from me in disgust when I revealed my secret. I waited for someone to tell me how I had let everyone down by lying to the group, but I heard none of the horrible things I was braced for. Instead, I heard only expressions of acceptance and support from people in the group. *I was honest and it paid off.* As a result, I felt as though an enormous weight had been lifted from my shoulders.

Today, I really work my Program. I have learned that a medallion is not the *goal* of the Program, but merely a symbol of *progress* in the Program. I no longer mark on my calendar when I think I'll get my next medallion, because there is no way I can really know that for sure. I *do* know that I *am* a sex addict and that I *am* powerless over my compulsive sexual behaviors. I can't promise that I will not act out next month or tomorrow; I only know that I can stay sober *today...and that I will stay sober today.*

What has helped me most in my recovery is paying attention to the Twelve Steps and really applying them in my daily life. Being in therapy and also being a professional social worker, I am sometimes tempted to theorize and "therapize" in my Twelve Step meetings. But I have learned that I really get and give the best kind of help when I keep my focus on the Twelve Steps. When I'm asked for help from another group member, I don't tell that person about the latest theoretical book I've read; instead, I tell that person about my experience and how I have used the Twelve Steps in my life. In fact, most newer group members don't even know what I do for a living. I am at the meetings only as another recovering sex addict, not as a trained helping professional. When I ask for help from other addicts, I don't ask them what they think their therapist would have to say about my problem; I ask them for suggestions as to how I can do a better job of applying the Twelve Steps and Twelve Traditions to my daily life.

One of the most surprising things I have learned about myself in recovery is that I was actually *afraid* of sex! (If someone had told me this during the years I was acting out, I would have said they were crazy.) Once I stopped fantasizing and began to pay attention to my body and my feelings *during* sex, I recognized the very real fear I was experiencing around sex. The concept of healthy, gentle, loving sex is a new thing for me and I'm just learning how to deal with it. Now I am also learning how to be playful and joyful in my sexual relationship with my wife.

Another thing about my recovery that surprises me is that I rarely want to act out now. *Acting out has almost completely lost its appeal for me.* No longer can I fool myself into believing that pornography will help me be less lonely or that an affair will prove that I'm a good person. When I am in a very stressful situation, addictive thoughts still come to mind. But now I know that I have group members to call; staying sober is no longer the terrible struggle for me that it was in the past.

When I tell people that I no longer struggle with my addiction, some of them ask me if I'm "cured" or fixed. I don't think I'm "cured"; I believe that I will *always* be a sex addict. I used to feel sorry for myself and sometimes even angry for having to rely on a group to help me get through life. Now I feel grateful that I have a group of people who care enough about me that they want to see me each week and hear about my life and how it's going. I think of the piece of paper I carry with me, an important phone list that contains the phone numbers of the members of my Twelve Step group. I am moved when I consider the collect calls I've placed from faraway cities, calls that were accepted because these people understood what I was feeling and that I wanted to talk to another recovering addict. With people like this in my life, why would I want to stop attending meetings? I used to say that I *had* to go to meetings; now I find myself saying (and thinking) that I *get* to go to meetings. I don't struggle with my addiction anymore, but that doesn't mean I am recovered. I am proud and happy to say that

I am a recover*ing* sex addict. The effort, pain, and time I invested in recovery has paid off in ways that I never would have believed possible. I truly hope that every person I share my story with will find the same joy and serenity in his or her recovery that I have found in mine.

Ryan's Story

*...I'm grateful that 99 percent of my life
is now recovery...*

(After thirty-six months in the Program; six months of sobriety.)

Sexual addiction has been a dominant force in my life for almost twenty years—more than half my lifetime. Looking back, I'd say that my compulsive sexual behavior began when I discovered masturbation at the age of thirteen. Soon after making that discovery, I was masturbating two or three times a day—often until I was sore and raw. As with other addictive behaviors I would develop in the future, masturbation was something I kept totally secret; I didn't even discuss it with my older brothers. I was reading a so-called "dirty book" the first time I masturbated and from that time on, reading or visual stimulation became important elements in my addictive ritual. By the time I was fifteen, I was buying pornographic magazines and bondage/ domination books. Whenever I bought these magazines, hid them at home, and used them, I was filled with feelings of fear, shame, and excitement.

At this same time in my life, I began wearing women's clothing while masturbating. I felt enormous shame and fear about this new behavior, and I became even more isolated and secretive. Then my compulsive behavior gradually began to take on new forms: window-peeping, exposing myself in public, making anonymous phone calls while masturbating, and burglarizing homes for lingerie. Window-peeping dominated my evenings and interfered with my school work. I still recall spending *hours* hiding in bug-infested bushes, sometimes drenched by rain, desperately waiting and watching for a mere crack of light in a shade or a curtain. I exposed myself in public two or three different times and I was just lucky not to have been caught and arrested for indecent exposure. For years, I also made anonymous phone calls on a regular basis, trying to get someone— anyone—to stay on the line with me while I masturbated. Because I didn't use obscene words or threaten anyone, I managed to convince myself that the phone calls I was making were not harmful. The burglaries I committed involved prowling the neighborhood, entering houses of friends or acquaintances when no one was home, and stealing lingerie from bedrooms. I knew that the things I was doing were all *very risky,* but I was in a compulsive daze, completely unable to stop on my own.

My feelings of shame, fear, and excitement grew more intense and I also developed feelings of *dread* and self-hatred. In brief moments of clarity, I'd think about what I was doing and it all seemed so sick and crazy. Drugs, I discovered, could "fix" the bad feelings I had about myself and my behavior. I started smoking dope and also began using liquor, barbiturates, and opiates—addictive substances that deadened my awareness and obscured my reality. During the five years I was using and abusing drugs, I had several relationships with women. But my addiction was apparent in these relationships; I had a constant need for sex. I used drugs and so-called "normal" relationships with women to cover up the pain and shame I felt about my secret activities. With *all* of my acting-out behaviors, I rationalized my sexual indulgences by telling myself that I was an adventurous and sophisticated person who just liked to try "different" things.

When I was twenty years old, some friends of mine confronted me about my drug use. As a result of this confrontation, I took a one-way plane ride to a distant city and spent six months in a chemical dependency treatment facility there. During my treatment, I first talked with someone about my compulsive behavior related to cross-dressing (wearing women's clothing.) My treatment for chemical dependency certainly represented a new beginning for me in many ways, but it didn't help me deal with my compulsive sexual behavior. In fact, my sexual compulsiveness was, at this time, as strong as it ever had been: even while I was in treatment, I continued to masturbate and use pornography compulsively. I also continued to make anonymous phone calls whenever I could.

During my first year of being chemically free, I realized that contrary to my hopes, my "weird" sexual practices were *not* a by-product of my drug use. And without chemicals to medicate me, my feelings of shame intensified. As soon as I got out of treatment, I got a job as a delivery person...and I located all the "adult" bookstores in the town I had relocated to. I even started another collection of magazines, pornographic pictures, and books. Of course, the extra hours I spent buying books, watching quarter movies, and masturbating created problems for me on the job. I'd lie and argue indignantly whenever my supervisor confronted me about being late with a delivery. Shopping for women's garments at thrift shops and rummage sales became part of my acting-out behavior at this time. I felt an ever-present combination of fear of getting caught and shame for doing things that I felt sure would be considered "weird." In those days, I had two large suitcases—one for the pornography I used and one for the women's apparel I used for cross-dressing. *I lived in fear of being discovered.* Even though I was living with roommates at the time, I resumed my anonymous phone calling. This behavior seemed very sick. When I found that I was completely unable to rationalize the phone calling any longer, I went to a psychiatrist and told him *everything*. Doing this helped me in some ways and, subsequently, I was able to stop making those phone calls. Unfortunately, though, this psychiatrist told me it was okay for me to use pornography. (I have since learned that because *my* use of pornography was part of my addiction, it is definitely *not* okay for *me* to use it.)

During the next three years, I had a series of relationships with women and again my addiction manifested itself in most

235

of these relationships. One woman was open to my cross-dressing and also tolerated some of my other compulsive behaviors. Usually, though, my secret life was a source of extreme anxiety and shame for me. Periodically, I still visited a few men I knew I could cross-dress around and who I could get oral sex from. The shame and guilt I felt intensified. Given my constant need for sex and my improving financial situation, I finally decided that visiting prostitutes would be a viable option for me. So I established contact with several female prostitutes who I subsequently saw at least four or five times a month. Eventually, though, this habit became so expensive that I actually had to *borrow* money to pay for the pornography I was buying and the services of prostitutes. It was then that I began to see how my compulsive sexual behavior resembled my chemical addiction—complete with obsessive thinking, rigidity, denial, rationalization, and hundreds of promises to myself, after acting out, that "I'll *never* do that again." In the few lucid moments I had in those days, I could see my sexual behavior for the addiction it really was. *But I couldn't stop.*

Then, four years ago, I began dating the woman I eventually married. A few months after we started dating, she found a large bag of womens' clothing in my closet. The confrontation between us that ensued resulted in my going into therapy again. While in therapy this time, I began my first *real work* on my sexual addiction. I began to see that the use of pornography and prostitutes, the cross-dressing, the window-peeping, the indecent exposure, and the anonymous phone calling were all acting-out behaviors that were harmful to *me*. Even though I gained some new insights into my behavior through therapy, I continued to visit prostitutes and adult bookstores. I also continued to have occasional sexual encounters with men.

Then my therapist told me about a weekend workshop and suggested that I attend. I went, and during that weekend, I shared a lot about my acting-out behaviors. At the end of the weekend, I was told about a Twelve Step group for people with addictions and acting-out behaviors similar to mine. I wrote to that group asking for help. When someone from the group called me, I felt excited yet sad and scared. I was excited to know that now I could get help on a day-by-day basis; I was sad when I thought about my years of struggle and pain; I was scared to think about not acting out. I attended a meeting of the group and there I met some people who had personal histories similar to mine. *It was then I knew I had found a home.*

Progress rather than perfection definitely characterizes the thirty-six months I've been in the Program so far. Through the Twelve Steps, I've been able to find some peace of mind, one day at a time. And through the fellowship of my group, I've been able to feel a sense of community with other recovering people. (I'm so grateful for these things.) My feelings of shame have lessened and some days now I go for hours without even *thinking* about sex. I've had some slips, but I'm grateful that 99 percent of my life is now recovery...at least for today. And since sexual addiction occupies only a very small percentage of my life now, I certainly don't intend to allow it to make me 100 percent miserable any longer. I've discovered that my hope lies in a foundation that is based on the Twelve Steps and regular contact with my group. These new spiritual resources in my life have helped me stop my constant fantasizing about sex. At first I had to force myself to stop my acting-out behaviors while "white-knuckling" through hours and days of fantasies and addictive urges. But Steps Two, Three, and Twelve have helped me find relief from those urges and fantasies. Remembering a certain phrase in the AA Big Book has also helped me so much: "We stood at the turning point. We asked (God's) protection and care with complete abandon" (p. 59).

Anyone in recovery will tell you that it's no picnic—there's so much work and pain involved when we change our thinking and behavior. And I believe that recovery from sex addiction is complicated by the fact that in our society, this addiction—even more than addictions to food, drugs, or alcohol—carries with it so much shame and fear. But the struggle has been worth it for me because now I have a new life that's richer, more enjoyable, and more fulfilling. The two years I've been in the Program mark the first real progress I've made in finding contentment and happiness. Recovery has given me relief from the feelings of anxiety, guilt, shame, and self-hatred that were so much a part of my acting out. I still have those feelings from time to time, but I no longer *fuel* them, nor do I allow them to *control* me. Since many of my acting-out behaviors seem to be related to my upbringing and my early family relationships, my recovery seems to improve as I work through my feelings about family issues and focus on the spiritual aspects of the Twelve Steps. My weekly therapy sessions are essential to my recovery too, because I find that getting help from people who are not sexually addicted has given me a better look at my shame, self-hatred, and self-judgment. In my Twelve Step group as well as in therapy, I learned that *first* I had to believe that I was loved and okay, *and then* I would stop acting out—not the other way around.

One of the by-products of recovery for me is that I've learned to like myself more. When I began to recover, every aspect of my life began to improve. As hard as I had tried to "compartmentalize" my acting-out behaviors, they eventually affected every aspect of my life. Unfortunately, my profession as well as my relationship with my wife and my child were big casualties. Now I find that I'm more productive in my job and more focused in my efforts to achieve my professional and financial goals. In the past, I was alienated from the people I loved because of the secret, furtive nature of my addiction. Now my personal relationships have improved and, finally, *I have peace of mind*.

Jamie's Story

My goal today is the same as it has been throughout my recovery—to merge sexuality and intimacy in one relationship.

(After three years in the Program; eighteen months of sobriety.)

As a young boy growing up in a small midwestern town, I was shy and artistically inclined. Most of the other boys my age regarded me as a "sissy" and I *did* feel that I was somehow different. I had great admiration for older boys—like my brother—who were proficient in sports. I was introduced to sex by a close friend of my brother's. I thought that if I let him fondle me as he wanted to, he would like me and eventually I'd be accepted by my brother's friends and possibly by my brother as well. I gave this older boy whatever he wanted sexually, but received nothing from him in return. Despite this one-sided relationship, I allowed him to use me for several years. I never really liked him; he was the town bully. We didn't even speak to each other in public and our only involvement was his use of me for his own sexual pleasure. A few years later, I had a similar sexual relationship with the older brother of my best friend. He was also my brother's age, about eighteen months older than I. I liked and admired this young man and felt sure that if I could satisfy him sexually, he would accept me and perhaps even *like* me. I also realized that the clandestine nature of my secret meetings with him was very exciting to me.

After high school, I enrolled at a large university. It didn't take me long to find secret places there where I could meet men. I also met a boy there who became my roommate. He grew fond of me, and even though I didn't care for him as much as he cared for me, I let him use me for his own sexual pleasure. After a couple of years in college, my behavior pattern was set:

239

I completely separated sex and intimacy. I had sex only with men who were strangers to me or men I didn't care about, yet I played it straight with friends and I even had a girl friend.

After I graduated from college, I started to cruise for sex compulsively. This acting-out behavior continued while I was in the army and later, when I worked in a large city. Sometimes I'd go on compulsive cruising "binges" that lasted half the night. While cruising in a public park one time, I was assaulted by a total stranger who became enraged when I refused to engage in the kind of sex he wanted to have with me right there in the park. Terrified, I ran away. My cruising continued, even though I had other frightening experiences and contracted venereal disease.

Occasionally I'd stay with one person for a short period of time, but still I'd cruise. For a few years, I had a relationship with a younger man, but eventually I left him and resumed my pattern of compulsive and dangerous cruising. Although I didn't realize it at the time, I had become addicted to my cruising activities. I ran away from this developing relationship because I couldn't tell the young man I was involved with the truth about me. I had never been completely honest with him and he knew nothing about my compulsive cruising. Though I thought I was restlessly looking for new conquests, all the time I was really *running away from myself*. At that time in my life, I was still in the closet as a gay person. In fact, I was dating women and playing straight with friends. My closest male friends as well as my roommate were straight; I had no gay friends. Actually, I felt superior to gay men and really despised the "obvious" ones, the "queens" and those who had so obviously "come out." Then I had a brief affair with a man and introduced him to my roommate. But even this man was not someone I wanted to get to know; to me, he was just another body.

When I was in my early thirties, I fell in love with a woman. We lived together for a year, then married. This woman had a son from a previous marriage and together we had two children of our own. I stopped cruising for awhile and, on the surface at least, my life seemed to be going quite well. When I wasn't acting out, I'd either "white-knuckle" my way through compulsive urges, or I'd tell myself that my cruising days were over, I loved my wife, and I had changed in some ways. *But life was still a tremendous struggle for me.* When I'd force myself to be sexual with my wife or just try to be affectionate with her, she'd say that she felt something was wrong. In response to her observation, I'd withdraw, make excuses to her, and pretend that everything was fine.

Periodically during our eight-year marriage, I resumed my compulsive cruising for men. But never once during that time did I admit to myself that I was gay. Toward the end of our marriage, my wife and I had some intensive therapy. Through it all, I was desperately trying to save our marriage and "cure" my homosexual urges. Outwardly, I blamed my wife for the emotional scenes we were having; secretly, though, I blamed myself. I felt guilty when I realized that I didn't really love my wife; my feelings of guilt were compounded when I realized I was also deceiving my wife and withdrawing from her. The two of us were becoming involved in a co-dependent dance, and each of us was abusing the other emotionally. She knew nothing about my cruising and I felt terribly ashamed of the lies I had told her in order to cover up my behavior. In fact, *no one* knew the lurid details of my cruising "binges." *I couldn't even face the details of this acting-out behavior myself.*

This basic denial affected my career, my social life, my family relationships, *virtually everything in my life.* I had worked to pretend that everything was fine for so long that I was worn out from the effort. For more than thirty years, I had carried with me a tremendous burden made up of secrets and feelings of shame—it was an enormous drain on my energy and productivity. The pain I felt about thinking I was a bad person and hating myself was so intolerable that I repressed it and denied it. And the pain and rage I felt ultimately surfaced in my marriage. Unwittingly, I took everything out on my wife and we tormented each other with shame and blame. My children suffered during their formative years because there was no way I could be honest and nurturing with them—not with all the shame I felt.

Even after my wife and I separated, I still had great difficulty coming to terms with my homosexuality. My compulsive cruising binges continued, alternating with periods of extreme loneliness. I was involved with a man for a brief period of time, but our relationship didn't work out—possibly because both of us were so emotionally needy. This pattern of behavior continued on for about six years. My therapist finally recommended a Twelve Step group for sex addicts. At that time, I had attended Al-Anon meetings for over a year and, therefore, had some knowledge of the Twelve Steps. Now I also had some hope that addiction might explain my dilemma. I longed for a solution or, at the very least, some explanation for my behavior and my lack of control. Even though I was scared at my first Twelve Step meeting, I also knew that I belonged there. I learned that sex addicts are ordinary people very much like me. Still, I was *terrified* about revealing my secrets to these people. Like all addicts, I felt enormous shame. I also held on to my "special" shame as a homosexual, even though I knew that other men in the group had acted out with members of the same sex, and one member of the group acknowledged that he was gay. Coming out as a homosexual required a long and difficult struggle. I had to learn not to hold back any secrets. I had buried the facts for so long I didn't even know how to reveal them. Finally, I wrote a detailed account of my cruising behavior and shared it with the group. The group encouraged me by helping me see that all of us shared a similar pain. Eventually the shame lifted and I felt enormous relief.

After three years in the Program, I had a slip. It all started when I gave in to my urges and turned to pornographic magazines and pornographic movies. One night, I was particularly low and felt that I couldn't stand the loneliness anymore. I went to a gay bathhouse—an activity clearly outside the boundaries I had set for myself in my Program. What I really wanted that night was affection and a chance to feel the touch and warmth of another human being. And because I wanted to be close to another person *instantly* and *easily,* I allowed a stranger to perform oral sex on me. We didn't even speak to each other during our encounter. I pretended that he cared for me and imagined that he was treating me like a god or a king by lavishing unlimited attention and affection on me. As soon as our encounter ended, I went home. There I confronted *more* loneliness. After this slip, it became even clearer to me how I had, for most of my life, confused intimacy with sexual activity. But the sex act had never brought intimacy into my life. And now, sex was even *less* satisfying to me because I could no longer fool myself—I knew that never again would I be able to settle for sex without intimacy.

Knowing that I'd have to give intimacy a chance to grow, I decided to be celibate for a period of time. I knew that I would have to get to know a person as a friend before I could have a sexual relationship with him. But after so many years of having sex only with strangers or people I didn't care about, I had some serious doubts whether I could really be interested in sex with someone I knew and *did* care about; the idea seemed unappealing, almost frightening, to me. I found that I needed a long period of celibacy to rid myself of the shame I felt, to learn to like myself again, and to learn to trust myself and others. As long as the sexual act was there for me, I knew I would be confused about what it was I really wanted: did I need warmth, affection and intimacy, or just relief from powerful sexual urges? Now I understand that the sex act cannot relieve my feelings—particularly feelings of pain, anger, or loneliness. I have come to believe that sex is not an act of taking and using; it is an act of love and sharing that satisfies the human need to reach out and contact another person in a caring and giving way.

Even though I have attended Twelve Step meetings regularly, recovery has been a very slow and painful process for me. For a long time, I actually *preferred* my addictive loneliness to reaching out. As it turned out, it was more than a year before I could telephone people and ask for their support. I set my boundaries: no cruising, no sex with strangers, and no pornography. I also set my goals: to merge sex with intimacy, to build a caring relationship with one person, to give up having sex with strangers, to accept myself and my partner, and to share our lives, especially our feelings. These goals are not easy and they all involve an ongoing process. But since I had that slip, I realize that I cannot settle for less. *Life is too short.* I have come out as a gay person. Attending a gay support group helped me to be much more comfortable with my homosexuality, but it was the Twelve Step Program that brought me back to sanity. I get support from the Program and I constantly seek a deeper level of spirituality. I have so much more confidence in myself now, and my career has prospered and grown. Also, I have been involved in a relationship with a man for more than six months now. This relationship has been a real challenge and I struggle with my co-dependency within it, but now I know that sex and intimacy *can* be combined and that I can be a loving person and receive love from others as well. I will always be an addict, but a recovering one, and my spiritual search will never end. I thank God for the Program.

(Postscript: After four years in the Program; thirty months of sobriety.)

When I think back over the last year, I think about how much I've learned. I am no longer with the man I wrote about a year ago. We worked on our relationship for over a year before we decided that it would be best for both of us to end it. When our relationship began, I had been attending Twelve Step meetings and had been sober for some time, but he was at a very early stage in his recovery. This man and I also attended the same Twelve Step group. I can now see that attending meetings together and being at different stages of recovery contributed to the difficulties we experienced. Although I still see this man as a friend occasionally, we no longer have a sexual relationship. The special gay group we attended together while we were sexually involved with one another has since disbanded. Looking back, I can see how the issues related to our sexual relationship affected the stability of that group.

Now I am a member of another group for men with gay concerns; this group is thriving. Our stories are so similar and our fellowship helps us build and reinforce positive images of ourselves as gay males. As a group, we have set a common boundary: no sex between group members. We remind ourselves of this at the start of each meeting. I am now a sponsor for newer members of the group. I was flattered and humbled when they asked me to be a sponsor but at the same time, I was concerned that I wouldn't be a good sponsor. Now I can see that my sponsorship of other people in the Program is my Higher Power's way of helping me stay connected to the group and helping me reach out to others who are struggling with their addictive behavior just as I did for so long.

When I was attending only a "regular" Twelve Step meeting, I projected my self-hate on to the other members in the group. Although the people in this group treated me kindly, I convinced myself that they secretly judged me for being gay; consequently, I distanced myself from them. But when I finally met other gay people who openly shared their experiences with me, I realized that I could no longer hide behind my feelings of being "different." When I really faced myself, I realized that

I had feelings of shame on two levels: being gay and being a sex addict. I came to understand that I could not comfortably or completely come out as a gay person until I faced my addiction and became a recovering addict. Now I can accept myself and my gayness. I like myself and I have found a spiritual connection which is renewed each time I do a Twelfth Step or attend a Twelve Step meeting.

I have a special friend in my recovery: my former wife. We face each other honestly about what our relationship was and is. Although we live apart, we are very close on an emotional level. In fact, we have a mutual trust that we never had during the time we were married. Now I am able to talk to my children honestly about my sex addiction and about my homosexuality. Now I can face these things about myself *without shame*. And the less shame I feel about my life, the easier it seems to be for my children to cope. I believe that my willingness to be true to myself will give them the strength and clarity they will need to be honest about me with themselves and their peers.

My goal today is the same as it has been throughout my recovery—to merge sexuality and intimacy in one relationship. I trust that if I stay in the Program, my Higher Power will always guide me toward that goal.

Phil's Story

*When I look at the past in light of the present,
I am reminded of the pain of addiction and the
grace of recovery.*

(After thirty-two months in the Program; twenty-seven months
of sobriety.)

There was a time in my life when masturbation, pornography,
and fantasy were the best friends I had. I first turned to masturbation as a way to relieve feelings of depression, loneliness,
shame, anger, and fear. Later on, I followed a compulsive ritual
of reading pornography, masturbating, and fantasizing about
women hurting me and forcing me to be sexual with them.
Whenever I questioned my preoccupation with sex, I had a
ready answer for myself: I just had a very healthy sex drive and
a good imagination. But hidden deep within me were feelings
that my sexual behavior was *not normal.* Secretly, I hoped that
my compulsive sexual rituals would end when I got married,
but they didn't and my secret life continued on. I masturbated
when my wife wasn't home or after she had gone to bed for the
night. When I had sexual relations with my wife, I usually
fantasized that I was with a prostitute.

Looking back, I now realize that I was completely unaware
of and uncaring about about my wife's sexual needs and desires.
Like the alcoholic's wife who buys liquor for her husband, my
wife bought pornography for me and joked with me about my
masturbation. As it turned out, neither of us was being honest
in our sexual relationship. Actually, I was very anxious about
our relationship. I simply didn't know how to deal with the
intimacy that is so important to healthy sexuality.

My sexual behavior became even more compulsive after I
completed my doctorate and then got my first job. In those
days, I was masturbating several times a day and sometimes

even in the middle of the night. After awhile, my health began to deteriorate because I wasn't getting enough sleep. By this time, my wife and I had a child and I was really struggling with my role as a parent. I was very impatient with my son and sometimes I'd yank him around in an abusive manner. My wife and I began fighting more. I was experiencing mood swings and at times I became depressed and suicidal. But I never once associated the problems I was having with my feelings of shame about my compulsive sexual behavior. *I just thought life was tough.*

One day a friend of mine told me that he was a sex addict. I listened to him carefully and thanked him for sharing with me. Secretly, though, I was *terrified* of what my friend was telling me, because my story was so similar to his. Even then, I just couldn't accept the possibility that I was sexually addicted. Nevertheless, I began talking to this friend of mine about my masturbation. It was the first time I had ever shared any information about my secret sexual life with another person. Fortunately, my friend did not judge me or offer advice. Instead, he listened carefully. Then he simply encouraged me to keep thinking about what I was doing to myself sexually.

Following an episode of severe depression, I finally decided to see a therapist who had some knowledge about sexual addiction. I told him that I wanted to find out whether or not I was a sex addict. (Prior to seeing this therapist for the first time, I tried hard to convince myself that he would say I was not a sex addict and that my fantasies and masturbation were, in fact, perfectly normal.) At our third session together, he asked me to make a commitment to not masturbate at all for the period of time I would be in therapy—weeks, perhaps even months. Anticipating very little difficulty, I made the commitment quickly and willingly. Then, soon after that session, I woke up one night with an intense urge to masturbate. I got up to complete my ritual, then remembered the commitment I had made to my therapist just three days earlier. I sat down in a chair and consciously made a decision to not masturbate. A few minutes later, I thought "to heck with the commitment" and went to get my pornography. Then I changed my mind and sat down again. This seesaw battle went on most of the night and *it was sheer hell*. Finally, at about five o'clock in the morning, I called my therapist and told him what a terribly difficult time I was having with the commitment I had made. Somehow, I got through that night without masturbating, but it was almost unbearable. In addition to the pain I felt, I was *horrified* to realize how difficult it was for me to control my behavior. If there was anything positive in the pain and horror I felt that night, it was this: I finally began to understand that my masturbation was compulsive behavior and that it really was *harmful* to me.

Soon after that terrible night, my therapist told me that he thought I was a sex addict. He recommended that I attend a special support group based on the Twelve Step Alcoholics Anonymous model. I was absolutely *terrified* at the first few meetings I attended. I didn't want *anyone* to know *anything* at all about my secret sexual life. My first impression of the meeting was that the sexual behavior being discussed was very different from my behavior. Again, I tried to convince myself that I was different, that I didn't have the same problems these men had and, therefore, didn't belong in this kind of Program. But as I listened more closely to the stories they shared that night, I heard some common themes and began to see my own behavior patterns: sexual compulsiveness, inability to stop acting out, mood swings, rationalizations, and secretiveness.

At the first meeting, I was given a list of phone numbers of other people in the group; I was encouraged to use this list whenever I felt like acting out. One day when I was struggling with a very strong urge to masturbate, I called one of the men on the list and told him that I felt I was close to a slip. We talked for a long time and I managed to get through that day without masturbating. There would be many more days like this, days when *not masturbating* was my primary goal. By this time, I was terribly depressed and just barely functioning in my job as a mental health professional. I had been told that I would go through a period of mourning, because in abstaining from masturbation, I was essentially giving up a friend I had relied on for years. *But knowing this didn't help me.* There were many days when I desperately wanted to give up and go back to my compulsive rituals. Many of the men in my Twelve Step group encouraged me to *keep trying.* They told me that the longer they stayed sober, the better things were for them. My marriage was in bad shape at this time. I assumed that since I was the addict in the family, the fighting that went on was *necessarily* my fault. I didn't yet understand that my wife was a co-addict who was struggling with compulsive and enabling behaviors of her own. Without realizing it, my wife and I had developed rituals within our relationship that helped us avoid emotional intimacy. In order to avoid coming to terms with our pain, we nurtured these rituals and competed with each other emotionally.

For months, I frequently thought to myself that if all this pain was what recovery was about, then recovery be damned! *I'd be better off acting out!* But then, slowly, I began to make some progress in therapy. I came to understand how ashamed I was of my sexual behavior and how I chose to be a loner caught up in my addictive behaviors, rather than reaching out and having *real relationships with real people.* I began to share with others my feelings about having lived with a sense of shame for so many years. I began to understand more about my family background and how the emotional neglect and abuse I experienced most likely led to my avoidance of feelings and my sexual compulsiveness. I also began to understand my powerlessness over my addiction and how I could not stop my acting out with will power. For the first time ever, I had a spiritual life that was based on my growing belief that God could do what I could not do for myself.

When I finally stopped masturbating, all the feelings I had denied for so long began to come out. These new feelings were difficult to accept and even more difficult to work through. Despite my progress in therapy, I felt a growing rage about my addiction and the way my parents had treated me. After struggling with these feelings of anger for a long time, I decided to masturbate again. But my decision was no spur-of-the-moment thing. Before I acted out again, I talked with one of the men in my Twelve Step group and told him of my plans. He encouraged me to make a commitment to stick with the Twelve Step Program, *even after my slip*. I was angry at him for suggesting this, but I *did* make that commitment.

In the past, masturbation had almost always given me some short-term relief from my emotional pain. *Not so after my slip!* My depression and despair were profound. I was suicidal and felt completely hopeless about my recovery. But even though I was depressed, I *did* honor my commitment to stay with the Program. At the suggestion of my therapist, I started attending four group meetings each week. As I worked the Program, my depression and despair gradually subsided. It seemed possible that maybe I *could* reclaim my recovery by continuing to work the Twelve Step Program. *Sometimes pain is really a gift in disguise:* my slip and the pain I felt afterward gave me the opportunity to learn that *I cannot afford to practice my addiction because to do so jeopardizes my mental and physical health as well as my relationships with the people I love.*

Subsequently, I got more involved in the spiritual aspect of my recovery program. I was raised in a Jewish home, but did not have a formal Jewish education. After my slip, I began attending synagogue, talked with a rabbi about God and Jewish life, and participated in a program of Jewish study. Eventually, I came to understand how I had been trying to orchestrate my own recovery instead of believing that my Higher Power would be there to help me if only I called upon that power. In the past, I had found it difficult to accept certain parts of the Program. I did not believe that God—if there was one—could help me in any way. My therapist helped me see how I was defining God in terms of my own will: if God didn't act the way I wanted Him/Her to, that just proved to me that S/He did not exist. Through my studies and my work in the Twelve Step Program, I found that I could look for God in places I hadn't thought of before: in the faces of my fellow recovering addicts, in the celebrations and rituals of my faith, and in the love I have for my wife and my child. Gradually, I began to see much more evidence of God's presence all around me. I started praying regularly.

My new spiritual values seemed to add new strength to my recovery. I used the phone to check in regularly with fellow addicts and I got a sponsor I trusted and could check in with on just about anything that happened to be going on in my life. *It felt good to be alive*! Instead of denying, suppressing, or trying to "fix" or forget my feelings, I used them as a *guide* in my recovery. I still experienced some depression and anxiety, times of wanting to act out and times of real despair. But at those times, I would pray, read about recovery, or reach out to recovering friends. As a result, those unsettling urges and feelings subsided more quickly than they had earlier in my recovery.

As my sobriety continued, my family life improved significantly. My wife and I were involved in marriage counseling for over a year and we worked together to untangle our emotional competitiveness and the unhealthy aspects of our interdependency. My wife joined a support group for co-addicts and got special support there. I learned to stop shaming and blaming her when I was upset and I learned to be more honest with her about my feelings. Together we learned to talk about our sexual relationship as honest and mature adults. I chose to spend more time with our son and found new ways to discipline him with *love*. I still have some tough days with my family, days when I feel as though I'm about to slip back into old ways of thinking and interacting. But I find that by praying and reaching out to friends, I stay in recovery.

At this point, I feel that my recovery is solid. But I'm also aware that I need to keep working my Program in order to maintain that recovery because *I will never be recovered, only recovering*. Checking in with fellow addicts, attending meetings, praying, working a spiritual program are things I must continue to do in order to maintain my sobriety. When I look at the past in light of the present, I am reminded of the pain of addiction and the grace of recovery. Even though I have not masturbated or used pornography for over two years now, I still struggle with the temptation to use sexual fantasy as an escape from life. I still struggle, also, to accept the powerlessness of my addiction. As I continue on in my recovery, I find that my definition of sobriety is evolving in two ways. First, I am beginning to include more subtle, "hidden" acting-out behaviors (such as sexual fantasies) when I define my boundaries. Second, I now define sobriety not only in terms of behaviors I *don't* engage in (masturbation, for example,) but also in terms of behaviors I *do* engage in to strengthen my recovery (praying, going to synagogue, reaching out to fellow addicts.) *I keep working to choose life*.

Margret's Story

Now I use my thoughts to keep myself grounded in reality, not to escape from it.

(After two years in the Program; two years of sobriety.)

The First Step of the Twelve Step Program for sex addicts is absolutely imperative to recovery. For this reason, I share my story within the context of the First Step. I can recall having some feelings of powerlessness about males even when I was in first grade. In those days, the boys in school would give me a dime each time I'd swing on the playground swings and let them see my underwear. When my mother found out about this, she lashed out in anger at me and called me a slut. But I remember that the *real* difficulty for me in this situation was having to go back to school and tell the boys I could no longer play the game. I felt guilty about dropping out of the "game" we played because I believed that I owed the boys something. Throughout my elementary school years, I was obsessed with boys. In fact, when I was in sixth grade, I spent so much time off in my own world and thinking about boys that I was labeled a "dreamer" by teachers and classmates.

By the time I was in junior high school, my primary activities involved my powerlessness relative to boys. In eighth grade, I was regularly playing "spin the bottle" games for sexual favors. I acted as if I enjoyed the activity, but the pain I felt about it affected me physically—sometimes I'd shake so hard during these games that I'd have to leave the room. But as frightened as I was, I could no more imagine removing myself from situations like this than I could imagine flying to the moon. By the end of ninth grade, I was known around school as a "flirt," or "easy." I'd already had sexual experiences with several boys. I assumed that each experience would eventually add to my feelings of accomplishment. In reality, though, my feelings of

255

shame grew as I became more and more experienced sexually. And when my shame intensified, my performance in school deteriorated as did my relationships with girls *and* boys. Drugs seemed to offer the only way to numb my pain and fear.

At the end of tenth grade, I began dealing drugs at another high school in town and got involved with new friends who were acting in irresponsible and destructive ways. In eleventh grade, my world came crashing down around me: I was failing in school and in danger of losing my part-time job because of my irresponsible behavior. I finally dropped out of school and then in a two-month period of time, I had seven car accidents and ruined three cars. I began losing friends who had been in my life since second grade. I became so powerless over my sexual behavior that I completely abandoned my own values and morals. At that time in my life, I felt that I belonged nowhere and had virtually no identity. I'd sleep with any man or boy who'd have me. My life was completely unmanageable and I was so desperate that I chose to be institutionalized for two months. But I didn't have any therapy or any program to follow there. In fact, my life *continued* to be out of control while I was hospitalized: I dealt drugs, had sexual contact with the male patients, and almost died after overdosing on drugs.

When my condition improved somewhat, I was released to a foster home. At that time, my sex addiction became even more nightmarish and overwhelming. On several occasions, I woke up in a filthy hotel room next to a man I didn't even know. When my foster parents finally threw me out and my own family took me back, I made a real effort to turn my life around. Almost immediately, though, I latched onto another man in an attempt to find a sense of security. But despite this new relationship, I was powerless to let go of the men I had been involved with in the past. I wanted all of the men I had known in my life to *always* want me. I couldn't bear the thought of any of them going away; I'd do *anything* to keep them in my life. At this point in time, I was emotionally numb; I could feel nothing but the constant dull ache of loneliness. When I was in twelfth grade, I transferred to another high school. My family tried to encourage me to put my life together again. At last, there was some stability in my life: I stayed with the same man for a whole year and finally succeeded in getting enough credits to graduate from high school. But even with this positive new start in life, feelings of powerlessness still overwhelmed me. I tried to harness my own will power in order to control my behavior, but my fantasies, flirtations, and obsessions always made me feel that I was destined to be one of the so-called "bad girls."

At the end of high school, I met another man. I was sure that this man was my knight on a white horse. The two of us went away to the same college together; for the first year, my life was fairly stable. But in my second year of college, my life was again unmanageable and dominated by my feelings of power-lessness. I entered into another relationship with an alcoholic man, then looked around to discover that I was losing friends and failing in school. I figured it must be time for a new begin-ning, so I left everything to go back to my parents' home and start all over again. Two months after I returned home, I was engaged to my "white knight"; eighteen months later we were married. But even before we celebrated our first anniversary, I left my husband for another man. My obsessions and fantasies became my only reality. Though I was three months pregnant at the time, I took a bus to another state in order to meet this man in the town where he worked. Each day for four weeks, I'd wait for him in his hotel room until he came home from work. But when it became clear to me that our relationship wouldn't work, I turned to this man's two best friends. I lugged my suitcase from room to room and in one night, I had sex with all three men. When I left the hotel later the same night and thought about my life, I broke down and cried. There I was— alone, pregnant, and in a strange town with nowhere to go. I checked into another hotel and stayed there alone for a few days, then called my parents and asked them to help me get back home.

When I got home, my husband and I moved back together and I entered therapy. But even with therapy, powerlessness continued to dominate my life; I had seven extramarital affairs in the next seven years. I also arranged clandestine meetings with new men I met. I arranged these meetings only to flirt and play games—to *pretend* that I had a relationship with a certain man. The relationships I *did* have were totally empty. My life was so unmanageable at times that I wasn't sure I'd even be able to take care of my family. I jumped from job to job. During the last extramarital affair I had, I didn't even care enough about myself to take precautions; consequently, I became pregnant again. I was carrying a child neither man in my life wanted. *My life was totally out of control.* During that time I had an abortion, even though it was completely against my personal beliefs to do so. I know that for the rest of my life I will carry with me the pain, sadness, and anguish of losing that child.

I realize that I talk about my past as if I lived in a vacuum, yet that's an accurate conceptualization of my life in those days. My addiction certainly compounded my feelings of being numb and cut off from others. All that time, of course, I *did* belong to a family and that family is an important part of my story. It is only through recovery and therapy that I have been able to "go back" to my family—*back to the core of my pain.*

I remember that when I was in sixth grade, my mother told me in great detail about her dissatisfactions with life. By the time I was in junior high, she was confiding in me about a variety of things: her sexual fantasies; the shame she felt about her sexual attitudes; her despair about her failing marriage; and her total lack of self-worth. In a sense, my mother related to me not as her child, but as her friend, her therapist, and her spouse: I felt locked into this unusual relationship because it represented the only intimacy I knew. I had no boundaries of my own and, as a result, my identity became totally enmeshed with my mother's identity. This childhood experience gave me an awareness of what a love/hate relationship is all about.

My father was a professional man and he was rarely home. I recall having very few one-to-one interactions with him during my childhood. I was always trying to get his approval; I tried to get him to like me in so many different ways. Everyone seemed to like *him,* so I always wondered what was wrong with *me* that I was unable to establish any kind of relationship with him. I used to dream about having the kind of father who'd hold me and reassure me that everything would be all right. Not long ago, I learned in a family therapy sesssion that my father had essentially rejected me when I was only four years old because he thought I was untruthful and incompetent. Looking back, I can see that I became a scapegoat in my family. I was frequently blamed for problems that affected individual family members as well as problems that affected the family as a whole. By working through the intense anger and grief I felt about my family background, I can now accept my past in the sense that I am no longer ruled by it. The reflection of my addiction can be seen in the mirror of my past, and this mirror has been an extremely useful tool in my recovery.

Since I began my recovery two years ago, I have developed a new sense of living, a new sense of hope, and a new sense of *myself.* My journey has been an incredibly tough one at times. When I began my work in the Program, I took a very basic step. I could see that my addiction was being fed by certain people, places, and situations. Bars, parties, and even certain *friends* seemed unsafe to me as I became more aware of what my addict was really getting high from. I even became uncomfortable with some regular daily activities, like going to the grocery store. I was so terribly afraid of men and the powerlessness I felt when I was around them. Most people are amazed to hear that there are withdrawal symptoms from sex addiction. When I finally chose recovery and stopped acting out, I felt so terribly empty inside. This feeling of emptiness scared me: How would I fill the emptiness? How could anything fill the deep and long-standing need I had to be cared about or even noticed? In attempting to answer these questions, I became friends with a slogan I still use in recovery: *Act As If.* In one way, I used to act as if *all the time* because I was a master of manipulation and deceit. But acting as if in recovery was an entirely different matter; the concept of acting as if was a useful tool that gave me a thread of hope that I could recover someday, too. I began to listen to the stories of others. As much as I was convinced that my story was the "worst" and that I was totally "hopeless," the ray of hope shed by my group helped me maintain my willingness to wait and *Act As If* I was recovering from my addiction.

Loneliness and isolation were still big traps for me early in recovery. Staying isolated from others, keeping "secrets" filled with shame, and other "wall-building" measures had been important parts of my active addiction. Slowly and cautiously, I began to let other people into my life. By choosing recovery, I also chose to know other people. To cleanse the deep shame within me was to share the "awful secrets" of my past. Early in recovery, I also chose to be celibate for several months. Even masturbation seemed unsafe and threatening to me at that time. I couldn't forget that when I was out of control, empty, and detached, sex was like a powerful and uncontrollable weapon. But as my recovery progressed, I realized that not all of my sexual feelings were addictive; some of the sexual feelings I had were based on mutual respect and they could give life-enhancing support to a healthy person. As more time passed, I realized that opposed to the sexual feelings that came only from my addict, I also have sexual feelings that are based on a spirit of sharing, giving, and nurturing. Gradually, I am finding the most appropriate place for sex in my life—a sharing between two equal people and a chance to honor and enjoy myself.

For the first time in my life, I could see where I ended and other people started. The word "boundary" became a valuable tool in recovery; for the first time, I could see myself as being separate from others. Whereas in the past, I never knew who to share myself with and who not to share myself with, I learned to develop a working sense of who I could and could not trust. In the same way, I also began to see that other people had boundaries of their own and rights to their own opinions and that I need not be threatened by that. My new awareness had some impact on my friendships: some people respected and celebrated my growth while other people walked out of my life because they were threatened by the changes in me. At the same time, my husband and I became increasingly aware of the challenges we were up against in our marriage. Each of us made a commitment to our individual Program and therapy, but we were still overwhelmed at times by the unhealthy aspects of our relationship. We came to see that some degree of separateness between people is essential to intimacy and that a loving relationship must be based on a fundamental equality of the two people involved.

As a result of my pain and discovery, my sexual values have evolved into solid convictions. I realize that I am not comfortable with sex outside of marriage; I am absolutely firm on that decision. Neither am I comfortable with flirtations of any kind. Flirtations feel manipulative to me now and feed into the feelings of shame that fuel my addiction. *Now I use my thoughts to keep myself grounded in reality, not to escape from it.* No longer are my fantasies filled with abuse or demeaning thoughts. Instead, my fantasies have become a support for the kind of love that nurtures the reality of a relationship. I have more respect for other people now and a sense of pride in myself instead of the old feelings of powerlessness and shame. I have consciously worked at "letting go" and I no longer try to be in control of everything. Now when I let go, I find a path toward serenity and an awareness of the choices I have rather than feelings of helplessness and loneliness. The emptiness I was left with after I chose to recover was soon filled with a wonderful new sense of spirituality. This spirituality gives me the opportunity to see that I have never been alone and never *will* be alone. My Higher Power has filled that emptiness to overflowing.

Now I know that I can live a *good life* with the help of: supportive people who teach me about giving and receiving; the Program and its many tools; a husband committed to his own recovery; and a Higher Power who loves me unconditionally and with gentleness. I no longer believe that the woman I used to be is the woman I am now; finally, we are separate. Now I am struck by how life-threatening my addiction really was and continues to be. The other thing that strikes me is that each year in my addiction was just another year, but each year in recovery is very special. I used to think about how difficult recovery was and how difficult it would be to start a new life. But now the changes I have made in my life are an integral part of my life and they seem very natural. I've learned to take risks and do things I never thought would be possible, and I've done these things with ease and confidence. When I was acting out sexually, I was so afraid of life. Now I turn my fear over to my Higher Power. These days I'm not just surviving life, *I'm really living it*.

Ken's Story

Recovery has helped me discard most of the negative things I learned within my family system.

(After twenty-six months in the Program; twenty-five months of sobriety.)

My childhood was filled with severe physical, sexual, and emotional abuse. When I was only four years old, someone performed oral sex on me; when I was eleven years old, I was forced to have sex with a forty-two-year-old woman. As a child, I was forced to chew and swallow the pages of a book to "learn respect" for them. Because of the physical abuse I suffered, I was always hiding the bruises on my body so that my playmates wouldn't see them. I believe that my home environment reinforced the negative self-image that led to my becoming a loner. Eventually, I became a sex addict and was totally out of control for the next twenty years. During those years, I survived two suicide attempts and spent more than a hundred thousand dollars on my sex addiction. Today I am a working professional, I am financially secure, and most important, I have peace of mind. I have now been sober for twenty-five months, thanks to my last two years in the Twelve Step Program and two years of weekly professional therapy.

I began acting out my sex addiction when I was in ninth grade. At that time, I started visiting houses of prostitution and pornographic movie theaters. I used this kind of acting-out behavior in a desperate attempt to "fix" my feelings of loneliness and sadness. The more lonely and sad I was, the more I'd act out; the more I acted out, the more I had to conceal my activities from others and the more necessary it was for me to be alone. My aloneness, in turn, reinforced my negative self-image. At that time in my life my self-image was so low that I felt I *deserved* the abuse I suffered. Already, I was caught up in a vicious and self-destructive cycle.

Through my family system, I somehow learned that I was a worthless individual who would never make positive or important contributions to the world. As time went on, my acting-out behaviors reinforced the necessity for me to isolate myself from other people. I got into a cycle of acting out in order to "fix" my loneliness. But after each incidence of acting out, I realized that I felt even lonelier than I had before. Despite the fact that acting out never "fixed" me or my feelings, I continued to do it. By the time I was in tenth grade, I was visiting prostitutes twice a week, reading lots of pornographic literature, masturbating, and attending pornographic movies.

After my wife and I got married, I'd always ask her to set the alarm to allow extra time for us to have sex before she left for work. Soon my wife and I were having sex four times a day; after awhile, she was so sore and uncomfortable that she had to consult with a doctor. In addition to the excessive sexual demands I made of my wife, I also demanded that she accompany me on my adventures to pornographic movie theatres, and I belittled her at every opportunity. Whenever my wife and I would drive anywhere in the car together, I'd choose a route where I knew we'd encounter streetwalkers. As we drove by these women, I'd berate my wife for her looks and point out women on the street who were particularly appealing to me. Every reference I made to a woman—even my wife—was sexual and hostile in nature.

My addiction eventually led to a complete lack of control. In fact, I believe that lack of control is one of the primary indicators of sex addiction. I first became painfully—and dramatically—aware of my lack of control one time when I was in a theatre watching a pornographic movie. Suddenly, the man seated next to me placed his hand on my belt buckle. Before I was able to refuse this man's advances, my addiction took control of me and I allowed this stranger to pull my pants down to my ankles and perform oral sex on me. What if the police had caught and arrested me? What if I had contracted a venereal disease during this brief and completely absurd encounter? These are important and rational questions, certainly, but they aren't the kinds of questions I took the time to answer—or even consider—as the power of my addiction took over my body and my mind. Due to my frequent visits to massage parlors, I was once visited at my home by members of the vice squad. Luckily, my wife was not home at the time. The investigators interviewed me and tried to get me to testify against certain prostitutes I knew. On one hand, I was *afraid* of the investigators; on the other hand, I was afraid of possible reprisals from the hookers and pimps I knew. What was I to do? *I was completely out of control.*

I started getting bored with massage parlors and instead began paying for sexually explicit phone conversations with "stars" of pornographic films. This activity seemed to work well for me; I'd share a fantasy on the phone and masturbate as we spoke. I even *taped* these conversations so that I'd get more mileage from them. My wife discovered what I was doing when she inadvertently opened the bills containing credit card receipts from these specialized phone services. Despite the fact that I knew she was terribly hurt by this discovery, I didn't curtail my activities; instead, I continued making my fantasy calls, completely powerless over my addiction.

Later on, I began placing and answering ads in "swinger" magazines. I was taking an enormous risk whenever I'd offer my address and phone number to strangers in responding to their ads. Regardless of the risk, I took it because I discovered that without this personal information, no one would even *respond* to me. My intense fear that someone might try to blackmail me was less powerful than my addiction. One time I answered an ad placed in a swinger magazine by phone and immediately made plans to visit the couple who had placed the ad. In order to make this visit, I lied to my wife and to my employer, drove hundreds of miles in a single day, and spent three hours being sexual with the couple who had placed the ad. I felt as though I was in a trance throughout the entire trip and encounter; it wasn't until I was driving home that night that I really thought about what I had done. It was then I finally realized that my life was completely out of control and that I was really at the mercy of my addiction. *I had actually driven seven hundred miles that day just to have another sexual experience that left me feeling even more sadness and loneliness.*

Then one day, I was asked to account for some long-distance phone calls I had placed from work. (I had done this in order to set up distant sexual encounters.) It was becoming increasingly difficult to explain my behavior; I had to be very imaginative and inventive with my lies. As my addiction escalated and I went in search of new and different "highs," I decided that I wanted to have sex with a transvestite—a man dressed as a woman. When my addiction has control of me, any fear I have is *insignificant* by comparison. At these times, I have a false sense of courage that is really a loss of reasoning ability. I remember being so completely out of control in seeking this new kind of sexual experience that I willingly drove to the worst part of town in a major metropolitan area and walked into an apartment that had just been broken into—in fact, the door had been ripped off its hinges and was still on the floor. A man dressed as a woman kept telling me that "she" was a man. This strange new experience was thrilling for me until I discovered it was, in fact, an elaborate setup to rob me. Through the entryway to this apartment came three large men carrying knives. As soon as I saw them, I broke out of that apartment building and I ran—stark naked—down a busy main thoroughfare. Try finding clothes in the middle of the night before returning home; try explaining to your wife how you managed to lose certain pants, shoes, or shirts she knows you own. I was completely at the mercy of my addiction yet my addict was desperate for an even stronger "high." Eventually I decided that I needed to add some variety to the things I was already doing, so I got involved with activities I'd never been involved with before. I started going to bathhouses where adult males had anonymous sex with each other. I knew that I was taking a tremendous risk in visiting these places—a risk that involved the possibility of contracting sexually-transmitted diseases. But I didn't care because I was totally out of control. I'd offer myself to all patrons at these bathhouses; it was just luck that I never contracted venereal disease.

I always traveled alone, so out of town business trips presented very real problems for me. During the flight toward my destination, I'd frantically flip through the yellow pages in my mind, visualizing what the ads for massage parlors and "personal escort" services would look like in the town I'd be visiting. Then when I got to my destination, I'd act out all night long until it was time to go to work the next day. I never slept during these out of town trips; instead, I'd sleep during the flight home. Then once I was home, I'd sometimes have to take two or three days off from work just to recover.

Whenever I was acting out, I'd spend an enormous amount of time looking for sex, fantasizing, and justifying why I should or shouldn't act out again. Eventually I was forced to become even more inventive with my lies because I had used the same stories too many times in explaining my behavior. People began to catch me in my lies and I could tell that they were having difficulty believing my excuses.

Of course, my addiction began to interfere with my work and with my marriage (I'd even act out during my lunch hours.) In time, I preferred acting out with strangers to being with my wife. I was taking virtually all of our family grocery money and using it to act out in some way. Family vacations were out of the question because we were always so much in debt from my addiction. At one point, I had charged the limit on several credit card accounts and had two mortgages on my house. My self-defeating cycle began: I'd pay off my enormous credit card balances with a debt consolidation loan, then use the credit cards again. I'd also take out additional loans to pay off consolidation loans and also to clear my credit card balances once again. For a long time, I was making monthly payments of more than one thousand dollars just on my credit card accounts. Finally I got myself and my family into one hundred thousand dollars of debt—"addiction debt," I call it. This addiction debt was more than twice what I had spent on my brand new home! I was unable to sleep. If I wasn't worrying about money, I was wondering how I was going to act out next. What new adventure could I try? I believe that when we are acting out, we sex addicts constantly seek new and more intense highs.

I attempted suicide twice and was nearly successful each time. Following each attempt, I was admitted to the mental ward of a hospital. One time I even *left* a mental ward so that I could act out. Then after I had been treated for manic-depression for six months, a psychologist finally diagnosed my problem as compulsive sexual behavior. At that time, however, few therapists knew much about sex addiction and the concept of a Twelve Step Program for this kind of addiction was brand new and being talked about in professional circles for the very first time.

Then one day I saw an ad in a newspaper for a program specializing in the treatment of female sex addicts. At this point, I desperately wanted some help. I realized just how unmanageable my life was and how out of control I had become. I actually thought to myself that this program might be a particularly good one for me because it would give me an opportunity to act out with female sex addicts. What could be better, I reasoned, than to get involved with a female who was as out of control as I was? At the same time, I wanted to stop the craziness that was ruling my life, so I called the number listed in the ad. A male therapist answered the phone; in his role as a therapist, he offered to help me. But he suggested that the first thing I could do was to become a member of a Twelve Step group for sex addicts. Then he gave me a mailing address for a specific Twelve Step group. (Unlike now, there was no hot line phone support then.) After three long weeks, someone from the group got back to me and Twelve-Stepped me. By the time I was Twelve-Stepped, I was reaching out with all my heart. I sensed that this was my last chance.

At my first Twelve Step meeting, other people in the group did "mini" First Steps to help those of us who were newcomers to the Program. This helped me see that everyone in the group shared the same affliction—everyone in the group had the same story, albeit with different words, different circumstances, and different degrees of severity. For the first time in my life, I realized there were other people just like me. Finally, I knew people I could talk with about all those things I'd never been able to tell *anyone*. One of the first things I did after attending my first Twelve Step meeting was to obtain a sponsor. Sponsorship is important in many ways—not the least of which is the opportunity to have a relationship with someone from the group that goes beyond attending group meetings. A sponsor can guide a person in working his or her Program and, believe me, *the Program is work*. The Twelve Step Program is difficult in terms of interpreting the full intention of Twelve simple steps. During my first few weeks in the Program, I wrote and rewrote my First Step several times. Each time I wrote my First Step, more details of my life and my acting-out behaviors were revealed to me. My feelings really began to surface when I did a First Step with my sponsor present.

Next, I tried to establish some boundaries for myself— "boundaries of sanity," I call them. Basically, these boundaries are controls I place on myself, parameters for my behavior. I have found that when I stay within my boundaries, I don't act out and I am able to maintain my sobriety. I try to remember that for me, breaking a boundary is acting out and that when I ignore my boundaries, I eventually have a slip. I was quite willing to establish boundaries around *most* of my inappropriate behaviors. "Most" is an important word here. At first, I didn't want to give up my visits to massage parlors because that behavior was the most powerful and dominant form of acting out for me. I felt that I could comfortably exclude all other acting-out behaviors from my boundaries; I felt confident that I could survive as long as I could visit a massage parlor now and then. But, then, much to my disappointment, I discovered that the most important boundary to set is the one that eliminates the most powerful and dominant acting-out behavior.

At first I did not set a boundary excluding visits to massage parlors—in some ways, I think that was a way of my addiction indicating to me that it still had firm control of me. But then, several members of my Twelve Step group finally forced the issue when they said that they would not support me unless I completely excluded visits to massage parlors with my boundaries. Establishing this particular boundary was one of the most difficult things I have ever done because I was fully aware of what it would mean to me: I'd have to completely give up something that I had always counted on to give me a "fix." I acted out the very same night I established this boundary for myself; but with the help of my Twelve Step group and professional therapy, I have stayed sober from that time right up to this day.

Recovery involves asking for help and reaching out to others—actions most people who are addicted to sex are not at all familiar with. Finally I have broken the isolation I have experienced for so many years. I no longer have to hide my activities when I'm sober because now I have nothing to hide.

This is one of the most important things that we sex addicts can do—break our self-imposed isolation from other people. I find that I cannot unjustly criticize myself as much when I'm not isolated. For me, "isolation" always produced a feeling of being "alone," a feeling of not being wanted or loved. Recovery has helped me discard most of the negative things I learned within my family system.

As I progressed in my recovery and curtailed my acting-out behaviors, I realized that my thoughts were no longer focused on sex as they had been when I was so completely out of control with my addiction. My fuzzy, irrational thinking began to vanish, and I found that sex didn't *have* to be an issue in every decision I made.

The Twelve Step Program helps me in the following ways: it keeps me off the streets; it teaches me to reach out when I'm in need; it teaches me how to establish boundaries; it rewards me when I stay *within* those boundaries; it comforts me when I make mistakes; and it teaches me to break my isolation, enhance my self-worth, and bring spirituality into my Program and my life. At first it was very difficult for me to bring spirituality into my life because my parents had always forced religion on me. I have since found that spirituality is important primarily because I can't work my Program in a vacuum. I find that I need spirituality in the same way I need other people. Spirituality was difficult for me even though in my recovery it was obvious to anyone that God was with me in strength, every step of the way.

I certainly felt the presence of God the time I was in New York City and planning to explore the area around Times Square. At the time, I'd been sober for about three months, so I told myself that I'd just casually look at what some of the local "attractions" were. I'd seen an ad in the paper about a live performance in the area where one could actually watch people engage in sexual activity. Just thinking about this opportunity created an irresistable urge; I had not yet experienced this kind of activity. As I stepped outside my motel room in New York that night, planning to attend this performance, the streets were completely dry and rain was not in the forecast. Then, without warning, a heavy rainstorm began. Not wanting my plans to be ruined by the weather, I bought an umbrella in the motel gift shop. Then when I opened the door to go outside, the rain suddenly stopped and I grumbled to myself about not needing an umbrella. Then, just as I stepped outside, the rain came down even harder than it had the first time. Even with my umbrella, I was completely soaked in just a matter of seconds. Finally, I gave up and returned to my room for the night. Shortly after that, the rain stopped and the streets dried.

One of the most memorable spiritual experiences I had came after my first year of sobriety. I was lying in a hospital bed and for some reason (I now believe it was my Higher Power), I felt that I wanted to contact a Presbyterian minister I had not seen or heard from for over fourteen years. I had avoided this clergy-man for so many years because religion had always been forced on me and I resisted discussing it with anyone. I finally got information on the church he was serving after making several long-distance calls trying to track him down. I called him and was told that he was gone for the weekend, so I left a message for him. I certainly didn't expect to hear from this man until the following week but, strangely enough, he called me back *within ten minutes*. He said he not only *remembered* me, but had always known that I'd reach out to him someday. He invited me to spend a weekend with him. The weekend I spent with this clergyman was truly a "spiritual awakening" for me. I told him the complete story about my sex addiction and asked him some questions that would be difficult for *anyone* to answer—questions like, "Why would God love me after the things I have done?" I was "drawn" to this minister's church no less than five times during my weekend visit with him. The church had a strength and a beauty that overwhelmed me. It housed a large pipe organ and when I heard that organ music, the deeply rich tones seemed to go directly through my skin and into my heart. I was simply overwhelmed. I started to weep at the same time my heart was saying "You may come in now." From that day on, spirituality has been an important part of my Program and, therefore, an important part of my life.

My recovery focuses on the Twelve Step Program as well as professional therapy. Now I realize that my addiction was an inappropriate medication I prescribed for myself in an effort to lessen the pain I suffered inside. Professional therapy is helping me get to the source of this pain so that it can be identified and worked through. I've now paid off most of my "addiction debt." Now my wife and I have a very good relationship and we are getting closer all the time. I am respected in my profession now and, more important, I respect *myself*. Now I really look *forward* to life. I am no longer a lonely person; now I reach out to bring activities and friendship into my life. As I walk forward with a positive self-image and with feelings of shame behind me, I know that I will always be a sex addict; but I also know that I am a *recovering* sex addict.

Mark's Story

...it's never too late to recover.

(After thirty months in the Program; twenty-eight months of sobriety.)

I was the youngest of four children born to parents of limited means. Even as a very young child, I spent most of my time alone or with older people. I remember my childhood, my adolescence, and even most of my adulthood as terribly lonely. When I was very young, an older neighbor boy sexually abused me. I remember that he took me aside and asked me to perform oral sex on him. I don't believe there was any coercion involved because I actually enjoyed being singled out and receiving attention from an older child. At the time, I didn't have any idea what was happening. A few years later, I experimented with masturbation with some boys my own age. Then when I was a young teenager, I was sexually abused by two older men.

Over a period of several years, I was sexually involved with one of these men. In fact, we continued to have a sexual relationship until I graduated from high school and he left town to take a job in another state. I missed this man when he left, but also felt a great sense of relief because I always had very strong feelings of guilt about our relationship. During the time I was acting out sexually with him, I was very active in my church. In the course of my religious studies there, I came to the decision that the kind of sexual behavior I was engaging in with this man conflicted with Biblical teachings. I had feelings of shame about the relationship, but I felt sure that this was just a phase in my life and I would "grow out of it." After all, I knew that I was attracted to girls. I had girl friends, I was attentive to them, and I had every intention of getting married someday.

After high school, I entered military service and subsequently had very few opportunities to be sexual with men. On the rare occasions when I *did* have a sexual encounter with a man, I was consumed with guilt and fear that someone in authority would find out about it. I think this is when my sense of "powerlessness" first hit me. Each time I engaged in sexual activity with a man, I vowed it was the "last time," but my resolve held only until the next opportunity. Throughout my years in the service, I continued attending church services regularly and when I was discharged, I even considered studying for the ministry. At that time, I dated only women who shared my religious beliefs. Of course, I never dared tell these women that I was having sex with men in order to deal with my feelings of loneliness and isolation. Sexual encounters with men provided momentary relief from the pain I felt, but these encounters always left me with almost unbearable feelings of emptiness.

Later on, I began my career in the human service field and essentially dedicated my life to helping other people. The work was demanding and even though I found some satisfaction in it, I always came back to feeling that I was somehow "not good enough." Periodically, I'd feel absolutely worthless. And those were the times I'd seek out sexual partners in public places like parks, rest rooms, and shopping centers. I knew that I was taking an enormous risk by engaging in this kind of activity, *but I couldn't stop*. After each encounter, I'd struggle with even stronger feelings of shame, guilt, and worthlessness.

During the time in my life when I was acting out sexually with men, I met the woman who became my wife. For the first few months of our marriage, I was able to put my "acting out" behavior aside. But as much as I loved my wife, I was unable to suppress my addiction for very long. I distanced myself from her by staying late at work and spending time in public places where I knew I had the best chance of meeting men I could act out with sexually. The situation worsened when we had

276

children: *any stress or disappointment* I encountered as a professional person, a husband, or a father justified acting out. On the other hand, any "honor" I received or any sense of accomplishment I felt in any area of my life also justified acting out.

When I look back, I now realize that throughout my life, many people have accepted me and sought out my friendship. But back when I was acting out, I always felt so *lonely*. I felt lonely in a crowd and I felt lonely when I was with one other person. I discovered that seeking anonymous sex with men in public places was the only way I could get some relief from my profound loneliness. What little self-control I *did* have soon eroded, and I started taking even greater risks. Seeking anonymous sexual partners became a way of life for me. I finally went beyond the limitations I had set for my acting-out behavior when I *paid* for sex. Then it wasn't long before I had a real *need* to pay for sex and began seeking out young male prostitutes in pornographic bookstores. The sexual encounters I had with these young men were never satisfying, yet I spent more and more of my time seeking out prostitutes in a desperate effort to fill the emptiness I felt within. Although I never spent a lot of *money* for sex, I did spend a lot of *time* juggling household funds to cover up the money I *did* spend on sex. I hid spare change until I had saved up enough to go to a pornographic bookstore. But soon, paying for sex was no longer enough. I began taking even greater risks in order to meet and have sex with men in parks or in the toilet stalls of rest rooms in shopping centers.

Finally, I was discovered and apprehended in a prominent public place. Because of my profession, there was a great deal of publicity about the incident and as a consequence, I lost my job. *My life was shattered* and the pain and shame I felt were unbearable. Suicide seemed to me the best solution for my problems, but my family and my therapist intervened and eventually deterred me. In my despair, I discovered the Twelve Steps and a Twelve Step group. I am absolutely convinced that a Higher Power came into my life with these discoveries. I had just turned sixty at the time, and I wept for all the years I had been alone and fighting my addiction. Other addicts in the group helped me understand that it's *never* too late to recover. They also helped me believe that I *deserved* to recover.

In recovery, *I am a changed person*—my group members remind me of this. I am much less depressed now and the feelings of emptiness I experienced for most of my sixty-two plus years are virtually gone. I am nearly content with my life now. Even with the important changes in my life, there are still moments of compulsiveness, but my friends in the Program help me stay grounded in my sobriety. Sobriety is rewarding and fulfilling; it brings joy to my life, intimacy to my marriage, and continuing spiritual growth. I believe that none of these blessings would have been possible without the loving help of my fellow group members and my ongoing *participation*—not just attendance—in a Twelve Step Program. I can't say life is easy; *I can say life is getting better*. I still feel profound loneliness at times, but I work through those feelings by calling another addict. I have learned to accept that I am a good and worthwhile person. Each day I work the Program, my recovery becomes stronger. But I am also aware that my old life of compulsive acting out is only a "slip" away. I maintain serenity and sobriety one day at a time with my Program and with the grace of God.

Liam's Story

*I no longer travel this life alone; now I travel
with many genuine friends and one very powerful Protector.*

(After three years in the Program; three years of sobriety.)

I believe that my life was shaped by the negative attitudes my
parents had about sex. As an example, one of my earliest
memories relating to my sexuality involved waking up one
morning with a wonderful sensation that I later learned was
called a "wet dream." When I told my father about what had
happened and how I felt, he made me feel so ashamed. I also
believe that I was physically, verbally, and perhaps even sexually abused by my mother. I have vivid recollections of her
obsession with the functions of elimination; she sometimes
shamed me and my younger brothers and sisters in the process
of toilet training us.

By the time I was four or five years old, I was fascinated
with the idea of girls and women urinating. When I was five
years old, I remember demanding that a young neighbor girl
"wet her pants"; in fact, I threatened to hit her with a pickaxe
from the garage unless she was willing to do what I asked.
When I was in kindergarten, I became sexually aroused
whenever a girl in class accidentally wet her pants. Even at that
early age, I was compulsive about trying to catch a glimpse of
girls' underwear. As a young child, I associated loss of bladder
control and exposed underwear with deep feelings of shame; in
terms of my own behavior, I was very anxious about these
things. When the teachers at the private school I attended
warned us about the sin of having impure thoughts, I began to
think about the *horrible* sin I was committing every day of my
life by having thoughts about urination and underwear. But
these deep feelings of shame actually *fed* my fantasies.

When I was about eleven years old, my five-year-old sister developed a bladder infection that lasted for more than six months. During that period of time, she frequently wet her pants. At this time, I was still fascinated with urination and discovered that I was sexually aroused whenever I *thought* about the next time she'd wet her pants. My arousal intensified when I felt her wet underpants. After I did this, I always felt so ashamed; I really believed that it was a sin to be fascinated with these things. But in spite of the shame I felt, I'd carefully etch the details of each incident in my memory so that I'd be able to use it to help me fantasize later on. Of course it's impossible to remember my physiological responses when I was aroused in this way—I think I probably had an erection. I know that I didn't masturbate at that time in my life because I was just too ashamed to do anything like that.

My sister subsequently had an operation to correct her bladder condition, but her problems with incontinence continued—and so did my expectation that I'd be aroused each time she wet her pants. Sometimes I'd even tickle her or try to scare her, just hoping she'd wet her pants. In fact this did happen on one occasion; I still remember the feelings of intense excitement and shame I struggled with afterwards. As disturbing and confusing as these feelings were for me, I never confided in my parents about my feelings because doing so did not seem safe to me. My parents never discussed anything related to sexuality and in retrospect, I feel angry that they never checked out what was going on with me regarding my developing obsession.

By the time I was a teenager, I had little more than memories left relating to my fascination with women and urination. But these memories were very graphic and powerful. (In fact, to this day, I can recall in vivid detail each incident from my childhood that aroused me sexually.) I attended a private high school and quickly became obsessed with my studies and with athletics. I was a good athlete and a good student as well. In fact, I channeled all of my sexual energies into athletics and academics. But at night when I'd try to study, my mind constantly wandered to thoughts of women, their underwear, and urination. I continued to try to catch glimpses of girls' underwear as they sat at their desks in classrooms and when I studied in the school library, I'd always position myself so that I'd be able to hear the toilets flush in the rest room next door. I'd become sexually aroused whenever I saw an attractive woman teacher go into the rest room.

I had my first real date several weeks after graduating from high school. Although I enjoyed being with this young woman, I was too shy and frightened to ask her out ever again. I attended a competitive university with an excellent academic reputation and as I soon as I got there, I felt a great deal of academic pressure. The school was co-educational, but the ratio of men to women was about five to one. While I was in college, I was attracted to a very pretty woman of my own ethnic background. As much as I wanted to get to know this woman, I was too shy to ever let her know of my interest in her. I attribute this reticence on my part to my feelings of low self-esteem and the shamefulness I felt about my sexuality. As fond as I was of this woman during the four years we went to school together, I never once asked her for a date. This inaction on my part perhaps symbolizes the saddest part of my story: there are so many people I never got to know as a young man because of my feelings of shame and worthlessness. I was rather withdrawn, even with my friends. I rarely disclosed my true feelings or had intimate conversations with people I was supposedly close to. During four years of college I had only two dates, both arranged for me by someone else.

Early in my college years, I began to wonder if there was a problem with my sexuality because of the things that did and did not arouse me. From my extensive reading and research, I learned that there were, indeed, other people who were interested in the same things that excited me. Soon my interest became my quest—to find out what was wrong with me by reading books. Now I'm convinced that my quest for information and self-understanding at this time in my life actually motivated me to major in psychology.

When I got to college, I discovered that when I studied in certain areas near the rest rooms, I could actually hear women urinating. Even though I felt it was shameful and perhaps even *sinful* to sit there and allow myself to be excited by these sounds, I continued to do it. I even found that newspaper advice columns were a source of sexual arousal for me, particularly when they carried letters dealing with the subject of urination. Sunday editions of newspapers were especially arousing to me because they often carried articles and ads relating to incontinence as well as photo ads of undergarments. I tried so hard to avoid looking at these advice columns and ads in the newspaper, but I always gave in to the temptation, then felt so shameful I'd proceed to punish myself for the rest of the day. I became more and more aware of my problems with sexuality. While taking a class with a clergyman who had counseling experience, I seriously considered sharing my problems with him, but could never quite bring myself to do it. I graduated from college with my secret intact and with the belief that I was a "pervert."

After college, I went overseas to continue my international studies. Even though I had been unable to initiate a relationship with a woman in America, I hoped that maybe I'd be able to have successful relationships with foreign women. In the developing country I worked in, I'd occasionally encounter women who were urinating in the fields. I was aroused by the sight of these women urinating and I'd stop and watch them whenever possible.

I returned to the United States planning to attend graduate school, but fearing the pressure I knew I'd encounter there. In time, my fear turned to depression and I finally consulted with

a psychiatrist in order to get some help in making a final decision about graduate school. Finally, I told this psychiatrist about
my shameful obsessive thoughts and he told me to stop thinking
about those things. *But that was exactly the problem; I couldn't
stop thinking about those things!* I spent hours each day searching in libraries for literature on urination. My head ached with
shame and self-hate. I was terribly lonely and lived in a succes-
sion of shabby, unsafe rooming houses because I felt that I
didn't deserve anything better. Then one day, I found blood in
my urine. My addiction even followed me to the urologist's
office: as I sat waiting for the doctor, I suddenly realized that
I was straining to overhear a female patient discuss her problems
with the doctor. At this point in my life, my nights were filled
with dreams of my sister and other women wetting their pants.
Sometimes I even wet the bed as I was dreaming. I was out of
control and at my lowest point ever; it was no coincidence that
I was also very lonely and had very low self-esteem. I knew
I'd never be able to have a real relationship with a woman. I
was tormented by thoughts that someday I'd be in bed with a
woman I cared about, discover I was sexually impotent, and
wet the bed. Then she'd know what a pervert I was, leave me,
and I'd be isolated and alone again.

As time passed, I spent more and more of my time searching
for books that would feed my addiction. When I discovered
some so-called "soft-core porn" books on "water sports," I was
overjoyed. I was delighted that a whole new world of vivid
fantasies was opening up to me and giving me some subtle
messages that it was okay to be aroused by urination.

My obsession with the idea of living overseas returned when
I was offered another work opportunity there—another job that
involved a great deal of pressure and responsibility. I took the
job and shortly thereafter I was again visiting libraries and
bookstores, compulsively searching for material that would
arouse me. As it turned out, the kind of material I was seeking

was not available overseas; this time I felt lonely, worthless, and insecure with my sexuality while I was there.

Throughout my life, I had assumed that my self-worth was based on my good deeds and accomplishments. I believe that I learned this from my father, who was a workaholic; the lesson I learned from him was reinforced through my own work experiences. My compulsiveness about work actually had a very powerful hold on me, but still my sexual addiction did not go away.

When I was in my late twenties, I had my second relationship with a woman. I wanted this new relationship to work out, but I was terribly afraid that this woman would want to be sexual with me and would then find out about my obsession. Entering into a new relationship, I also had a terrible fear that I wouldn't be stimulated by "normal" sexual things and that I would, in fact, be impotent. I decided to consult a therapist about my fears. After I told him about my life and my sexual history, he suggested that I read the Big Book of Alcoholics Anonymous and substitute the words "sexual behavior" wherever the text referred to "drinking." Even after reading the book the way he suggested and consulting with him again, I found it very difficult to think of myself as a sex addict.

Nevertheless, I finally took my therapist's suggestion and attended a Twelve Step meeting. As I sat at that first meeting, I was angry to think that I was giving up an evening when I could be relaxing at home instead. But I found that both my embarrassment and my shame actually lessened as I described my thoughts and behaviors to the group. It was very difficult to hear other people in the group tell their stories. I wondered how I could possibly get the help and support I needed by listening to them recount their pain, shame, and agony. At first I didn't make many phone calls to other members of the group. I told people in the group that I wouldn't feel comfortable calling them for help because of the lack of privacy in my housing situation; the real reason I didn't want to make those calls was that I didn't want to "bother" people.

I continued to be skeptical of the Twelve Steps, even after I began attending meetings regularly. I had always been told that the Twelve Steps were really a spiritual program. To me, the Twelve Step concept sounded like a "quick fix," and it brought back negative memories of my religious training. But with the help of the group, I was able to set my boundaries: I would avoid reading things that aroused me—material in commercial bookstores and certain sections of the newspaper. But because much of my acting out was in the form of obsessive thinking, it was very difficult for me to fully identify all of my acting-out activity early in my recovery. Finally I did my First Step in the group. I told people about my powerlessness, my shame, and the unmanageability of my life. Of course I was very nervous about doing this—I was afraid that people in the group would confront me for not being specific enough about my behavior and for not disclosing the most shameful things I had thought and done. But somehow I managed to work through my fear about sharing with others. In the process, I was able to convince myself and my "brothers" in recovery that I am a sex addict. When I accepted that fact myself, I felt as if a massive weight had been lifted from my shoulders.

I decided to tell my girl friend about my sex addiction. I was terribly afraid she'd reject me as soon as I told her the truth, but I didn't want to keep secrets from her any longer either. After I told her my story she told me—much to my surprise and delight—that she still accepted and supported me. But as I went through the anxiety and pain of early recovery during the next three months, my girl friend made it clear to me that she didn't wish to continue having an exclusive relationship with me. I felt sad, lonely, and abandoned; there were times when I desperately wanted to act out sexually—go to a pornographic bookstore and lose myself and my feelings there. But this time

I didn't act out because I knew that I had a helpful and supportive group of people to share with during this struggle of mine. The group helped me acknowledge my fears and express them and I managed to stay sober. I subsequently decided not to accept a challenging position overseas that had been offered to me. Despite the fact that I had participated in therapy and in the Twelve Step group in order to *accept* this assignment, I could see that my own recovery had just begun at this point. Because of that, I decided not to leave. Although this choice was very painful for me, it was an extremely important part of my recovery, particularly in terms of my accepting and working the Second and Third Steps. I began to view recovery in a new way: I no longer thought of it as representing things I was giving up; I thought of it as something gentle and loving I could do for myself. My parents and my colleagues put a great deal of pressure on me to return to my work overseas. It was very hard *not* to do this, but I finally decided that my recovery was much more important than running away again. I finally realized that I had to help *myself* before I could help others.

At this point in my recovery, I began to recognize some of the aspects of my life that I believe strongly influenced my sexual development. I finally understood how my family and my social environment erroneously taught me to ignore and even *deny* my natural feelings and instincts—including my sexuality. When I saw how I had been abused as a child, I went through a period of grieving. After the grieving, I made an effort to take better care of myself. I took more responsibility for my own life and became much less dependent on my family. Then as each month passed in recovery, I gained more trust in the group members and began to share my innermost feelings and thoughts with people I was learning to trust. I joined a new group and asked someone in that group to be my sponsor. The relationship I have with my sponsor has helped me so much in recovery.

After some time in recovery, my intense feelings of fear and inferiority regarding women subsided and I even had an intimate relationship with a woman. This relationship was very enriching, but sadly—and against my wishes—it recently ended after we had been together for more than two years. I still get very tense and anxious about sex. When I came to the Program, I had not yet engaged in sexual intercourse. In fact, it is only recently, within this first intimate relationship, that I have been sexual in ways other than hugging and kissing. Any form of sexuality beyond those activities was always terrifying for me to consider because I always held on to the self-defeating and powerful belief that I would be impotent because of my addiction and my feelings of shame about sexuality. My therapist confronted me with the facts of my life and urged me to become more aware of myself, my needs, and my body. He also said that I needed to learn to love myself and appreciate my body. He suggested that I might consider masturbating occasionally in order to learn to feel okay about my sexuality. At first I discovered that taking time to do this was at least as difficult as taking time to meditate. Also, because of my religious background, I found it very difficult to give myself permission to do some of the things the therapist suggested I do. Even now, when I'm being sexual, I still become quite tense; tension, in turn, affects my ability to have an orgasm.

Even now, under relatively normal circumstances, I am sometimes unable to ejaculate. There is, however, one ironic exception to my problem: when I am extremely tense, I sometimes ejaculate *without any stimulation at all*. In some ways, this irony symbolizes the incongruity that we sex addicts know so well. Early in my recovery, I feared that my sexual dysfunction would always be with me, but now I feel much more hopeful. In recovery, I'm learning that it will be possible for me to experience an orgasm, sexual fulfillment, *and* healthy sexuality besides. For me, the key to all this is learning what

287

it is I want, giving myself permission to be sexual, and learning to become more relaxed about my sexuality.

My life today is not perfect; I am not forever "cured." Sometimes I'm still filled with shame and sometimes my addictive urges return while I'm reading the newspaper or spending time with women. Other days I feel terribly lonely and wonder if I'll ever have an intimate relationship with a woman again. When I feel this way, the grace of my Higher Power and the members of my group help me avoid a slip. These two sources of support have helped me maintain two years of sobriety while enhancing my self-esteem and giving me peace of mind.

Lately I have come to realize that I still am patronizing in the way I treat women. When I was in a healthy relationship, my addict wanted me to look at other women. In fact, I have come to realize that I have a core addict that goes much deeper than sex—an addict that tries to inject self-doubt and self-hatred into almost everything I think and do. I found that in order to work my Program effectively, I had to put some distance between myself and my family and I had to put my career plans on hold. I now realize that I am—by nature—a workaholic. Now I realize that it is sometimes important for me to distance myself from people who only do, do, do, and never take time to pause and reflect. With the help of my group and my Higher Power, I am moving toward a more spiritual existence. While I am still concerned about politics, social justice, and poverty, I realize that there are other struggles in my life and in recovery that I must work on. If I ultimately decide to continue on in a career in the human services, *taking care of myself must come first*. This means taking time for meditation, prayer, maintaining a journal, accepting those things in my life I cannot change, and applying the principles of the Twelve Steps in all areas of my life.

Gradually, I am preparing myself for another intimate relationship. I am taking some time to grieve the end of my last relationship and I'm also learning to be more comfortable with my sexuality. Finally I realize that I will need to be clearer about what I need and want from an intimate relationship and what kind of partner I would like to have as well. In order to do this, I know that I'll need to take some risks: I will need to approach, spend time with, get to know, and learn to be comfortable in the company of women who I am interested in.

At this stage in my recovery, I finally know the difference between being religious and being spiritual; I try to let go of the former and embrace the latter. Turning my will and my life over to my Higher Power once seemed so frightening—a tremendous and questionable sacrifice. Now *turning it over* represents to me the end of death and the beginning of life—a way to let go of the feelings of shame as well as the illusion of control. I now see my God as a gentle and compassionate being who is waiting to be there for me. To know Him, all I need to do is let go. The spiritual Steps (Two, Three, Seven, and Eleven) represent the most significant elements of my recovery at this time. I find that spirituality is freeing and liberating, and it offers me the opportunity to serve, to love, to receive forgiveness, to be truly human, and to experience peace. I am very grateful to my Higher Power and my group for these things. *I no longer travel this life alone; now I travel with many genuine friends and one very powerful Protector.*

Alvin's Story

Now I know that it isn't what happens to me but what I do with it that makes the real difference in my life.

(After twenty-eight months in the Program; six months of sobriety.)

My name is Alvin. I am a sex addict. Several years after I was ordained a minister, I discovered I was a sex addict. I'd like to share what my life was like before that discovery, how I got into the Twelve Step Fellowship, and what my life is like now. As far back as I can remember, I have been a lonely, scared person filled with shame. Very early in my life, I discovered that there were two ways I could successfully avoid reality: perfectionism and sexual preoccupation. Each of these avoidance techniques led me to a secret world that offered refuge from the pain of reality. After a time, these two secret worlds were the only reality I knew. I believed that if only I could achieve absolute perfection in my work, then either I would get all the sex I wanted as a "reward" for my professional achievements or my preoccupation with sex would simply disappear.

The first stage of my sex addiction lasted from childhood throughout my college days. During those years, I masturbated at least once a day and often many more times than that. I liked pornography, but never purchased it. When I was still living at home, I secretly used the pornographic materials that other family members had purchased and stashed away in what they assumed were good hiding places. I also searched for sexual stimulation in family and women's magazines I found around the house, in newspapers, and on television. I remember once when I was in tenth grade, I spent an entire Sunday afternoon masturbating in my room as I looked at some pornographic magazines that belonged to my brothers. I'd spend *hours* in

291

front of the television watching for something—anything—my addict could get high on.

My addiction intensified after I was ordained. I realized that as a minister, I had a position that commanded respect and trust; my addict proceeded to use that respect and trust in a number of seductive, manipulative, and abusive ways. For example, in counseling situations and as a "friend of the family," I crossed sexual boundaries with many women in the congregation I served. After I had established my career in the ministry, I began buying my own pornographic books and magazines and started attending X-rated movies. I always did these things with intense fear that I'd be seen by someone who knew me. Each time I bought a pornographic magazine or attended an X-rated film, I promised myself that it was *the last time. But this behavior continued.* In fact, on several occasions I "needed" pornography so much that I bought it right in the neighborhood where I worked. By doing this I was, of course, taking enormous risks with my reputation, my career, and the well-being of my family. But my addict wasn't the least bit concerned about my professional reputation or the stability of my family. My addict has no boundaries around women: my addict does not care that I am married; my addict does not distinguish between adolescents and adults; my addict does not distinguish between married women and unmarried women.

Eventually I had an extramarital affair that lasted for several months. I was willing to do *anything* within that relationship in order to have sexual activity. As a result, when I was with my mistress, I denied the tremendous gap that existed between my responsibilities as a minister and a family man and this secret sexual affair. In some ways, I think I was actually *hoping* I'd get "caught" by someone. Acting out was my self-destructive way of dealing with anger—anger at God, the church, my co-workers, my family, myself, reality...you name it. I sought out psychological help while I was still involved in this affair. I started attending Al-Anon and also began seeing a counselor.

After six months in counseling, I managed to end the affair. Then, a few months later, I told my counselor about my behavior during a week-long retreat I'd recently returned from. I told the counselor that even though the retreat I attended was very relaxing and not at all stressful, I still craved pornography while I was there. One night I actually left the retreat setting, bought some pornography, then took it back to the retreat with me and masturbated. I even considered going to a pornographic movie during the week. I knew that I couldn't "justify" my acting-out behaviors with my usual excuse (that I'd had an especially hard day at work or was under a great deal of pressure.) *I realized that I had been preoccupied with sex that week for reasons I didn't understand.* After I related this story to my counselor, he suggested that I might be a sex addict; based on what I had told him, he believed that I was powerless over my sexual thoughts and behaviors.

I went to my first Twelve Step meeting fearful that I wouldn't be able to *prove* that I really was a sex addict. After all, I had *never* been arrested for my acting-out behaviors; I had *never* been to a prostitute; and I *hadn't* physically harmed anyone. At that first meeting I found—for the first time in my life—a place where I could talk about what was really happening in my life with people who understood what I was saying and respected me for having the courage to say it. My Twelve Step group was then and still is a place where I feel I belong. This group is made up of people I like, respect, and admire and *all of us are dealing with the same addiction.* The group helps me move out of shame and secrecy into self-respect and fellowship.

My awareness of my addiction has continued to grow since the time of that first meeting. My initial goal was to stop masturbating and using pornography. Several times after that first meeting, I acted out by purchasing pornographic magazines and/or masturbating. After a while, I found that I was also powerless over looking at covers of pornographic magazines and scanning newspapers for X-rated movie ads. I now realize that I need to maintain very clear boundaries regarding these behaviors: no matter what happens in my life, I cannot allow myself to look at these movies and ads. I've also learned that I need to be very careful not to use television to fuel my addictive behaviors. When I catch myself changing channels just to see what's on, I know I'm into my addict and looking for a "fix." Since I've been in the Program, I've also become aware that I carry in my head an endless supply of images from the pornography I've read, from my fantasies, and from my sexual encounters with women. My addict loves to spend time with these stimulating images; I once learned that I could "solve" all my problems and take a vacation from reality for *hours* by dwelling on these things. Now I realize that obsessing about these images cheats me out of my feelings, distracts me from doing what I need to do, robs me of time I could spend productively, and leaves me feeling lonely and shameful. When I allow myself to spend time thinking about these things, I am setting myself up to act out in other ways. Now when I find my mind cluttered with these images, I ask God to help me stay sober; I read Twelve Step literature; and I call on other recovering addicts.

I have also learned in the Program that I need to be very careful with my thoughts about women. I have discovered that I can get into my addictive obsession just thinking about a woman's body, her smile, her clothing, the sound of her voice, or the way she carries herself. My addict uses all these images and impressions to perpetuate the addictive behavior. I used to spend the entire service focusing on attractive women in the audience and telling myself that they were there only because they wanted to have sex with me. Even though I still have fantasies about women while I'm in church, I now have a behavioral boundary that helps me: I focus on people who are "safe" for me. My addict is compulsive about trying to get women to feel sorry for me and take care of me. I used to be so obsessed with these women and what I "needed" to do to have sex with them that I completely lost touch with what I needed and wanted in my real life. I shudder when I think where I'd be without the Program. Of course, my addict would love to act out by having sex with an adolescent girl or with the wife or girl friend of a member of my congregation. Now I know that what my addict wants for me could easily cost me my reputation, my family, my career, and my self-respect.

Since I first came to the group, I have found a new life. I used to be constantly exhausted and depressed. No one around me could meet my unrealistic expectations and I hated them for that. The only "friends" I had were the women around whom I would show my inadequacy in a desperate attempt to get them to be sexual with me. Work was drudgery and a burden for me. I used to wonder why other people had so much energy and how they could enjoy life so much and maintain friendships too. My life has really turned around since I've been working the Steps. Now I have some genuine friendships and a growing sense of self-respect; I live life as a stronger, more competent person. Because of my own experience and the experiences others haved shared with me, I have hope that the promises in the AA Big Book will continue to be fulfilled in my life. Gradually I am regaining my sense of humor and my ability to really live life and have fun; I'm also learning to enjoy real intimacy with my wife and family. In learning to accept my own limitations as well as the limitations of other people, I am learning to like myself and others—just as we are. Now my boundaries also exclude sexually-oriented conversations with women and use of any form of pornography. When I talk with women now, I am careful never to characterize myself as lost, lonely, abused, or pain-filled.

During my first year in the Program, I acted out several

times. During that time I also had stretches of unbroken sobriety—ranging from a couple of weeks to a couple of months. After a while, I started attending two meetings a week to help me maintain my sobriety. I was surprised when I first understood how pervasive my addiction is and how deeply it affects me. I continued to learn more about my addiction and how it has worked and continues to work in my life. I also learned to break out of my isolation during that first year. In order to stay sober, I found I had to make many phone calls to other people in my group—sometimes I made up to five calls a day.

It is very clear to me now that the Twelve Steps constitute a spiritual Program. Many times each day, I ask God to help me stay sober because I know I can't do it on my own. Many times each day, I also ask God to give me knowledge of His will for me and the power to carry it out. I know that God answers these prayers. Working the Steps is a real adventure. It's challenging to live one day at a time, keep life simple, and let go and let God. As I do these things each day, I feel a growing sense of fulfillment and serenity. *Now I know that it isn't what happens to me but what I do with it that makes the real difference in my life.*

Sobriety is now the most important thing in my life and I find that Twelve Step work helps me maintain that sobriety. I now attend three Twelve Step meetings every week. I added a third meeting after I'd been in the Program for nineteen months and had a slip. I added the third meeting as a way of making amends to myself; adding the meeting for that reason represents a change in attitude. In the past, I had seen "extra" meetings as a form of punishment. Now as I make that additional forty-five minute drive to another meeting each week, I remember that I care about myself and that going to Twelve Step meetings is simply one of the caring and loving things I can do for myself.

At the present time, I'm experiencing some new benefits of sobriety I hadn't experienced after my first year in the Program.

In many ways, I feel like a new person now and that change leads me to a re-examination of my basic life commitments. This re-examination is at once terrifying and exhilarating, but I know the process will strengthen my sobriety. Another new benefit of my maintained sobriety is that I'm finding a healthy sexual identity. During my active addiction, I did not have access to my sexuality in healthy or nurturing ways. *For months, it was so much easier to talk about acting out than it was to talk about my healthy sexual feelings.* The Program has helped me to accept my body as well as my sexuality.

There is a passage from the Big Book of Alcoholics Anonymous that continues to be very helpful to me. This passage reminds me of my delusions regarding my addiction as well as my many unsuccessful attempts to control that addiction: "Most of us have been unwilling to admit we were real alcoholics. No person likes to think he is bodily and mentally different from his fellows. Therefore, it is not surprising that our drinking careers have been characterized by countless vain attempts to prove we could drink like other people. The idea that somehow, someday he will control and enjoy his drinking is the great obsession of every abnormal drinker. The persistence of this illusion is astonishing. Many pursue it into the gates of insanity or death" (p. 30).

Recovery has given me a new life for which I am extremely grateful. I wish everyone well in recovery.

297

Jean's Story

Recovery is never easy, but it is always possible...

(After three and a half years of recovery.)

As a co-dependent to a sex addict, my story is also one of pain, loneliness, and acting out. For years, I spent so much of my emotional energy looking for just the "right" man—a man who could change my world from the miserable confused place it was to a place where I would always feel good about myself. As long as I knew that someone desired me, I could accept myself and my world. At the time, I felt that sex was the only thing I had to offer a man. I felt "loved" only when someone was sexual with me and I felt comfortable in a relationship only if sex was the most important element. It was not clear to me at the time, but because my self-worth was based solely on my sexuality, a sex addict was really the perfect match for me.

Nine years ago I met the man who is now my husband. When we met, I knew that he had a reputation for "sleeping around," even though he was engaged to be married at the time. I decided that if I could somehow get this man to be sexual with me and *no one else,* I could at last *prove* that I was special. Even as a child, I always longed to be special to someone, anyone. When this man subsequently broke off his engagement and started a sexual relationship with me, I honestly believed that I was the only woman he was involved with sexually. Even though I was thrilled to know that he wanted me, I was fearful that sooner or later he would lose interest and leave. Because my addiction is to the sex addict, I couldn't bear to think of my life without him; I was sure I'd *die* if he ever left me.

For the next six years, our sexual acting-out behaviors intensified. Even though I had no desire to do many of the things he asked me to do, I never felt free to say no to him. I managed to convince myself and my friends that the things we were doing sexually were fun, or trendy, or sophisticated. *I had to justify what I was doing.* I was sure that he would act out sexually whether he was with me or not. Knowing this, I decided it was best to always be there with him and control the situation as best I could. When he told me that he wanted to include other women in our sexual activities, I suppressed my real feelings and agreed to go along with the idea. Instead of telling him what I really thought, I denied my own needs and instincts and told him I thought it would be interesting and fun to include other people in our sexual activities. But I did manage to retain some measure of control: I always made sure that the women we invited to share our sexual activities posed no real threat to me in terms of their appearance. Everywhere we went in those days, I compared myself to the other women around and even "ranked" myself. If I thought I was the most attractive woman at a party, *I was on top of the world.* But if I thought that another woman at the party was more attractive—particularly to the man in my life—I usually withdrew, then started a fight with him about an issue completely unrelated to my feelings about the other woman.

I felt distant from this man even though we were living together. But I was reluctant to acknowledge my feelings about the emotional distance between us because our relationship was so very fragile; I just couldn't rock the boat and risk losing him. Our relationship was based on sex, so as long as I was being sexual with him, I knew where he was and what he was feeling. As always, I felt that it was *my* responsibility to change or work on whatever was causing problems in our relationship. I reasoned that if I were prettier, or smarter, or sexier, he would love me enough to stay with me or to change in the exact ways I wanted him to change. I never trusted him when he was out of my sight, yet I rarely confronted him about my lack of trust in him. I found that it was always less frightening to start a fight with him about something that really had nothing at all to do with my feelings about his behavior.

After we had been together for six years, I felt as if I was dying inside. *I knew that I should leave this man.* I felt the need for more feelings and more sharing in my primary relationship; I needed to have someone in my life who I could feel closer to; *I needed to know myself again.* Throughout our relationship, I had given up my own activities and interests just to have time and energy for *him.* I no longer wanted to be sexual with him, but I knew if I refused him our relationship would end. In order to cope with this conflict between my feelings and my fear of sharing those feelings, I began to engage in a sort of "passive" acting out. For example, I'd agree to be sexual with him when he asked. I'd then fall asleep, or intentionally think about other things while we were being sexual so that I was not "present" or really aware of what was going on. I simply didn't want to *feel* how meaningless and disconnected our sexual relationship had become.

I could see that I wasn't getting what I wanted from this relationship or from my life, *but I didn't know how to change things.* Then one day he mentioned a group he had heard about for people with sexual problems; he even talked about joining the group. I was afraid when I heard him say this, because I had assumed all along that the only sexual problem he had was his "sleeping around" behavior during the period of time when he was engaged. And as far as I knew, that activity had ended *years* ago. So what was going on that I didn't know about? Why did he need to join a group like *that*? All the time I had been with him, I was under the illusion that I could actually *control* him. *Now I wondered if I had been wrong.*

The night after his first meeting with the group, we had a big fight. Following that, he went to the phone and called someone in his group. When I overheard him say, "She doesn't know...," I felt crazy. He got off the phone, sensed my anxiety, and told me that he had been masturbating compulsively for many years. I was so relieved—at least he hadn't slept with other women during our time together. He also told me that there was a special group for people in relationships with sex addicts. When I said I'd attend one of their meetings, I felt as though I had agreed to visit another planet! I had absolutely no idea what this group would be like. *I wondered what kind of people actually stayed in relationships with sex addicts.* I expected to encounter crude, immoral people at the meeting, perhaps even characters like those portrayed in porno movies. *But to my surprise, at that meeting I found an intelligent and loving group of people.* As each co-dependent in the group introduced herself, my anxiety subsided; I felt secure and comfortable with these people. Each of the personal stories shared with the group that evening focused on some common themes that I was all too familiar with: the inability to say no; extreme fear of losing a relationship; feelings of isolation and loneliness within that relationship; subordination of individual needs to the needs of another person; and a persistent feeling that the sex addicts in our lives would stop acting out *if only we* (co-dependents) *were more attractive, more perfect, more sexually appealing.* As I listened to the stories, I also came to understand that I had acted out my co-dependency in other relationships in my life, too. Before I met my husband, I often dated men I had very little in common with. But regardless of who I was dating or how few interests we shared, I would routinely abandon my own interests, friends, and school work just to focus all of my energies on the current man in my life.

Early in my recovery, I had some serious doubts about my relationship with the man who had at that time been in my life for more than six years. Eventually I got in touch with the feelings of anger and resentment I had toward him. I realized that I was uncertain about what our relationship really *was,* other than a sick and destructive mess. In order to collect my feelings and really confront them, I moved away for a few months. Time and distance helped both of us see that *despite our addictions, we really liked each other*. We began to discuss marriage. Then, just one week before our official engagement, my husband-to-be told me that he had been sleeping with other women up until the time he got into the Program. *I was devastated*. During that period of time, I had assumed I was his only sexual partner—supposedly because I was "the best." Hearing the truth from him was like having the foundation of both my identity and my self-worth suddenly ripped out from under me. The members of my group were the only people who could understand the depth of my pain.

When my emotional pain finally subsided, I could see the powerful truth of the First Step reflected in my relationship with the man who would become my husband: I realized that I had *always* been powerless over his acting-out behaviors because he was an addict. During the three and a half years I've attended Twelve Step meetings, I have learned to use the Steps in direct relation to *my* addiction to the sex addict in my life. Now when I look back over my life, I can see how powerless I really *was*, not only in relation to the sexual acting-out behaviors of the man in my life, but also in relation to my own feelings of insecurity. I began to see how the sexual and physical abuse I was subjected to as a child actually taught me to act out; I had learned to be cooperative and conciliatory to the point of being submissive and completely denying my own needs and interests. Now, whenever I find myself wanting to experience the high of that false control again or my life really *is* unmanageable, I go back to my First Step to see that I learned co-dependent behavior early in my life and that *I am not a bad person*. I now have a relationship with my Higher Power who, I believe, was there all along and who got me through those horrible times in the past. Now when I'm fearful about the future, I find that I have to let go and trust that my Higher Power will let me know, through my feelings, what is right for me. I must trust that my husband has a Higher Power too, and that I cannot modify, deter, restrain, or otherwise control his acting-out behaviors.

For me, recovery has been a time of feeling pain and anger for the first time; recovery has also been a time of feeling real joy and closeness for the first time. My husband and I continue to work on our relationship in recovery with the help of the Twelve Steps and therapy. And I find that as I gain confidence in myself as a person with much more than sex to offer, I am expanding and enriching my life by making time for my own interests, activities, and goals. The early stages of recovery are the toughest. The same Program that promises so much asks us to give up powerful addictive beliefs about ourselves that may have shaped our lives; the Program asks us to love ourselves and believe that we *deserve* love and respect; the Program asks us to look honestly at past behaviors and relationships and reach out for the feelings we have tried to run away from for so many years. Most important, the Program asks us to let go of trying to understand, analyze, or fix everything and, instead, trust a Higher Power to get us through the process of recovery in our own way and at our own pace. Recovery is never easy, but it is always possible with the help and support of a Higher Power and a Twelve Step group. My road to recovery has been a rough one, but it's getting easier all the time.

A Personal Message
from the Authors

We share the following thoughts with you whether you have read all or part of this book or have chosen to glance through it only:

If you have questions or concerns about your sexual thoughts and behaviors, we want you to know that *we understand how you feel.* The isolation, the secrets, and the shame you might be struggling with at this very moment are well known to us because we have struggled with isolation, secrets, and shame ourselves. We have tried our best to share the experience of recovery in this book because we have found, through that recovery, a way to live a different kind of life. Above all, we want you to know that you can find a way to live a different kind of life too.

We understand that you might be very frightened and perhaps even angry right now. Based on our own searches for help and our early experiences in the Program, we encourage you to do several things as soon as you make the decision that you want and need help:

First of all, *be persistent.* Because of the anonymous nature of the Program as well as a public relations policy guided by the Twelve Traditions and based on attraction rather than promotion, you may find that at first it is very difficult to obtain information about the Program, even more difficult to obtain information about specific groups and meetings. *You may find it helpful to refer to a phone book, or to consult with a social service agency or a community mental health referral service for information regarding anonymous groups based on the Twelve Step Program.* Even though awareness is growing and there are currently Twelve Step groups for sex addicts throughout the country, it is possible that there is not yet a specialized

Twelve Step group available in your area.

If you are unable to find a Twelve Step group for sex addicts in your community, we encourage you to attend other Twelve Step group meetings and consult with people there about establishing a special Twelve Step group to address the needs of sex addicts. (For meeting suggestions, see pages 319-322).

If you find that there are several Twelve Step groups for sex addicts in your community, attend as many different meetings as you like, but select one of them to attend regularly so that you will have an opportunity to get to know the people there. When you have selected a Twelve Step meeting that you wish to attend on a regular basis, make sure that you get yourself a sponsor immediately, and then make use of the support that he or she offers you.

Ask questions, lots of them. Don't hesitate to ask recovering addicts in the group to share their stories with you—the nature of their acting-out behaviors; the event, situation, or feeling that finally led them to seek help; how they set their boundaries and continue to monitor them; ways they are different now; and how they continue to grow in their recovery.

Also, *read the personal stories in this book* (pages 131-304) *and respond to the questions* in the Appendix that are designed to assist you in examining your sexual thoughts and behaviors (pages 311-318).

As you do all of these things, try to focus on similarities rather than differences. As often as possible, discuss the Twelve Steps with recovering addicts and consider the many ways you can use the Steps in your daily life. There are bound to be elements of the Program that you do not fully support or agree with, particularly at first, but don't allow yourself to waste time and energy *debating* with others, focusing on your disagreements, or trying to change portions of the Program that you think need "fixing." Instead, we suggest that you make a conscious effort to focus on the elements of the Program that you agree with and the elements of the Program that feel affirming and positive to you.

Above all, be patient and gentle with yourself and remember that there are people who understand what you have been through and who will care about you and give you support every step of the way. You can do it...you can recover. We pray that recovery will be the choice you make.

Appendix

Questions to Consider

As we shared our personal stories with each other, we became aware of some similarities in our thinking, behaviors, and experiences. Drawing on these similarities, we developed the following list of sixty-five questions as a guide for others who might have some concerns about their own sexual thoughts and behaviors. These questions do not constitute a standardized test designed to diagnose addiction. Instead, these questions reflect our own experiences; our point is simply that those people who answer "yes" to a number of these questions have histories that are similar to ours. It is our hope that those who respond affirmatively to any of these questions will carefully consider the effects their sexual thoughts and behaviors have on their lives *today*. Those who do have concerns about their sexual thoughts and behaviors need to know that, like us, they can get help and support through the Twelve Step Fellowship.

_____ 1. Do you sense that your sexual thoughts and/or behaviors are causing problems in your life?

_____ 2. Have sexual thoughts interfered with your ability to function at work or at school?

_____ 3. Do you worry that your sexual thoughts and/or behaviors are more powerful than you are?

_____ 4. Do you sometimes think that you are the only person who has certain sexual thoughts or engages in certain sexual behaviors?

_____ 5. Do you fail to meet commitments or fail to carry out responsibilities because of your sexual behaviors?

_____ 6. Do you struggle to control or completely stop your sexual thoughts and/or behaviors?

_____ 7. Do you fantasize about sex, or masturbate, or engage in sexual activity with another person in order to escape, deny, or numb your feelings?

_____ 8. Do you think about sex either more or less than you would like to?

_____ 9. Do you think of yourself as a person who has no sexual thoughts or desires whatsoever?

_____ 10. Do you think that there is something wrong regarding the frequency of sexual activity you have or wish to have?

_____ 11. Do you spend more money than you can afford to spend on sexual activities?

_____ 12. Does it seem as though there is another person or force inside of you that drives you to be sexual?

_____ 13. Do you have two standards of fidelity—one for yourself and one for your spouse or partner?

_____ 14. Do you think you would be happy if only you had enough sex and/or just the right sex partner(s)?

_____ 15. Do you feel empty or shameful after engaging in sexual activity or having sexual fantasies?

_____ 16. Do you feel obligated to have sex?

_____ 17. Have you ever promised yourself that you would never again have another sexual relationship?

_____ 18. Do you find it necessary to fantasize during sexual activity?

_____ 19. Do you set rules regulating the frequency of your sexual thoughts and activities?

_____ 20. Do you dress in such a way as to make your body appear undesirable?

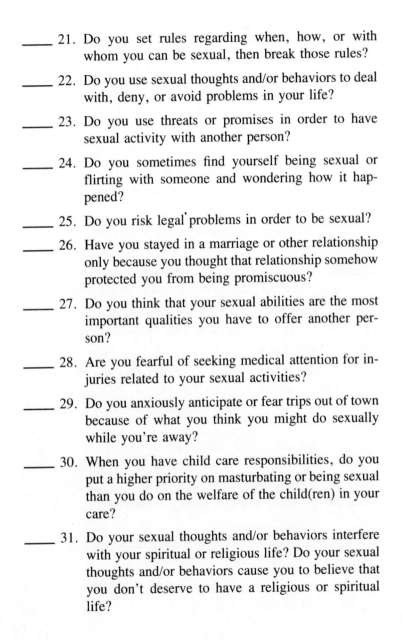

_____ 21. Do you set rules regarding when, how, or with whom you can be sexual, then break those rules?

_____ 22. Do you use sexual thoughts and/or behaviors to deal with, deny, or avoid problems in your life?

_____ 23. Do you use threats or promises in order to have sexual activity with another person?

_____ 24. Do you sometimes find yourself being sexual or flirting with someone and wondering how it happened?

_____ 25. Do you risk legal problems in order to be sexual?

_____ 26. Have you stayed in a marriage or other relationship only because you thought that relationship somehow protected you from being promiscuous?

_____ 27. Do you think that your sexual abilities are the most important qualities you have to offer another person?

_____ 28. Are you fearful of seeking medical attention for injuries related to your sexual activities?

_____ 29. Do you anxiously anticipate or fear trips out of town because of what you think you might do sexually while you're away?

_____ 30. When you have child care responsibilities, do you put a higher priority on masturbating or being sexual than you do on the welfare of the child(ren) in your care?

_____ 31. Do your sexual thoughts and/or behaviors interfere with your spiritual or religious life? Do your sexual thoughts and/or behaviors cause you to believe that you don't deserve to have a religious or spiritual life?

_____ 32. Are you afraid to be left alone with children, for fear of being sexual with them?

_____ 33. Have your sexual thoughts and/or behaviors ever led you to consider suicide, castration, or self-mutilation?

_____ 34. When you are in a relationship with someone, do you try to make sure that another sex partner will be available to you immediately in case anything goes wrong with your current relationship?

_____ 35. Do you stay in unsatisfying, painful, humiliating, or otherwise unhealthy relationships only so that you can continue to be sexual with someone?

_____ 36. Do you spend time with people you don't even like or respect, hoping that you will have an opportunity to be sexual with them?

_____ 37. Do you have sex with your partner even when he or she is ill?

_____ 38. Does your sexual partner complain about your need for sex or your sexual behaviors? Does he or she refuse to participate in certain sexual activities with you?

_____ 39. Do you either minimize or exaggerate the facts when discussing your sexual life with others?

_____ 40. Have you ever tried to stop your sexual activity in an effort to end a painful relationship or behavior pattern?

_____ 41. Do you initiate sexual activity with a partner before he or she is awake?

_____ 42. Do you have chronic medical problems with your sex organs?

_____ 43. Do you put yourself in danger by not taking reasonable precautions or by going to unsafe places in order to have sex?

_____ 44. Have you lost a job or risked losing a job because of your sexual behaviors?

_____ 45. Do your sexual behaviors cause you to violate the ethical standards, principles, and/or oaths of your profession?

_____ 46. Do you scan printed material (novels, newspapers, magazines) or change channels on the television set just to find something that will stimulate you sexually?

_____ 47. Do you regularly engage in fantasies involving self-abuse or other kinds of physical abuse?

_____ 48. Do you trade material things (dinner, drugs, money) for sex?

_____ 49. Do your sexual behaviors lead you to risk injury, illness, or death?

_____ 50. Have your sexual behaviors led to treatment in a hospital emergency room?

_____ 51. Do you masturbate after having sex?

_____ 52. Have you injured yourself due to the frequency, intensity, or nature of your masturbation or other sexual activities?

_____ 53. Would you rather masturbate than be sexual with a partner?

_____ 54. Do you spend time looking through windows hoping that you might see something that will stimulate you sexually?

_____ 55. Do you follow people on the street, pick up hitch-hikers, or drive around (cruise) hoping that these activities will lead to sexual encounters?

_____ 56. Do you undress, masturbate, or engage in sexual activities in places where strangers are likely to see you?

_____ 57. Do you feel compelled to dress a certain way or take part in certain rituals in order to masturbate or be sexual with another person?

_____ 58. Do you seek out crowds so that you can rub against people or otherwise be in close physical contact with strangers?

_____ 59. Do you make phone calls to strangers in order to talk about sex or masturbate?

_____ 60. Do you masturbate while driving?

_____ 61. Have you ever been sexual with animals?

_____ 62. Have you replaced a collection of pornographic material after destroying one collection and vowing never to purchase pornography again?

_____ 63. Do you masturbate or engage in sexual activity with partners in public places?

_____ 64. Do you steal money in order to engage in sexual activities?

_____ 65. Has an important relationship in your life ended because of your inability to stop being sexual outside of that relationship?

First Step Questions

Along with the Questions to Consider *(page 311), the following questions helped prepare us to work the First Step:*

Powerlessness – *what does it mean to me?*

- How have I attempted to stop, limit, change, or otherwise control my sexual behaviors?
- How have I been dishonest with myself and with others regarding my sexual thoughts and behaviors?
- What promises regarding my sexual behaviors have I made to myself, to my Higher Power, to members of my family, and to other people?
- How have I tried to hide my sexual behaviors?
- How have I tried to explain, justify, or rationalize my sexual behaviors to myself and to others?
- In what ways have I been sexual without planning to be? (For example, going to the store for groceries and stopping at a pornography shop instead.)
- In what ways are my sexual behaviors *different* from how I would like them to be?

Unmanageability – *what does it mean to me?*

- How has my sexual behavior affected the following aspects of my life:
    - my education?
    - my career?
    - my feelings?
    - my relationships with family and friends?

- my financial situation? (Consider money spent on prostitution, pornographic material, fines, bail, etc.)
- my spirituality?
- my physical health? (Consider accidents, abuse, and/or diseases resulting from sexual activities.)
- my mental health?
- my integrity?
- my self-respect?
- my morals and values?
- my life goals and objectives?

"Hitting Bottom" – *What specific event in my life has convinced me that I've hit bottom*—that I cannot continue to live as I have been living? Based on what I know about my past behaviors, what could happen to me in the future if I choose not to seek help now?

Meeting Suggestions

In keeping with Tradition Four, each group is autonomous and may operate any way it chooses, providing it operates within the guidelines of the Twelve Traditions. Following is a list of procedures that are being used in various Twelve Step meetings. Take what works for you and leave the rest. Whenever people ask for guidance regarding Twelve Step meetings, we give them the same general advice: feel free to experiment within the Traditions, but always remember to "Keep It Simple."

I. Opening

- Someone in the group reads The Preamble and "How It Works" (pages 323-326).

- Stand for a moment of silence for those people who still suffer.

- While holding hands or linking arms, everyone says the Serenity Prayer in unison (page 327).

- Trusted servant or other person in the group asks for two minutes of silent meditation.

- Trusted servant begins the meeting by saying "Welcome to the meeting. I'm *(first name)*; I'm a sex addict." Group answers "Hi *(first name)*" or remains silent.

- Each member introduces himself or herself *by first name only*. After his or her introductory statement—"I'm *(first name)*; I'm a sex addict," some people follow up by sharing a brief descriptive phrase about their feelings at that moment—"and I'm feeling...(grateful, relieved, sad, happy, proud, lonely.")

II. Business

- Keeping the Twelve Traditions in mind and, accordingly, issues that are appropriate and inappropriate for meetings, the following information is shared among people in the group:

    –details about special meetings, upcoming retreats, newly formed groups, or the need for new groups;

    –updates on group finances (confirmation that rent is being paid, etc);

    –information about current Twelve Step opportunities—names of people or organizations requesting speakers, special resources, or Twelve Step calls.

- Consistent with the Seventh Tradition, a basket or envelope is passed among those present for *voluntary donations*. People are reminded that money collected at this time helps to pay the rent and also helps to establish and maintain an active post office box, a phone line, and printed material that will be helpful to individuals as well as to the group as a whole.

- Medallions are presented. Many groups offer medallions or some other appropriate token to those people in the group who have maintained sobriety for specific periods of time. Some groups give medallions to people in order to mark the following periods of sobriety: *thirty days, three months, six months, twelve months, and each year thereafter*. Often the sponsor of the individual receiving the medallion says something about that person's progress at this time. In response to the sponsor's remarks, the person receiving the medallion may then choose to share with other group members some thoughts about what the last few months have been like and how recovery has changed his or her life. In some groups, there is sufficient time at this point for other people in the group to comment about the changes they have observed in this person.

If a person who has received a medallion has a slip, he or she is not asked to return the medallion. It is understood that any medallions a person has earned represent periods of sobriety *already* achieved. When a slip *does* occur, a person simply changes his or her sobriety date and begins again—"One Day At A Time".

III. Step Presentation

- Someone in the group initiates discussion about a particular Step and a particular Tradition. Some groups structure this discussion somewhat by selecting a different Step and Tradition for each meeting and then the group as a whole discusses that Step and that Tradition. Or they might choose to form smaller groups in order to facilitate discussion. Dividing into smaller groups is usually seen as an option if the entire group has grown to the point that it is difficult or impossible for everyone to have an opportunity to talk.

- Some large groups break into *squads*, permanent small groups that include the same people from week to week. Other large groups ask people to number off each time they meet and then break into different groups.

IV. Check In

- Each person takes a couple of minutes—either in the large group or in one of the smaller groups or squads—to let others know how he or she is doing in regard to his or her addiction and recovery.

- In some groups everyone just listens as individuals share. In other groups, people are encouraged to interject references to specific Steps they feel might provide special help and guidance to the individual who is sharing. Regardless of how this give-and-take is handled, everyone makes a concerted effort not to tell others what to do and not to allow the meeting to become a therapy group.

V. Closing

- The Trusted servant reads a closing of the group's choosing or The Promises (page 326).

- The Serenity Prayer is spoken in unison (page 327) or some other ritual particularly meaningful to the group is used.

Preamble*

Ours is a fellowship of women and men who share our experience, strength, and hope with each other that we may solve our common problem and help others to recover from their sexual addictions. The only requirement for membership is a desire to stop compulsive sexual behavior. There are no dues or fees for membership; we are self-supporting through our own contributions. We are not allied with any organization. We do not wish to engage in any controversy, endorse nor oppose any causes. Although there is no organizational affiliation between Alcoholics Anonymous and our fellowship we are based on the principles of AA. Our primary purpose is to stay sexually healthy and help other sex addicts achieve freedom from compulsive sexual behavior.

* Preamble reprinted for adaptation with permission of the AA *Grapevine*.

How It Works*

"Rarely have we seen a person fail who has thoroughly followed our path. Those who do not recover are people who cannot or will not completely give themselves to this simple program... They are naturally incapable of grasping and developing a manner of living which demands rigorous honesty... There are those, too, who suffer from grave emotional and mental disorders, but many of them do recover if they have the capacity to be honest.

"Our stories disclose in a general way what we used to be like, what happened, and what we are like now. If you have decided you want what we have and are willing to go to any length to get it—then you are ready to take certain steps.

"At some of these we balked. We thought we could find an easier, softer way. But we could not. With all the earnestness at our command, we beg of you to be fearless and thorough from the very start. Some of us have tried to hold on to our old ideas and the result was nil until we let go absolutely."

"Remember that we deal with sexual addiction—cunning, baffling, powerful! Without help it is too much for us. But there is One who has all power—that One is God. May you find God now!

"Half measures availed us nothing. We stood at the turning point. We asked God's protection and care with complete abandon.

"Here are the steps we took, which are suggested as a program of recovery:

The Twelve Steps

Step One
We admitted we were powerless over our compulsive sexual behavior—that our lives had become unmanageable.
Step Two
Came to believe that a Power greater than ourselves could restore us to sanity.
Step Three
Made a decision to turn our will and our lives over to the care of God as we understood God.
Step Four
Made a searching and fearless moral inventory of ourselves.
Step Five
Admitted to God, to ourselves, and to another human being the exact nature of our wrongs.

Step Six
Were entirely ready to have God remove all these defects of character.
Step Seven
Humbly asked God to remove our shortcomings.
Step Eight
Made a list of all persons we had harmed and became willing to make amends to them all.
Step Nine
Made direct amends to such people wherever possible, except when to do so would injure them or others.
Step Ten
Continued to take personal inventory and when we were wrong promptly admitted it.
Step Eleven
Sought through prayer and meditation to improve our conscious contact with God, as we understood God, praying only for knowledge of God's will for us and the power to carry that out.
Step Twelve
Having had a spiritual awakening as the result of these Steps, we tried to carry this message to other sex addicts and to practice these principles in all of our activities.

"Many of us exclaimed, 'What an order! I can't go through with it.' Do not be discouraged. No one among us has been able to maintain anything like perfect adherence to these principles. We are not saints. The point is, that we are willing to grow along spiritual lines. The principles we have set down are guides to progress. We claim spiritual progress rather than spiritual perfection.

"Our understanding of sexual addiction and our personal adventures before and after make clear three pertinent ideas:

a) That we were sexually addicted and could not manage our own lives.

b) That probably no human power could have relieved our addictive behavior.

c) That God could and would if God were sought."

* From "How It Works," Chapter 5 of *Alcoholics Anonymous*, reprinted for adaptation with permission of Alcoholics Anonymous World Services, Inc.

The Promises

"If we are painstaking about this phase of our development, we will be amazed before we are half way through. We are going to know a new freedom and a new happiness. We will not regret the past nor wish to shut the door on it. We will comprehend the word serenity and we will know peace. No matter how far down the scale we have gone, we will see how our experience can benefit others. That feeling of uselessness and self-pity will disappear. We will lose interest in selfish things and gain interest in our fellows. Self-seeking will slip away. Our whole attitude and outlook upon life will change. Fear of people and of economic insecurity will leave us. We will intuitively know how to handle situations which used to baffle us. We will suddenly realize that God is doing for us what we could not do for ourselves.

"Are these extravagant promises? We think not. They are being fulfilled among us—sometimes quickly, sometimes slowly. They will always materialize if we work for them."

Alcoholics Anonymous (pp. 83-4)

The Serenity Prayer

God Grant me the serenity
To accept the things I cannot change,
Courage to change the things I can,
And wisdom to know the difference.

This prayer is read at most group meetings and often analyzed
in group discussions. It also serves as inspiration to individuals
for their daily meditations.